# BOYS AND OIL

ALSO BY TAYLOR BRORBY

*Coming Alive: Action and Civil Disobedience*

*Crude: Poems About Place, Energy, and Politics*

*Fracture: Essays, Poems, and Stories on Fracking in America,*
with Stefanie Brook Trout

# BOYS
## AND OIL

*growing up gay in a fractured land*

## TAYLOR BRORBY

LIVERIGHT PUBLISHING CORPORATION

A Division of W. W. Norton & Company

*Independent Publishers Since 1923*

Several portions of this book appeared in a slightly different form in
*Southern Humanities Review*, *High Desert Journal*, *On Second Thought*,
and the *Huffington Post*.

For information about permission to reproduce selections from this book,
write to Permissions, Liveright Publishing Corporation, a division of
W. W. Norton & Company, Inc., 500 Fifth Avenue, New York, NY 10110

For information about special discounts for bulk purchases, please contact
W. W. Norton Special Sales at specialsales@wwnorton.com or 800-233-4830

Manufacturing by Lake Book Manufacturing
Book design by Ellen Cipriano
Production manager: Lauren Abbate

ISBN 978-1-324-09086-1

Liveright Publishing Corporation, 500 Fifth Avenue, New York, N.Y. 10110
www.wwnorton.com

W. W. Norton & Company Ltd., 15 Carlisle Street, London W1D 3BS

1 2 3 4 5 6 7 8 9 0

*For Tanya and Kirsten*

There's a place for us,
Somewhere a place for us.
—STEPHEN SONDHEIM

Families are a thin skin quickly shed once flight from
the prison of home became possible. . . . I am not about
closure. I am about reopening wounds and slashing
through the scar tissue to the place where the dreams
sleep and wait to come back to life.
—CHARLES BOWDEN

# CONTENTS

# SEA

B EFORE IT WAS an ocean of grasses, the prairie was a shallow sea. Salt water sloshed for millennia, as rounded grains of quartz sand were swept from the dry land into the surf. When the quartz finally settled—down into the beds thousands of yards thick—trilobites, those bottom-feeding arthropods, crawled onto the large shelf of sand.

Generation after generation of trilobites, a number stretching to near infinity, would die, covered by sediment, sludge, and mud. Weight and time then would transfigure the trilobites into a massive underground sea of gas- and oil-rich rock.

As the sediment settled, a large delta emerged—swamps, lagoons, meandering rivers, and vast forested floodplains. Trees—expanding twelve feet in diameter and more than one hundred feet tall—grew like a prehistoric version of the Everglades.

Plants growing in the swamps, lagoons, and marshes perished. They, too, were submerged underwater. Oxygen could not exist in the shallow bowls of plant debris, so the plants were broken down, slowly but inexorably, by anaerobic bacteria. But a thick layer of plant material did not fully decompose, and vast beds of peat accumulated.

The surrounding streams changed course and, when they did, sprinkled sand and silt atop the peat. Layer upon layer—some more than fifty feet deep—weighed down the peat beds that, over time, transformed into seams of lignite coal only a few feet thick.

Volcanoes shot ash into the atmosphere. The ash floated on the airstreams. Ancient waterways flowing north and east carried silt and clay. *Tyrannosaurus rex*, triceratops, and other dinosaurs roamed the ancient, verdant land.

When a meteor struck what is now Mexico, the Age of Dinosaurs abruptly ceased, a blanket of dust and sand covering these creatures' thewy flesh. Ferns wilted and died. The weight of it all pressed the coal and oil down.

Then came the great sheets of ice—miles thick—from the north. Boulders were picked up like tennis balls and dropped along the way. The middle of what would become the North American continent was bulldozed and reshaped into a vast, open plain.

# SOIL

# 1.

CENTER IS A PLACE where people only end up. Socked in south-central North Dakota, located in the middle of Oliver County, Center is a stone's throw from the 100th meridian, the rod of aridity that cleaves America between the luscious greens of the East and the mottled browns of the West. My hometown is where great trapeziums of buttes begin to break against the wash of sky. It's the small county seat and the only incorporated town. Center is where farmers begin to get supplanted by ranchers. Fields flow into mines; it is where dust kicks up. Center is an ecotone, a transitory region of change. As the town motto reminds visitors, "It's better in Center."

There is no stoplight in Center, no grocery store. Such necessities as milk, Hot Stuff pizza, and two-liter bottles of Coke are purchased at the Corner Stop, the one gas station in the county. When I was small, growing up in a trailer house on the south side of Center, it took me all of ten minutes to pedal my bicycle across town to Grandpa and Grandma Brorby's. I went to the one school in the county with the same twenty-two other students in my grade—a lopsided division of six girls and sixteen other boys. There are two bars, a bank, a courthouse, and the small Coal Country Community Health Center on Center's main street. There are three churches but not even a motel.

As a child, though, my world didn't feel small. I played baseball and spent my afternoons with Grandpa Hatzenbihler fishing for bluegills or picking tart chokecherries. I wandered the grassy banks of the small Square Butte Creek, a squiggly stream that eventually empties into the wide Missouri River, looking for muskrat, heron, or beaver. Sometimes I'd spot a coyote loping in the distance.

The prairie I grew up on teaches you to notice, to pay attention—the yolk of the sun as it slides across the dome of sky, streaking the world orange and indigo, the swish of grass in the afternoon breeze, the screech of a grackle.

During the "golden hour" on the prairie, the North Dakota palette reveals the subtle differences between ocher and umber and sienna.

And North Dakota can also be biblical in terms of the weather—hailstones hurl from the sky, rain floods fields, tornadoes rip across the hills, blizzards kill cattle, heat chars crops.

To the west of Center, a large dragline lumbers on as it breaks the soil, ripping lignite coal from underground.

The men in Center fill the pews on Sunday, and on Monday are back at the mine or at the power plant, digging in the ground, heaving coal into large boilers, sending electricity to eastern North Dakota and western Minnesota. The men call Oliver County God's Country—a land filled with ring-necked pheasants, deer, red-winged blackbirds. It's Eden, it's brimming, it's full of life. But each Monday, and every day after, the men stumble into the two bars, their sooted hands grip cold beer, warm whiskey.

Each year North Dakota ranks first in binge drinking. High schoolers sneak bottles to hidden bonfire parties, someone shoots off the road, is memorialized by a flowered wreath and, if they were nice, a crude wooden cross, on a cottonwood tree on Highway 25, just before crossing the county line.

Drinking is a way to numb the pain, the dissonance, the sound of the dragline, the rumble of the boiler. The blasphemy of the work that lies ahead.

THE STORY OF NORTH DAKOTA is then the story of self-destruction. Everything leaves North Dakota full and comes back empty. The only way I've understood my home is by getting out, escaping its crushing weight, watching the destruction, now from the outside.

In childhood, when I escaped to the hills with my tackle box and drawing paper, I told no friends. I kept it a secret, like a coal burning in my gut. Boys liked playing smear the queer, king of the hill, and cowboys and Indians. I played, too, to fit in, hurled my body against other small-boned bodies atop lumpy snow mounds. I was reminded by my father that *Brorbys never tap out.*

But the prairie I escaped to was a supple whirlwind of grass tilting in the wind, a symphony of sage-grouse song. Beaver tails slapped the water. I would cast spoons for northern pike in the Square Butte Creek. When the casting became boring, I pulled out my sketchbook and pencils and traced the bend of the creek against the white paper.

I tried to create the world I wanted rather than the world as it was—a world of broken lignite and all-too-often broken people.

On the playground, I asked friends to play tag or an imaginary game of pirates. Instead, the other boys sized one another up, divided into two lines, and threw footballs. They ran back and forth across the asphalt playground, slammed the ball hard against the ground when they scored a touchdown. I watched, from a distance, wondering where I fit into the place I lived.

I still cringe when I say I played with girls, since I was constantly called a girl because I wanted to create my own games. I wanted room for my imagination.

Throughout elementary school, on Halloween those boys dressed like police officers, firefighters, and football players. I dressed, not as Barbie, but as Dracula, or a wizard, or a pirate.

Even then, I wanted a larger world.

My classmates played a preconceived game in a world that was preordained for them—chase a ball under Friday night lights, grow into men who dig coal from the ground. Save for the Mexican cruise you've always wanted. Retire when your body begins to break.

There was something I, too, craved in that landscape, something soft, something I couldn't see in the human-made world. So, I headed for the hills where badgers roamed, where pheasants tucked into marshy grass. There was diversity to the natural world that I could not find in my hometown. *He's a dreamer, he's not a hard worker, he doesn't want to play football.*

# 2.

THE PRAIRIE IS A TAPESTRY of intermingled roots woven together. One hundred acres of prairie may support over three thousand species of insects. Yet, when overlaid with extractive economies, it becomes simple, reduced to bloodless words: flyover country.

When you grow up knowing you come from a place no one visits, your dreams settle for staying put, for digging in the earth, for doing the act you've been trained to do: make your money by destroying the world. Though you don't see it that way, you become a pawn in someone else's story, a story of *That's the way it is, this is the way it has to be.* The illogical violence wrought upon the prairie is propelled by powerful men destroying lives to line their own pocketbooks.

And yet, the prairie, like memory, is powerful, too: it is a collection of single, varied grasses woven into an interlinked tapestry that secures soil in place. That's how I think of this book, like the woven roots of a symphony of grass.

# ROOTS

# 1.

THE PRAIRIE IS BEST rendered in fall. In a land where light—its length, its clarity—is abundant, it is only in fall when its sheer intensity, its radiant glory, is felt. In late afternoon, as the sun slides lower in the western sky, the buttes blaze copper; the harvested fields of wheat turn tawny. The sky slowly streaks to calamine. Shadows lengthen and the world rushes toward the close of day, the golden light lasting a mere hour. It is as if you are within the brushstrokes of a fiery painting.

As the ferocity of the crepuscular light fades and darkness seeps across the vault of sky, stars shroud the edges of the wide world. It is as if fireflies are lodged into a large black sheet. Once, when I was in elementary school, while my family drove home in winter on a cold, clear night, the aurora borealis leaked into my periphery. Lime ribbons began to swirl higher and higher until the ionosphere pulsed. Vertiginous, my father pulled over and we enjoyed the silent fireworks sweeping across the sky—it felt like I was inside the birthing of a nebula.

The ocean of the prairie is too large to be captured in any one image. However much I've tried, no panoramic lens can give the scale of the prairie's magnitude. The prairie cannot be summited; we cannot even go, like a forest, into it. To truly experience the prairie, we must lower ourselves and submit our bodies to the ground. We must be comfortable with soil, with earth, with dust.

For hours in childhood I would lie down on a hilltop beyond the wheat field behind our house. The sky washed with clouds that slowly shifted like a trail of smoke. The earth below me seemed to move, but maybe it was because of the wheeling of a hawk or the whirling of a turkey vulture high above me. I felt unmoored, floating across the sea of sky.

The prairie, too, can become unmoored. The chalky soil of western North Dakota was, in the early days of European immigration, cut into bricks to build sod houses—brick by brick, layer by layer, crude houses rose across the ocean of sage, milkvetch, and little bluestem. Like a fishnet, the grass's roots held the sod bricks together yet were still permeable. Sometimes bull snakes fell from the ceiling onto dining tables.

But the prairie is fragile. To be *of* the prairie is to recognize its fragility. To some, what feels harsh and open is, upon closer examination, delicate and sensitive.

The prairie of western North Dakota does not heal. On my sojourns in southwestern North Dakota, near Amidon and Marmarth, I've rubbed my hands along wagon tracks still rutted in the land from Custer's fateful trip west.

Before growing upward, grass tests the conditions to see whether it can make a home in place. Before sending up its bright blade, as much as two-thirds of the plant will vein through the soil, spreading outward and down like the branches of a tree. The grass is patient; it can take years before it decides to pop up and emerge.

This patience has been broken throughout history by various animals—horses and cattle whose hooves aren't shaped for the arid soil of western North Dakota—and by excavation of oil and coal, which rips the roots and breaks the fibers that bind and secure soil in place.

The prairie needs time to flourish. The empire of fossil fuels moves swiftly. The prairie I know is not like the forests of New England; it does not regenerate quickly. In a culture where we spend, lose, save, and buy our time—where time is an economic transaction—the prairie teaches us that to flourish, we need patience.

When a mountaintop is removed, we see its rubble cast into the valley. When a forest is clear cut, we see the stumps like fibrous tombstones. But when the prairie is overturned, we fail to mourn because, to most of us, the prairie is dirt, a patch of grass, nothing remotely remarkable. What we cannot recognize we oftentimes will not protect.

Perhaps it is because of intimidation. Since the prairie spreads, instead of builds, we view it as no great wonder, as something we have no control over, as something that's around and beneath us, as something we cannot conquer. But so often, at least to our way of seeing, we fail to notice what's right at our feet. By looking down, instead of up, an entire universe reveals itself. A community of microbes, miles of roots twisting and wrapping, field mice and badger burrows.

To live on the prairie is to be hunted, whether by a coyote, by a pack of boys, or by the sting of loneliness. There is no other way to say this: the prairie *reveals*. Like a painting viewed at a nose's length, layer upon layer of color, of grass, of our very selves, is exposed on the prairie. It is a place that tests us spiritually, even existentially.

The prairie is humble—supple and gentle, a purl of stiff stalks in the wind, pulsing and swaying: a large, undulating wash of brown and green against the air that, not so very long ago, was brackish and heavy. The prairie begins in stillness and slips through the soil of my imagination, a great canvas against which to paint the ideas of history, the possibilities in a broken world, a vast space that makes enough room for any idea, for any wish—a biotic community of possibility and rootedness.

The prairie is perceived as barren, and the only way to deal with emptiness is to fill it up. Space is what the prairie provides. By seeing space, we might better know the spaces within us, and how to hold and carry space. To see space is a matter of sight. With enough space, ideas have room to take root, grow, and blossom.

The prairie, for millennia, was not perceived as empty; it was a riot of life. Throngs of bison ambled across the prairie. Elk, grizzly bear, and gray and red wolves lived as far east as the Missouri River. Cougars hunted the plentiful pronghorn antelope. And then Europeans, desperate for food and clothing—and, later in the nineteenth century, for sport as well as in a systematic attempt to starve Native Americans—began a multispecies slaughter. With the megafauna of the Plains reduced, a spiritual inanition replaced a region that had once vibrated with life. The symphony of the prairie quieted.

The prairie trains the eye to be attentive. The dome of the sky smolders cerulean, sapphire, indigo, crimson, amber, saffron, lavender, periwinkle, and plum.

The level of noticing that the prairie teaches is only achieved through attentiveness and stillness, and it's often found in solitude.

Perhaps this is why many Native Americans went on their vision quests atop buttes. It is by looking out that we can finally see within.

The boundary of the mixed-grass prairie is supple. Over dozens of miles the tall grasses, such as big bluestem, which can grow to more than six feet in height, lose their grip as they are replaced by the short grasses. There is a gradual change—there is no strong boundary, but rather a gentle flow. The mixed-grass prairie of North Dakota is the geographical center—the heart—of the continent.

Yet we are a culture that plays to the edges. We are fascinated with coastal cities, with density, with, as the writer Gretel Ehrlich says, building *against* space. But in the great middle is the core from which everything flows. It is the center upon which everything depends. When a wound in the heart festers, rot sweeps through the body—and this rot, in a place where little attention from the wider culture is given, can replicate, if not fester, over generations, spreading to the rest of the bioregions slowly, methodically, if not metaphorically, until we all are reduced to a stubble.

# 2.

Each year during childhood, Dad and I went to Borenko Coal, near Nelson Lake, four miles from our house, to get coal for our fireplace. I was his small helper.

Dad lifted me into our silver Dodge, a two-door pickup with a shiny ram's head atop the hood. A scratchy blanket with southwestern patterns prickled my legs as we rumbled across the roadway, a blue slice of Nelson Lake water coming into view, breaking the velvety, brown hills.

Once there, Dad, trim, with a red handlebar mustache, pulled the pickup under a large chute, glanced between mirrors to make sure the bed was centered. He put the truck in park and gave a thumbs-up to the man working in the trailer ahead of us.

Large black chunks of coal tumbled into the bed, which bucked and jolted as it filled. On occasion, Dad looked over and sometimes smiled. His hair was still red; no crow's feet then around his eyes. The chalky smell of smoke from his clothes perfumed the cab.

Once the rocking stopped, Dad put the truck in gear and we drove away, heavier with the weight of coal, Nelson Lake slipped behind flaxen hills. At home, he propped open the entryway door leading to a bin built of two-by-fours and plywood. He handed me a pair of his large leather work gloves and then smaller pieces of coal to haul into the entryway and plop in the bin.

The chunks were luminous. As if flecked with jewels, the coal glistened in sunlight. Piece by piece the bin filled with the promise of winter warmth, of us gathered around our coal stove heating the living room. Sometimes, in winter, I was allowed to go outside, make a snowball, and bring it inside to place on our hot, black stovetop. The snow steamed and crackled, and a pool of water grew, soaking up the smaller and smaller globe of snow.

Hot and cold, hot and cold. Even my parents must have known then the costs of this warmth—black soot flaked across the floor; ashes were hauled outside to cool.

Coal is dirty. But it put food on our table, it kept us warm, it paid for ski trips to the Black Hills and Bozeman, Montana, or family vacations to Disney World and Key West.

# 3.

ONE DAY, I SAT at Grandma Brorby's vanity, in Aunt Shelia's old room, while Grandma fiddled with her pearls and asked, "Would you like to have some fun, honey?"

I never said no to Grandma, the woman who peeled my apples and cut my bologna sandwiches into little triangles without the crust—she knew I didn't like crust.

Grandma lifted me up and plopped me on her lap. She unscrewed the lid of a small vial; her acrylic nails clicked against plastic.

"Do you like how my nails look, Taylor?"

Oh yes, I told her. I liked them a lot.

"Would you like your nails to look like mine?"

I closed my eyes to think about it (we liked to keep each other in suspense). I opened my eyes and looked into the bright light of the vanity.

Grandma rested her chin on my small shoulder, her curled brown hair tickling my ear.

"Yes," I said.

Grandma's white teeth glistened behind me; her eyes glittered behind her large glasses.

We sat and she hummed as, stroke by stroke, my nails turned crimson—one, two, three, until all ten shined like bright little apples. And then Grandma held my hands, one by one, and blew.

WHEN DAD CAME to pick me up, I bounded up the green-carpet stairs like Daisy, my Grandma's black dachshund. Dad saw me, and I stopped. I knew that look. His eyes flashed to Grandma.

"Go back downstairs," he said, and I slid on my butt, bounced harder and harder on each step because I knew I had done something wrong.

I went and sat in front of the vanity and stared into the mirror.

"Mom, I have one son and one daughter, not two daughters," I heard him yell.

Each word jolted me as I sat in my small chair. I held my cheeks with my fingers and then peeled the paint from my nails.

# 4.

THE FIRST MEMORY I have of my sister, Tanya, is of her lying down on her back on the ashen-colored carpet in our trailer house, her long red hair fanning out from her head, a wide smile spread across her face. Ten years older than me, Tanya was like a third parent in my life. She'd lift her legs straight up from her pelvis, bend at the knee, and tap her femur. "Hop up here, Nerdbomber," she'd say.

I, still in a diaper, cruised over toward her, gripped her hands as she slid my small Jell-O body on top of her legs. I never let go of her. She'd rock me up and down; her bangs, secured in place with hairspray, bounced as the weight of me pulled her legs toward the ground. I slid back and forth across her acid-washed jeans, her Hypercolor T-shirt changing colors before my eyes. I'd start giggling, knowing what was about to happen.

"One—"

I'd start to smile, my tuft of red hair flowing up and down.

"Two—"

I'd let out a cackle.

"Three!"

I'd shoot over her like being shot from a trebuchet. I somersaulted above her head, Tanya's hands firmly gripped mine, and I'd stick a landing, the force of which made me shoot from side to side as if I was balancing on a waterbed. Woozy, I'd laugh as Tanya slowly let go of me. Sometimes I tumbled, other times I stayed right side up, my diaper a little lower on my hips. She'd help me hoist it back to its proper place before I'd crow for her to launch me again and again and again. And all the while, my big sister never let me go.

# 5.

As a child, my father often made me cry—his loud, gravelly voice always seemed tinged with anger. Even saying good morning could provoke me to tears.

Once, while zipping up my jacket so I could go play in the snow, I accidentally looked down as the zipper rumbled up my belly. It caught my neck.

I wailed, and large tears fell onto my mittens.

My father stood up and pointed down at me. "Remember," he said, "Brorby men never cry."

But whenever I wanted to draw something challenging—a toy gargoyle or a triceratops—I would always take it to Dad. Usually it was in the low light just before bed, just before he would leave for the graveyard shift at the Bobcat factory, where he worked as a welder, forty miles out of our small town in coal country.

Dad would take my sketch pad, set down my toy, grip my pencil, and make light strokes across the page—never hard, never committed lines. As I sat by his frame, hardened by manual labor, perfumed by cigarette smoke, I watched gentle lines flow across the page.

My father's large fingers gripped my small pencil, the sound of the graphite against the paper mesmerized me. Later, his strokes could be pressed upon by me, tracing his movements, apprenticing to make something beautiful in his wake.

But my father fumed when I wouldn't grab him a leech or worm while we fished for walleye. I played with a toy Arctic tern, leashed on a short plastic rope alongside our boat. As we trolled against the current, and I held the rope, I watched the decoy make gentle rings in the hypnotic water. I daydreamed, which, in my family—where I was always encouraged to be in movement, to be doing something— was a type of sin.

Whenever I was caught reading a book, my parents would tell me to go and *do* something, which was a euphemism for *go outside*: to play baseball, to go fishing, to be like the other boys.

Outside was an amber world of wheat, gentling rolling hills where I'd sometimes be chased by angry ottomans of fur—badgers. Outside was where I escaped with my tackle box and sketchbook, walked past a weathered, abandoned farmhouse, weeds choking the scoria roadway leading to its now glassless window frames. The house, I thought, was certainly haunted.

The Square Butte Creek was my babysitter then, a twig of a stream I'd meander along as I hunted northern pike, watched musk-rats cruise along its grassy banks. No other children wandered in this watery world. My classmates played video games, worked on the family ranch, and didn't escape to the musical world of western meadowlarks and ring-necked pheasants.

Nature was the great god I sought. In nature, there was time for stillness, for me to sketch a great blue heron as it stalked small minnows. In nature, I relished how close I could crawl toward a beaver before the great paddle of its tail walloped the surface of the water.

All this was for me, mine for the savoring. The world beyond my small town fueled my mind on the page. I drew largemouth bass and northern pike lurking under cattails. I couldn't see that watery world below the surface, but I trained my eye to notice the opalescent clams glimmering through the cocoa-colored creek or the shortening tails of tadpoles in small, shallow pools.

But farther downstream was Nelson Lake, the only lake in North Dakota that never freezes. It's a man-made reservoir whose water cools the coal-fired turbine engines of Minnkota Power, the power plant where my mother spent her career as an administrative assistant.

Beyond the loamy hills near the Square Butte Creek swung the large dragline that ripped lignite coal from dusty North Dakota soil. The dragline was a part of the mine where Grandpa Brorby worked—the mine that supplied the coal to Minnkota Power.


THE EARLIEST WRITTEN account of lignite mining in Dakota Territory, to the best of my knowledge, is from 1873, when small mines were developed along the main transportation routes in what, in 1889, would become western North Dakota. To get to the coal, settlers tunneled into outcrops or simply dug the lignite out from the land—a technique like that used in modern strip mining.

By 1900 there were seventy-three "wagon mines" in the state—small, seasonal mines where farmers and ranchers brought their buckboards to the site and filled them with coal before making the trek back to their sod houses or tar-paper shacks.

In 1918, the Whittier Coal Company and Truax Brothers began strip-mining with horse-drawn elevating graders and dump wagons. The wagons disposed of till and hauled lignite to a loading site, where it would then be transported by rail.

Over the next half century, mining spread from northwestern North Dakota and followed the miry Missouri River east, as far as Underwood, fifty miles upstream from the capital of Bismarck. Later, because water is required to generate electricity, large electrical generating stations began to develop along Lake Sakakawea, the two-hundred-mile-long reservoir in western part of the state, as well as the main artery of the continent, the Missouri River. Mining had arrived in south-central North Dakota.

Grandpa Brorby began in the coal mines in Divide County and then, when coal was discovered in the late 1960s, moved his family— my grandmother, my father, and his three siblings—south to Center, in Oliver County. Others moved from Noonan, a coal town in Divide County, cutting the population in half, for it was a company town, and this new exodus drained Noonan of money, of people, of story. The city of Center, though, spread, if gently—new houses, a larger school, new Scandinavian names, in a community of farmers and ranchers that were Germans-from-Russia.

The Square Butte Creek, just outside Center, was dammed. The dam was made of jagged rocks that, when wet, looked like the newly discovered coal but still held the water back, creating, over time, Nelson Lake.

AND THEN, by November 1970, a power plant was completed. The Milton R. Young Station, owned by Minnkota Power, featuring a five-hundred-foot smokestack, was a high-rise on the surrounding prairie. Visible for miles, it chugged while burning coal like a lit cigarette—a Polaris for me on late-night rides home from Bismarck.

From a distance, the power plant looked like something built by a small child with blocks—large squares against the rolling, tan hills. The top of each block had a clear rim of black, as if drawn on by a marker. The base of each block of the building was a crisp white, a type of almost-camouflage in winter, when the sky smeared gray and white on overcast days.

Metal gates wrapped around the entrances to the plant—no barbed wire—and if you tried to pass through the front entrance gate, a voice would issue from a silver box with punched holes, after pressing a button, like an old telephone, the voice asking who you were and whom you wanted to see. If you answered correctly, the metal gate jolted back, allowing passage like some medieval entrance to another world.

On the grounds of the power plant, small industrial four-wheelers zipped across the cement, darted between garages, carrying men in hard hats, wearing plaid or denim shirts. It seemed like a city to my callow young eyes—one, though, without windows and that was all too often covered in soot.

# 6.

I N MY CHILDHOOD BEDROOM was a varnished oak box lined with
red felt that Grandpa Brorby had made for me. This small chest
was where I kept my treasures: a Morgan silver dollar, some marbles
(one black and one blue), and a jagged lump of coal.

In quiet moments, I'd open the box and roll these gems in my
cupped hands. I felt the weight of a history I did not yet know.

For me, it begins with coal—a black, speckled not-quite rock
that looks as if stars streak across its surface, this black hole that pulls
the whole world, as if gravitationally, to its center.

There, in my palm, I'd hold the universe in the making, layer
upon layer of Earth's history—one part dinosaur bone, two parts
bird feather, many parts mystery, compressed by millennia.

So much remains seen and hidden in North Dakota.

As I turned it over, I'd wonder what the coal could tell me about
the Stygian underworld from which it was created. I held it up to the
light, rotated it like a diamond, only to set it back in the box.

# 7.

M Y MOTHER AND I often sat in the kitchen-cum-dining-room
of our trailer house at my squat plastic Playskool table with a
white top and forest green legs. I'd pull off the lids of my Play-Doh
containers, and out wafted what smelled to me then like the ocean.
Between our hands we'd roll red and green and blue, warming it to
make the dough pliable, smiling at each other.

I remember my mother's fingernails—how the nail was not
smooth and round, but made up of planks of cartilage dovetailed
together like something from a fine woodworker's shop. Sometimes,
I'd roll my small fingers across the ridges of her nails.

"You are going to have large, beautiful moons under your nails,
just like your father, Taylor," she'd say, smiling.

Sometimes, when I was alone in the bathroom, where the light
was bright, I'd hold my hand up just right, so it would catch the light.
I'd twist my head and squint, checking to see that I had my mother's
ridges and, underneath, my father's moons, a type of celestial landscape blending to become one in me.

———

ONE NIGHT, MOM AND I made a volcano, the green dough rising off the white tabletop. Mom helped me press down with my thumb to make a huge hole in my volcano. Then she rolled the blue dough paper-thin and wrapped it around the volcano's base.

"Look, Taylor, it's a lake."

We rolled the red into tubes and folded them down the sides of my volcano. I imagined *Tyrannosaurus rexes* or stegosauruses running for the hills.

"Look, Mom—it's *lava*," I said, my hands beside my head as I bared my teeth and snarled. We laughed, and then I launched from the table and bolted past our fireplace and down the long, dark hallway to my room. I flipped on the light, ripped off the top of my large plastic toy bin, and grabbed a Batman action figure and a velociraptor. I darted back down the hallway, burst past the counter, and broke into the kitchen.

"Ta-da!" I cried.

"Oh, Batman and that dinosaur are going to make this look *so* good," Mom said. She then held up her hand, looked shocked, and said, "But wait—let's make your volcano erupt."

I sat in my small yellow plastic chair and kicked my legs back and forth under the table. This was always my favorite part.

Mom went to the sink and snagged a bottle of soap.

She returned and hovered over the volcano, dripping some liquid into it. I looked up at her and she winked.

She glided over to the cabinet and retrieved some baking soda and vinegar. I shot up from my seat and rushed over to a drawer to snatch a spoon.

We both took our places. We knew what to do.

Spoonful by small spoonful, I ladled the soda into my volcano. Mom popped open the vinegar lid. She held the bottle above the volcano. I bit my lower lip as a small stream began to shoot through the air and then, suddenly, the volcano erupted.

I squealed as the suds slid down the side and slipped around the ankles of my velociraptor and wet Batman's cape.

# 8.

ON A SUNNY DAY under a cobalt sky on the Missouri, we shoved off from the United Power Association's boat landing in my grandparents' blue Sylvan fishing boat, churning the beautiful ocher-colored water as we plowed upriver. The minnow bucket, filled with fatheads, swished in the stern, wetting the navy carpet.

Grandpa Hatzenbihler slowed the boat and we glided up and against the current, no longer having to hold on to our hats. Cottonwood leaves twitched like silver coins in the noonday sun. I heard a *thwack* in the distance. Grandpa, silver hair shooting out from his trucker hat, gripped the key with his sausage-sized fingers and shut off the motor.

"Come give me a hand, Taylor," he said.

I tromped to the bow of the boat, wrapped in my orange-and-yellow lifejacket, my head topped with a bucket hat. I'm sure I wore jeans, for that was the Summer of the Jean, as my family dubbed it, a summer when I only wore jeans because I, at seven, played baseball and did not want to sunburn my legs.

"Help me toss the anchor, will you?" Grandpa chimed.

I grabbed the nylon rope with Grandpa as we waddled toward the front of the bow, the heavy, blue plastic anchor swinging like a putter between our hands. My hands rubbed against Grandpa's belly, large and round from years of dough and cream—German-from-Russia cooking—and homemade chokecherry wine.

"Ready?" he asked. "One, two, three."

The anchor made a loud *ka-plop* and quickly disappeared into that muddy and watery world. Grandpa chuckled and patted me on the back.

"Grandma, can you hand me my pole, please?" he said to his wife, who was dressed in polyester pants and a sleeveless blouse.

"Taylor, can you take this to him?" she asked as she passed me the fishing pole with her liver-spotted hands.

I shuffled from the stern to the bow.

We rigged up, and I got to put the minnows on everyone's hooks. I had learned that it's best to place the hook right under the minnow's mouth, press upward quickly, and pull the hook back around. This usually doesn't kill the minnow, which you want to swim and look normal on the hook—you want to trick coveted walleye into swallowing those suckers, Grandpa had told me.

Sometimes he asked for a big fathead, by which he meant a spawning male—large, black about the body and head. I hated putting these ones on Grandpa's hook; they sounded like crunching chips when I pushed the hook through their heads.

Eventually all three of our lines were in the water, and we sat back and waited for that quick *bam-bam* of a walleye bite.

"Dollar for the first, the most, and the biggest," shouted Grandpa from the bow.

Soon after, Grandma set the hook, and a smile curled around

her thin lips. We heard, "*Scheisse, scheisse, scheisse,*" from the front of
the boat.

Grandma and I giggled.

I got the net as Grandma reeled slowly and methodically.

"There it is, Taylor," she said, and a white belly with that beautiful golden-green scale side sliced up from under the surface.

I plunged the net into the water and scooped underneath the
fish.

"It's a good eater," Grandma laughed to Grandpa, who had
kicked on the live well to fill it with water.

A few fish later, I had already grown tired. I ate a homemade
summer sausage sandwich on homemade buns and juneberry kuchen
and played with my decoy of an Arctic tern alongside the boat.

"It's okay if you want to take a nap, Taylor," said Grandma.

I took off my life jacket, used it as a pillow, and curled up in the
shade behind Grandma's chair. I slept, the gentle purr of the trolling
motor and the soft smack of the river against the bow of the boat
lulling me to sleep.

Later, I woke to the sound of Canada geese blasting above me.

"Grandpa, can I fish up front?" I asked.

"You bet, buddy. Let's pull anchor and troll for a bit, it'll be easier
for you to fish away from the motor anyway."

I put on a sleek silver-green minnow and thought about how
much it must hurt to have a hook through your head, then be
plunged into the murky Missouri, only to be chomped on by a walleye. I swung my pole over the river, opened the reel, and watched
the sinker take the minnow to the bottom. After a few seconds, I
clicked the reel closed and watched the tip of my rod *tick tick tick* as
the weight dragged along the bottom.

A moment passed, an eternity.

My rod bent into a mighty U.

"Grandpa, I think I might have snagged a tree," I yelled.

"Yah, yah, let me come see. Grandma, can you hold my pole?" he asked.

Grandpa lumbered toward me, a wrinkle of sweat on his upper lip.

"Oh, no, that's moving. If it is a tree, keep reeling, but it might be a big something, Taylor. It isn't moving like a walleye."

I kept reeling. I pulled back my rod when I could, like those great saltwater fishermen I watched on television fishing for marlin or sailfish. My hand went tense, so I sometimes did a big pull, took my hand off the reel, opened and closed my fist quickly, then returned to reeling.

"Grandpa, let's pull our lines in just in case Taylor does have a fish on," said Grandma.

Their lines came in and skittered across the surface of the river like dragonflies. My grandparents watched me. Grandpa came toward the bow.

"Slow and steady, Taylor. This might be a wall-mounter."

*Don't break the line*, I said to myself.

Even if it was a tree, I wanted to see it.

And then it came. It was no tree. A snout broke the surface, four barbels dripped with water, coal black eyes looked at me from an ashen body.

"Grandpa, it's huge!"

"Cecelia, I need a knife," said Grandpa.

I looked up at him, but he didn't look at me.

"Here, Monsadius," said Grandma.

I kept reeling. The large fish's gray snout sliced out of the water. Its belly was white. Its tail looked like a shark. Its side was wrapped in gray armor.

My eyes widened.

Grandpa grabbed the fishing line out from the tip of my pole, pulled it toward him, and slashed the line. My pole snapped straight, and the ghost submerged back into the water.

"Why did you do that? Why couldn't we bring the fish in the boat?" I cried.

"We can't, Taylor, it's illegal," said Grandpa.

"Why?" I wailed.

"Because it's against the law; we'd get in big trouble if we kept it."

"But we don't get in trouble for keeping walleye or crappie or bass."

"That's a pallid sturgeon. They're endangered—it's why we can't keep it."

"What does 'endangered' mean?" I asked.

"It means it might go extinct," said Grandma.

"What does that mean?"

"It means that there are so few of them left that, if we don't put them back to protect them, there'll be no more," she replied.

I set down my pole, grabbed my toy tern, and tossed it in the water. As it bobbed against the boat, I thought about the monster of a fish I had just seen—about it lurking down below me, one of so few in number. I wondered if it was lonely, if it felt as alone as I often felt. And then I wondered—now that I knew—what else in my life was at risk for passing away.

# 9.

LIGHT FILTERED THROUGH my blinds on an early Saturday morning. It was Earth Day 1995. I hurled from bed in my Batman pajamas, hustled toward my chest of drawers, stood on my toes, and opened the top drawer. I worked my hand from right to left. From the drawer I pulled my black Batman cape, complete with Velcro patches, tossed it around my shoulders, and squished the Velcro to my pajama shirt.

Mom and Dad were still asleep. I tiptoed past their room and scooted on my butt down the fourteen steps. Past the front door and the dining room was the large living room—at least, it seemed large to me. We had just moved from our trailer home to a blue split-level across town. We now had a basement. I had both a bedroom and a room for the drafting table Mom and Dad bought me so that I could draw in solitude. Reams of unused printer paper Mom brought home from work bricked the room's walls.

Outside, it was late April; a few patches of snow streaked the ground. I touched the knob on our wood-paneled television and static snapped my fingertips. My hair stood on end as I clenched and

unclenched my feet in our soft ashen carpet. I turned the larger knob
to the number 13—Nickelodeon.

I plopped down on the carpet and criss-cross applesauced my
legs. On the screen, a large yellow bull began to sing. The cartoon
was about Rocko, a wallaby, and his friend Heifer. That day, there
was a new character, Captain Compost Heap. CCH, as others called
him, told the residents of O-Town (where Rocko lived) that the
dump, which looked like a large muffin top, was too full of trash,
and that the local corporation, Conglom-O, was dumping its waste
in the local river. CCH began to bob and sing to the menagerie of
animals about recycling and composting, warning that if the residents of O-Town didn't take care of the planet, they would get what
they deserved.

The compost heap reached toward the sky, its eyes strained, as if
to sacrifice a virgin to a volcano god. Pink chemical compounds rep-
resenting fluorocarbons darted across the screen and blasted toward
the ozone layer. They chomped as if devouring donuts. Captain
Compost Heap pulled out a magnifying glass and sang, "They're too
small to be seen with normal vision." And a choir of fluorocarbons
harmonized in shrill voices, "But there's getting to be more of us
each year."

The frame cut back to the O-Town dump. Captain Compost
Heap's voice rang from the background when a dark character came
into view.

Heifer said, "Look, it's the Grim Recycler!" And the Grim Recycler said, "No autographs, please." A wolf and pig bounced, making
farting noises. I giggled.

Outside our large bay window, past our evergreen tree, rose the
white and gray spire of smoke from the power plant.

# 10.

To the west of Center, a large dragline swings back and forth every day as its mammoth bucket, weighing over one hundred tons, maneuvers with a boom, scrapes away the grass and soil of the prairie.

Grandpa Hatzenbihler, a hard-up farmer, lamented that the Baukol-Noonan, Inc., mine moved west instead of east—surely there was coal under his farm. The dragline made other families wealthy while he struggled with the yearly harvest.

Once the overburden—the rock and soil atop a coal deposit—is removed, the trucks come to transport coal from the strip mine to Minnkota Power. Large clouds of dust kick up. As a child, I loved watching the trail shoot up and hover as the trucks rumbled toward the power plant.

The coal feeds massive boilers in the belly of the plant, which turn the chunks of earth into electricity and heat. Because the coal burns so hot, Nelson Lake water is needed to cool the power plant's boilers. In winter, steam snails into the air from the lake. Fishermen wrapped in snowmobile suits hurl lures through ropes of mist, hoping to catch largemouth bass.

Between the mine, which we refer to as BNI, and Minnkota Power are overflow ponds—backwater that gathers from marshes and small, unnamed creeks the size of twigs. The ponds, rimmed with emerald-colored reeds, are the size of football fields.

A gunmetal gray farmhouse, worn from wind, water, and snow, marked the entrance to these ponds. When I was young, my mother told me that an old man lived there, but in all my hunting for fish along the cattails, I never saw a vehicle pull up to the farm, much less a light through its windows. I kept looking over my shoulder as I cast lures along the reeds, just in case.

The ponds were a nesting ground for carp, whose small, supple mouths, when they came up for air, looked like belly buttons. Their large black backs broke the surface and eventually one would roll among the cluster and shine his belly, the color of creamed corn, against the pale, fading light.

At eleven, after catching Brad Pitt casting in the movie *A River Runs Through It*, I asked my father what he was doing. "Fly-fishing," Dad said. And that year, on Christmas morning, a fly rod was waiting next to my velvety stocking.

The ponds were where I taught myself to fly-fish. A large hill rose in the southern pond near a tawdry beaver lodge. I cast my large nest of feather and fur back and forth; after it broke the serene glass of the pond, I stripped the line to help the fly submerge and cruise along the cattail reeds.

This was a warm, murky aquatic ecosystem of muskrat, fish, and amphibians. The chorus of northern leopard frogs was so loud that it sometimes felt like a subwoofer in my ears. I would see whitetail deer come to the water's edge at twilight—ever so slightly, the deer descended the steep southern hill's embankment. Near the edge, they would crane their necks; the flicking of tongues sent gentle ripples across the pond. Ears twitched, first this way, then that. If I threw a stick in the pond, the deer, half a football field away, jolted. They stared at me as the stick bobbed in the water.

It was a serene world, and we all, the deer and I, sensed danger lurked in the distance.

# 11.

By his actions and decisions, James J. Hill, the Empire Builder, shaped early life from Minneapolis to Seattle after Europeans arrived. Building his great western railroads in the decades of the 1870s through the 1890s, Hill opened the last remnants of the Homestead Act to cultivation and commercial interests. European settlers then bought their land through Hill's Great Northern Railway with the assurance that their crops and goods would be transported on Hill's railroad, securing the magnate a monopoly on the commerce across the northern Great Plains.

With land on their mind, my ancestors left the boreal air of Norway for the sea of tall grasses in Minnesota. The Homestead Act, originally passed and signed into law in 1862, had opened vast tracts of land—160 acres for any white man, white woman, or freeman who would make a go of it. The stiff stalks of grass waving in the afternoon breeze must have exuded the scent of possibility. Once cut and plowed, the land exposed the rich, brown soil of the Red River Valley of western Minnesota, a newly minted state.

The Brorbys settled near Rothsay in Otter Tail County, two

hundred miles northwest of Minneapolis, in the 1860s. Our name—
*Brorby*—is rooted in place: a farm name meaning "brother city," with
no paterfamilias ties, like other Norwegians. A name taken from the
farm my family must have longed for or longed to remember.

Describing the reaction of his protagonist, the recent immigrant
farmer Per Hansa, to the western tallgrass prairie in his novel *Giants
in the Earth*, Ole Rölvaag wrote, "Such soil! Only to sink the plow
into it, to turn over the sod—and there was a field ready for seed-
ing. . . . And this was not just ordinary soil, fit for barley, and oats,
and potatoes, and hay, and that sort of thing; indeed, it had been
meant for much finer and daintier uses; it was the soil for *wheat*,
the king of all grains! Such soil had been especially created by the
good Lord to bear this noble seed; and here was Per Hansa, walking
around on a hundred and sixty acres of it, all his very own!"

But the Brorbys didn't take to Minnesota, on the eastern edge of
ancient Lake Agassiz, that tabletop flat land. Two generations after
settling in the United States, in the 1910s, my great-grandpa Melvin,
like the characters in Rölvaag's novels, uprooted his family and left
the Red River Valley, moving farther west to the pothole prairie of
northwest North Dakota.

Socked in the corner of the state, Divide County borders Montana to the west and Saskatchewan to the north.

I grew up in the house that coal built. Great-Grandpa Melvin
started up the family practice of digging for coal. Coal provided. It
fortified our psyches and lined our bank accounts.

Fossil fuels flow through my veins.

# 12.

I REMEMBER JEERING CIRCLES on the asphalt playground in the early morning light. Boys and girls, cupped hands over their mouths, egging Charlie and Andrew on. *Hit him. Take him down. Put him in a headlock.*

I looked on from the periphery—Andrew, three years older than me, trudged like a mini-Quasimodo, his weight behind every hook or jab. Charlie, trim and wiry, lunged, hurled haymakers. The two boys eventually locked, rolled on the hard ground; sharp gravel cut their skin, a crimson trail on the elbow, above the brow, a swollen purple flower blossomed on the cheek.

In first grade Charlie had invited me to his birthday party, along with six other boys. No one went. He got into fights, my parents said. I couldn't play with boys who got into fights.

I walked to the slide, sat, and waited for the bell to ring. Mrs. Sheetz came out through the sleek metal doors and snagged each boy up by the ear. The circle scattered like ants.

———

I'D BE LYING if I said there wasn't a part of me on those early mornings that wanted to step into that circle, to test my mettle—but there
was something else burning in both those boys, some deep-seated
anger churning in their bodies, something that needed to be exor-
cised. They both were raised by family members.

The fights were because Charlie would pick on Andrew's younger
brother; Charlie called him *retard stupid idiot dipshit.*

When each boy was yanked up by the ear, it wasn't anger I saw.
It looked like some billowing sadness, a dark mantle of clouds gathering on the horizon of their lives.

# 13.

WHILE WAITING FOR Mrs. Schmidt, our third-grade teacher, to reveal our spelling words for the week, I crossed my right leg over my left, just like Matt Lauer, the host of *Today*, whom I watched every morning before school. Sleek and dapper, I wanted to be composed, put together, just like him.

"Only girls sit like that," said Wesley.

Boys, Wesley told me—if they crossed their legs at all—were supposed to rest their ankle on the opposite leg's knee, making a type of triangle gap between the crotch and legs.

I protested. "My way feels more comfortable."

"What?" asked Wesley. "Because you don't have a penis? Only *girls* sit like that—because they don't have penises."

I uncrossed my legs, slid my tibia along my knee until my ankle rested on my kneecap. I grimaced as a sharp pain shot through my pelvis. It hurt to sit like this.

———

YEARS EARLIER, when I still lived near Wesley, he and I rode our bicycles on the abandoned driveway next to his trailer house. There must have once been a trailer there, but it was long gone, a square of broken cement the only remnant of any previous residence. Weeds shot through the cracks. Sometimes they'd smack against our skinny shins as we whirled into a tempest, circling around the driveway, pumping our legs to pass each other.

I screeched to a halt, the black rubber of my tires streaking the cement like a line of charcoal. I told Wesley to wait right there.

I dropped my bike, ran through our crisp, clean grass, and bolted into the entryway of our trailer to snag an ice cream bucket. I shot soap into the bottom of the bucket, zipped outside, and cranked on our garden hose. Suds frothed and, nearly full, I turned off the hose.

I waddled over toward Wesley, my right hand holding the bucket as my left arm, perpendicular to my side, jutted out to balance me. Worried, I walked slowly so I didn't drop my soap brew.

When I reached Wesley, he was yanking weeds out of the cement, tossing them like carrot tops into the grass. I asked him if he had seen the ant mounds while we zipped around the driveway. Of course, he hadn't. He was too focused on pedaling hard and trying to beat me.

The anthills looked like gunpowder—volcanic little mounds where red or black ants disappeared and reappeared through a pin-sized hole.

"Watch," I said. Tipping the bucket carefully, I poured a thin line of soapy water from high above the hills, directly into the holes.

A grin spread across Wesley's face.

Suds bubbled atop the mounds like lava. The water gurgled.

I stopped. We waited. No ants appeared.

I ran back to the house and filled three separate ice cream buckets. I hollered from the front yard at Wesley to come from the abandoned lot and help. We stationed ourselves around more anthills. Our plan now was less precise—no sudsy waterfalls this time. It was time for full-on floods.

We ran around the driveway. Water gushed from our buckets as we squealed. Soap foamed and glistened across the wet pavement.

When my buckets were empty, I ran toward the house, turned on the hose, and pulled it as far as possible, folding my small thumb over the nozzle. A great wave of water shimmered in the air before falling like thunderbolts across the anthills.

I needed some way to assert my power, to show that I was in control, that, like a general, I could give orders and others would follow. Wesley had emasculated me earlier in the week, and, in the realm of boyhood, there is no sharper insult than to be called a girl.

We insult those we plan to control, those we seek to overpower. Our insecurities and weaknesses transfigure into attempts at domination—that's what Wesley did in class, whether he knew it or not. The detail of how I sat became an opportunity for control, a moment to remind me that, to fit in, I needed to conform—that *we* don't do *that* here. To sit properly, you must sit like *this*.

It was a whittling moment, an opportunity to chisel me into an acceptable form, to see if I would follow someone else's orders, to do as I was told.

Now, I needed those ants to die—to drown them, to show Wesley that I could kill with something as gentle as soapy water. I needed to show him that I was in control over whether something lived or died, that I could order Wesley to be an accomplice, to do my bidding— that he, too, would enjoy seeing the small red and black bodies bubble to the surface, char in the afternoon sun, that he would help bring about the apocalypse as I ordained it.

I *needed* to show that I also possessed power, that I was a powerful little boy.

BERN AMBLED DOWN Prairie Avenue, shaded by elms, bookended with ranch homes and fertilized lawns. He held a paper bag in his suntanned hands. Adam and I were practicing T-ball, my Louisville Slugger over our right shoulders. We tried to wind it in a circle like Kirby Puckett, before unleashing hellfire against that little ball on a stick. Usually, we missed, spun around in a circle, and then looked back to make sure the other wasn't laughing—and tried again.

That day, Adam cracked it—a line drive right at Bern, who caught it. Did he giggle or cackle?

We pulled our caps close to our eyes and kicked at the grass.

Bern sauntered toward us.

"You have to get it from him. You hit it," I said and pushed Adam toward Bern, who looked as big as a barn.

"Sorry, Bern," said Adam, and Bern stretched out his arm, pockmarked from cigarettes. He let the men from the coal mine put out their smokes on his scaled skin down at the bar: one butt for each snifter of bourbon.

Bern nodded, grunted something into the air, and moseyed along, step by step, and we turned to practice once more, to dream of the Major Leagues, of getting far away from here.

# 14.

THEY LIVED TOGETHER in a tawny house on the south end of town, across from the Corner Stop. The biology teacher and the home ec teacher, track coaches too—they shared a house together. One had curly hair the color of sand, the other straight black hair, typically tied in a bun.

Later, when I got older, I heard rumors about how they liked to linger in the locker room after meets, talked with the players who stripped and got in the shower, who washed the sweat and salt from their game-tired bodies. I only knew the teachers in passing—on my way to the library in first grade, marching in alphabetical order for Mrs. Sherwin. We scurried as the bell rang and high schoolers flooded the hallway. I remember that their smiles looked the same—gaps between their front teeth; big, warm grins, mild bemusement behind their spectacles.

Later, they moved, together, to a larger town.

# 15.

WHEN I WAS TEN, my parents and I took a vacation to Key West, Florida. I remember hordes of people bustling down Duval Street on a warm day.

We passed by Ripley's Believe It or Not, moving in a thick crowd. I stuck close to my parents, sometimes holding their hands to make sure I wouldn't get swallowed up by a drove of strangers. A large man, taller than Dad, resplendent in a sequined dress, fake eyelashes, and blond wig, sashayed alongside us.

"Hey, sugar, wanna come take a walk on the wild side?" he said to my father.

As we walked, I whispered to Dad, the man having now lost pace with us. "Dad, why did that man say that to you?"

"I'll tell you when you're older," he grunted, tightening his grip around my hand.

EVERY SUMMER BEFORE I reached middle school, my mother and I, along with Aunt Raylene and two of her children, traveled out to my uncle Scott and aunt Trudy's house in Billings. The dry heat of August meant that the Tongue and Powder Rivers had already turned to dust as we blazed across eastern Montana.

These trips were to see family, but they were also for back-to-school shopping, my aunts and Mom lugging us six cousins to Old Navy to buy clothes in a state with no sales tax. In this memory I'm thirteen, and my cousins and I laid out our new school clothes on the basement floor. My cousins—on my orders—decided to host a fashion show for our parents. I must have seen glimmers of runway shows on television. Aunt Raylene's children, Katie and Evan—eleven and six—joined Scott and Trudy's three kids, Grant, Chase, and Paige—seven, four, and one. Before us were piles of new blue jeans, T-shirts, polos, and shorts.

"Uncle Scott, we're almost ready," I shouted from the bottom steps. "Can you lower the lights and turn on the music?"

"Got it, buddy!" Uncle Scott bellowed.

We put on our first round of clothes and began to march up the stairs one by one. I instructed my younger cousins to wait until the person in front of them got back to the steps before tromping up to our parents and modeling for them.

"Remember," I whispered, "turn your head from side to side, twist your hip. Stop in front of them, twirl, and march back down. When you get down, change into your next outfit as fast as you can." I looked away from my cousins and yelled up the stairs. "Everyone ready up there?"

The music started to pump.

"First, from preschool just down the road," I announced and paused. "Chase! Chase is sporting athletic blue shorts from Old Navy, paired with a green polo top! Whether he's coloring outside of the lines or kicking a soccer ball, this four-year-old is ready for whatever the day throws at him!"

I heard a wash of laughter as Chase, who was out of sight, worked the crowd. Downstairs we could see flashes from our mothers' cameras as Uncle Scott clapped to the beat of the music.

"Next up is Evan!"

I announced for everyone. I announced because it meant I was in control, that I controlled the narrative. The narrative I already had from family trips to Florida, the narrative that I was the only grandchild who loved musicals, the only one who hid out in his art room rather than joined grown men in garages to discuss the mechanics of trucks and rifles and football, like my other male cousins.

There was an affection I sought, a type of recognition I knew I needed, one that, at least at my aunt and uncle's place in Billings, was rooted in being an announcer, rooted in entertaining people.

I knew then, as I know now, that if you make people laugh, if you can amuse them, they won't beat the shit out of you, they won't suspect you of being gay.

# 16.

On a sunny Saturday, Mom dropped me off at the Civic Center for art class. Me, eight women, and Jack, our art teacher. Elfish, wire-browed, Jack, at sixty, was my height in middle school.

Easels dotted the cold white room. The radiators rumbled. We rubbed our hands. The women were ecstatic that I, a boy, was taking art lessons. Some painted mule deer, others bouquets of flowers; a woman named Carla was painting from a black-and-white portrait, rendering her pastel version in color.

"My dress was actually green, but purple is my favorite color," she said as she slid a stubby pastel out of her box.

Later in the day, Jack and I went into a storage room, which was filled with faux wooden tables and gray metal chairs. Somehow, it felt like a slaughterhouse.

Jack flicked on the projector, on which we then placed the picture of a brown trout I wanted to sketch. Jack turned the dial. In and out of focus went the trout, a brown creel next to its plump body.

Jack looked as if he were about to tell ghost stories when out came his pencil—a slash here, a mark there. The pencil jolted across the bumpy pastel paper. Jack's eyes narrowed. The projector whirred while I pulled at the collar of my shirt, because there was no airflow.

I watched his hands, colored with pastel; his gaze never left the image.

He stepped back, held the pencil near his mouth as his other hand, free, went limp at his side.

And I wondered if he knew, wondered if he could tell. A boy and a man, silence between them, making art in a dim-lit room on the prairie.

He sketched differently than Dad—Jack held the pencil firmly, made committed lines on the paper. He had spent his twenties, the women told me over lunch, sketching tourists down in Florida rather than welding boilers in Iowa, like my father had.

And then the door opened, and a chill filled the small room.

# 17.

WE GRAPPLED, WESLEY AND I, wrapped thin arms around each other's heads. Wrestling, it's what boys do. We swayed back and forth like bluestem in the breeze, tried to throw the other down; on our backs we tried to wrap our feet and pull the other forward, make him fall onto the hard brown carpet.

That's what we wanted—to be on top, to hold the other in place, to wrap our arms around the other's armpits and press down on the back of his neck to do a full nelson, or snap his forearm behind his back and lift it up into a chicken wing, or to get on the backside, wrap legs around stomach, and pull—we wanted breathing to be hard, to whisper, *Hurts, doesn't it?*

We didn't grab each other's head and slam the neck onto our shoulder to do a Stone Cold stunner, but we'd body-slam each other on the couch. We didn't lift each other up by the chest and smack down to do a Rock bottom, but we'd snake an arm around the other's neck, pull back toward ourselves, and do a sleeper hold. It was our way to show we were men, to show that, if we ever wanted to, we could hurt each other.

In second grade we, just the two of us, played ball tag. I kept getting the ball, hurled it like a stone at Wesley, kept taunting, "Tag, you're it!" and then ran and got the ball again. Over and over. "Tag, tag, tag, tag!" And finally, Wesley, who was larger and slower than me, picked up my baseball bat and whipped it like a tomahawk. When it knocked me back into the cold grass, I cried, "Jesus Fucking Christ!" for the first time.

By eighth grade, our bodies had changed. Stronger, lower voiced, we pushed harder, sweated more, our faces a welter of crimson. Wesley played ball, ran track. I did speech and practiced saxophone. But that day, we tossed and tumbled, and when I pinned Wesley, we both saw it, couldn't unsee it—that our bodies had changed, and mine had betrayed me.

In eighth grade Henry grew baseballs in his arms. In swimming class, I had to turn away, had to keep from fading into a daydream— how he'd wrestle cattle into the cold mud, hold them down, arms locked around their heads, hot iron pressed into their velvet coat, branding them for life. A small coal in my gut told me to look away, told me that the prairie could also burn boys who liked boys—that's what we teach rural children. To be true, move away; find a home elsewhere; move along like a turtle slowly scraping away soil to reach the river, where you belong—someplace, but, no, not here. By eighth grade the boys were already lifting weights, heavy ones, too, but I knew to keep my head down as they snapped towels at testicles, their croaky, pubescent voices cackling with delight. I kept swallowing the coal even though it hurt, hoping, one day, the growing pain inside me would go away.

# 18.

I CAN SEE MYSELF AT FIVE, when I close my eyes, slipping my small feet into my mother's sleek, gray high heels, especially when no one else was around. How I'd traipse around our trailer house like a newborn egret, my arms flapping and flailing to help me stay balanced. I'd also wear Mom's old plum-colored silk pajama top; it flowed down past my apricot-sized knees. I'd jolt and flow around the room, steady myself as my feet shot around in the shoes. I'd say over and over a word of my own invention: *somabeechysomasafa*. I said it whenever my fingers rubbed silk, some euphemism akin to *This feels so damn good*.

Or maybe I'm three, outside with my father—he's trim with thirtysomething metabolism. He's holding shiny pruning shears as he manicures our shrubs: a little taste of English gardening in our coal country life.

I'm in a small gingham apron; my cheeks look as if they're stuffed with chestnuts, my hair is nearly crimson, not yet fired gold from days in the summer sun. I have my candy apple Fiskars scissors and a determined look on my face: I'm helping Dad cut the world to fit my form.

It is the last time there is a picture of me outside of our house in an apron.

Or perhaps I'm six, stomping and somersaulting to my Disney Sing-Along videotapes, the Mickey Mouse head bobbing along to the beat of "That's What Makes the World Go Round" from *The Sword in the Stone*. I became a fish, like Arthur and Merlin, or tromped along to another Disney song when the Genie sang "Prince Ali" from *Aladdin*.

Throughout my childhood I wore down my black, gold, and red pencils. I crumpled sketchbook paper, which grew into small hills, as I obsessively drew Jafar, the villainous grand vizier. Something in his voice, his sense of style (a long, dark flowing robe), his snappy mannerisms, his witty musical lyrics, appealed to me more than the dishwater story line of another Disney hero—in this case, Aladdin—pining for a princess.

I didn't believe in erasing—erasing was for mediocre people. I craved perfection from the start. I'd hold my paper away from me and gaze at the near perfect black line shaping Jafar's robe: not perfect enough. And I'd squish the sheet into a ball before blasting it across my faux wood-paneled room.

I'd launch from my slumped state, sketchbook and colored pencils in hand, barrel down the hallway, break into Tanya's room. I knew, just like she always did, that she would help me draw Jafar. There she'd be, bobbing on her waterbed watching *The Breakfast Club* or listening to Sir Mix-a-Lot or Vanilla Ice. She'd pause her movie or shut off her music, and turn to me.

"Yes, Nerdbomber?"

Exasperated, I'd sigh.

"I just can't get Jafar right! Can you show me how to draw him one more time?"

"One more time," she'd say emphatically, but there never seemed to be a limit to her one-more-times.

Tanya would take my sketch pad from me, turn to a clean page, and take out the black pencil. I'd retrieve my copy of the book version of *Aladdin*, snap it open, and snuggle up next to my sister. Slowly, perfectly, Jafar took shape. I'd watch her eyes dart back and forth from the book to the sketchpad. Under the spell of my big sister, I'd watch her draw his hat, his long face, his robe. I'd steal a glance at her face. Her eyes seemed to hover somewhere in the space between the book I held and the page she drew on. I wanted that type of concentration. I wanted to be as good at drawing as she was.

Suddenly, there he was: Jafar. Tanya would then exhale, slip the pencil back into my hand.

"I'll even let you color him in this time." She smiled at me and tickled my stomach.

I'd snag back my sketchbook, shut it, and huff toward the door.

Before leaving, I'd turn back toward her as she unpaused the movie or unmuted the music.

"Thanks, Consuela."

"No problem, Nerdbomber. Last time."

She knew I'd be back within the hour.

ONE DAY IN SECOND GRADE, Mrs. Fryslie asked us what we wanted to be when we grew up. The other sixteen boys in my class said police officers, farmers, miners—professions they would one day become, their futures set. I said I wanted to be a Disney illustrator.

My classmates laughed.

My lunch box with Timon and Pumbaa, from *The Lion King*, chilled in the large, steel fridge with other boys' Dallas Cowboys or Green Bay Packers lunch boxes.

I'd gaze around at the small bookshelves underneath the windows, up at the reading corner, complete with beanbags, and over to the wall where the class pet hermit crab, Harold, was kept. Mrs. Fryslie, middle-aged with chestnut hair and large glasses, read to us from *The Boxcar Children*, her lilting voice painting the world of the Alden children who kept their milk cold in a waterfall. I found that world amusing. But there was some understanding threaded through my DNA that told me I would always be a misfit if I never left where I came from—there was some desire for a different world, one where I could dance and sing. And in that faraway world, there must be others like me. I hoped there were.

# 19.

A T FOURTEEN I WATCHED, through our dining room window, our neighbor Mark, only two years older than me, soap up his Dodge Stratus. He was shirtless. Mark, like his older brothers Travis and Hunter, was a wrestler. Mark was kind to me, though we never hung out, and he was the youngest of a group of upperclassmen.

Muscled from lifting rusted weights in our small school's wrestling room, Mark sunned his body and moved around his car so unselfconsciously. He made me shiver. Mark had abs. He swaggered when he walked, as if he had the right kind of body that simply belonged to him. He had a large cross tattooed down his spine and across his wide shoulders.

One day, after beers with Mark's dad, my father cracked up when he told me Mark had to have the tattoo artist stop. The pain was too much for him when the needle stung his spine. The tattoo wasn't yet done, and Mark was scared to get it finished.

I didn't care. To me, Mark was strong—and he wrestled.

I wanted to wrestle to be strong, just like Mark. I wanted a strong body, to be in a sport that, at least from the outside, would make middle-school bullies think twice before messing with me.

But my body. My body, that of a redhead, was a landscape easy to read. My body flushed red when I was embarrassed and flared with hormones. Sometimes, I felt I just had the wrong kind of body.

I couldn't wrestle. I couldn't risk rolling around, mounting boys who were older, stronger—my body would betray me. The manifestation of what I knew to be a sin on my silent prairie revealed: that I *liked* other boys.

Years earlier, in elementary school in summer, I'd swim at the school pool, a large, echoey room with high and low diving boards. Even before I jumped in, my eyes watered from the chlorine. As I pruned in the water, some days Mark would come to swim.

I don't remember if he swam laps, or if he soaked in the pool to cool down from lifting weights.

What I do remember, even back then, was my amazement at the freedom he felt in wearing a tight black Speedo. A boy in my own class wore a speedo, but Steven was as large as a bison and on the swim team. Mark wasn't on the swim team. There wasn't a socially acceptable way for boys to reveal their chiseled bodies. Speedos were taboo. But Mark was a wrestler, and no one messed with wrestlers.

I asked my mom to show me Speedos in the JCPenney catalog. When she asked me why, I stammered in my shy way that I was thinking of going out for the swim team and wanted to know if they really did make you swim faster.

"Well then, let's look," she said, confirming what I already knew back in those days before I even hit puberty: I needed to hide what I really liked, what I wanted, or to make up excuses for things—even clothing choices—so that I could fit in where I lived.

I didn't go out for the swim team. I didn't make my mother order a Speedo then.

In middle school, I stewed in my embarrassment over my changing body, over its repeated confirmation of being different. I no longer wore gym shorts to school. I quickly changed in the locker room, my head down. Sometimes I felt a terror and crossed my legs, hard, in class. While I still was the fastest in my class and could do the most pull-ups, after seventh grade my body didn't put on muscle as quickly as the other boys. I stopped growing in eighth grade; at five and a half feet, I was one of the shortest boys on the basketball team. While I grew hair at an alarming rate, the other boys, even when hairless, were filling out in ways my body didn't. That was the year I stopped playing sports and focused on speech and playing saxophone.

One night, on a trip to Bismarck, I quickly roamed the swimsuit section of Scheel's Sporting Goods. I scanned and searched, the way other boys surreptitiously search to buy condoms, for what I hoped would be there.

And it was.

Hidden on a small rack, the closest rung to the ground, were a few black and blue Speedos. Mark wore black, but even then, I knew navy would look better on my slight, Nordic body.

I dashed to the register, plopped down the Speedo, and when the checkout clerk raised an eyebrow, as if I were buying a condom for the first time, I told him I was on the swim team. He nodded, shoving the scrap of nylon into a plastic bag

Before meeting up with my parents, I dumped the bag and the receipt—there was no going back now. I crumpled my new swimsuit into a ball and stuffed it into a pocket in my jacket, where it would stay secreted.

For the next several weeks, when Mom was out shopping for groceries or Dad was upstairs sleeping, preparing to go in for his graveyard welding shift, I slipped it on. I walked around the living room, savored how it fit against my body, imagined my seamless strokes through pool water. Me, cruising along, no drag, not being held back.

But I never went to the pool with my Speedo. Weeks after buying it, I took a scissors and cut it in half, and cut it again; smaller and smaller strips fell into our trash can. I shoved the scraps of Speedo lower, burying them below the garbage.

THAT YEAR, MR. ERHARDT, my middle-school English teacher, a gangly middle-aged man with brown hair, who resembled Ichabod Crane, quietly took me to a bookshelf in his classroom.

"Taylor, I've been enjoying reading your pieces for class," he said, "and I have a book here that I think you'd enjoy."

From the shelf he pulled out a thin volume with an aqua-colored spine. He flipped the book over and showed me a cover with an old man and his chocolate-furred poodle, sitting under an oak tree near a lake. The man was squinting and didn't smile. In large block type the book was emblazoned JOHN STEINBECK, and underneath the author's name *Travels with Charley: In Search of America*.

"I think you'll like this book," Mr. Erhardt said, smiling.

I nodded.

"Are we reading this next?" I asked.

Shaking his head, Mr. Erhardt handed me the book.

"No, I just thought you might enjoy it—he even writes about North Dakota. It's on page 118."

I took the book from my teacher's hands, flipped open its well-worn pages, and thumbed to the spot. My eyes sped across Steinbeck's sentences. "Someone must have told me about the Missouri River at Bismarck, North Dakota, or I must have read about it. In either case, I hadn't paid attention. I came on it in amazement. Here is where the map should fold. Here is the boundary between east and west."

I stopped. My eyes shot up to meet Mr. Erhardt's gaze.

"Good, isn't it? I knew you'd like it."

I nodded again.

"How long until I have to get it back to you, Mr. Erhardt?" I asked.

"It's yours," he said, smiling once more. Then he turned his head ever so slightly and leaned toward me. "And, Taylor, I think if you really wanted to, you could write like that."

My eyes widened. Scared, jolted with what seemed then like the terror of responsibility, I nodded quickly, feigned a smile, and shoved the small book in my backpack.

"Thank you, Mr. Erhardt," I said, dashing out of the room.

In my backpack I had a book by a man I had never heard of, someone long dead, but who wrote about where I came from, saw my home the way I saw it, the ecotone of lush green grass and broken brown buttes. He had documented it, taken the time to write about my part of the world, and, for me, echoed that it was important, a way of understanding the country I called home.

# 20.

CIRRUS CLOUDS FEATHERED the cerulean sky. I walked home a little after school had let out. I had stayed late to practice music.

In eighth grade my band teacher, Mr. Rooke, would write me notes to get out of study hall so that I could get away from classmates and play music. I stayed after school and practiced in a dinky practice room so that I didn't have to tiptoe around Dad as he slept before going in for work. I could wail and rock on my horn without worry. The practice room was next to the office of one of the school secretaries. Whenever I finished, packed up my saxophone, and closed the practice room door behind me, Mrs. Miller would crack her door and say, "It sounded even better than yesterday, Taylor."

On this day, my saxophone bobbed up and down in its hard-plastic case as I rounded the corner onto Prairie Avenue, I glanced to the west, past the stubble field and toward the weathered farmhouse with its rusty weather vane, the place I sometimes still passed whenever I needed a break from the reality of school to sink into the security of fishing for northern pike or watching red-tailed hawks circle high in the sky.

I walked past Eric Johnson's house. Eric, who was in love with basketball, and with whom I played on the team since fifth grade, had recently fallen in with Kai Martin, a pint-sized bully whose mission it was to mock me. Austin Berger, whose grandpa was a decades-long friend with Grandpa Hatzenbihler, filled out the trio.

Throughout eighth grade I had started to be called *gay* or *faggot*, but I didn't really know what those words meant. I knew it wasn't good to be gay or to be a faggot from how the boys said it.

I didn't shut down so much as I tried to avoid. I asked teachers not to put me in groups with Kai, Eric, or Austin.

Kai's stepdad, Walter, was the wrestling coach. Mark, my neighbor, stood up to Eric, for me, but said he couldn't do anything about Kai since his stepdad did so much for him as his coach on the wrestling team.

"I told Eric I'd take his Adidas shoes and shove those stripes sideways up his ass," Mark told me.

Eric, eventually, left me alone, for a while—but after cajoling from Kai and Austin, he joined back in.


THROUGHOUT EIGHTH GRADE, my mother drove me to Bismarck for saxophone lessons. At the power plant, one of her coworkers had recommended a college student in Bismarck.

"He's certainly made Zac better at saxophone. Zac actually enjoys practicing now," Mom's coworker had said to her.

When Mom asked Mr. Rooke, he told her that private lessons could do more for me than anything he could do in band class.

On some level my parents must have known I was struggling to fit in, that I looked forward to going away each weekend to speech competitions. In hindsight, I'm not sure they could afford my saxophone lessons, but my mother drove me an hour each way every week to sit in her car for a half hour, whether it rained or snowed, while I tried to master the A-flat or F-sharp scales.

WHEN I GOT HOME from school that day, I slowly opened the door. I floated like dust to not risk waking Dad. With a quiet thud, I put down my saxophone and backpack.

The house was still, the lights were off. The trees in the backyard had begun to bud and the rooms inside the house had a matted glow.

After a few minutes, I went downstairs to Dad's large safe in our hobby room, what Dad sometimes called our Man Cave. The safe didn't have a combination, only a large lever-handle. He left it unlocked so I didn't even need the key.

Over the past year I had taken up fly tying. Pheasant feathers, deer fur, small and large hooks, were strewn on the forest green counter where I practiced making nymphs, caddis flies, and streamers.

I pulled down the lever and swung the safe open. Inside, in neat rows lay our shotguns and rifles. My twenty-gauge Winchester, which Dad had bought for me in fifth grade to take me pheasant hunting, rested at the front. I rubbed my hand along its sleek forearm.

Earlier in the year, after I asked Mom and Dad if I could start taking lessons, they'd bought me an electric piano.

"I hope you have a better teacher than I did," Dad said. "She used to hit me on the wrists with a ruler."

I'd come home, turn the volume low or, if I sensed there was something in the air that might wake Dad, plug in my headphones to practice. I'd lay my fingers across the instrument's sleek plastic keys, adjust the volume, and practice my scales. In my own muffled world of music, I could pound out the pain I felt pulsing throughout my body.

But music wasn't working anymore.

Behind my shotgun were Dad's twelve-gauge and deer rifles. Uncle Greg, my father's older brother, had left Dad his pistols when he died a year earlier.

I opened the black plastic case that held Uncle Greg's sleek black nine-millimeter pistol. I checked the chamber and slipped a bullet in; I made sure the safety was on for the moment.

I don't remember crying; I don't even remember feeling particularly sad as I came back up the stairs. The kitchen was warm and the dining room still.

I went over to my backpack. Each pull of the zipper sounded loud. I stopped to make sure Dad hadn't woken. I pulled out my yellow science notebook, opened it to a new page, and drew two columns:

| Reasons to Live | Reasons to Die |
| --- | --- |
|  |  |
|  |  |
|  |  |
|  |  |
|  |  |

I sat for a few minutes and began to fill each column; the process wasn't quick, but it wasn't ponderous either.

I remember listing *Mom*, *Dad*, *Tanya*, and *Music* under "Reasons to Live."

The only item I listed under "Reasons to Die" was:

*Because I am gay.*

# 21.

M Y PARENTS KNEW something was awry. Throughout that school year I spent more time in the basement, more time practicing music, more time rehearsing my speeches. I got my driver's license at fourteen, so I could start barreling in my grandma's old '89 Buick Park Avenue to towns twenty, thirty, or sixty miles away, where I could visit the friends I'd made at speech competitions.

One night, my parents told me how they were inviting Kai's stepdad, the wrestling coach, a short man with a sturdy frame and mahogany hair, over. They had had enough. They wanted to know why Kai had a problem with me.

Mom and I sat at the table. There was a firm knock against the door. Mom tapped her finger.

I didn't say a word. My parents laid out how Kai had been bullying me. I tried to not look the coach in the eye, but, in my periphery, I could see a vein pulse in my dad's neck.

When Dad asked the coach why Kai was picking on me, the coach leaned back in his chair, looked at my father, and said, "Your son didn't invite Kai to his second-grade birthday party."

My father flushed. He then rubbed his handlebar mustache, puffed-up like a sage grouse, and told the coach to get out of our home.

THE FOLLOWING YEAR, while I qualified for state in speech and continued to practice my piano and saxophone, I gave my parents an ultimatum: either we moved forty miles away to Bismarck, a town one hundred times the size of my hometown, or I'd commute each day for high school. I shook whenever I thought about spending the rest of my high school sentence in Center. A girl three years older than I was, who had been on the speech team with me, commuted each day to a private school in Bismarck. I knew getting out was possible. I suggested that I could stay with one of Dad's siblings, Uncle Jody or Aunt Shelia, during the week, that I could get a job and pay them rent or chip in on groceries, that I wouldn't be any trouble, that I just needed someplace bigger, someplace where I felt like I could disappear rather than be noticed, singled out, made an example of what happens to you when you don't fit in where you're planted.

Instead of seeing Bismarck in the rearview mirror after my private saxophone lessons, I wanted to live there—a town with two colleges, a symphony orchestra, art galleries, a large public library, two malls, a Red Lobster, and two public high schools. I wanted to be in a town where I sensed there could be room enough for me to grow.

I wouldn't need to commute. I didn't need to fight my parents; they were invested in me. I wouldn't have to wait for yearly pastel classes with Jack, wouldn't need to commute for my saxophone lessons, could take Advance Placement classes, even take classes at one of the local colleges. My parents had tried to make the world of Center work for me as best they could but, as I ended my ninth-grade

year, my parents listed their house for sale so that we could make a
new life together in Bismarck.

NEAR THE END of that school year, at the end of a long workweek,
Mom and I hopped in the car and zipped to Bismarck, its flaxen
bluffs sweeping down to the tawny Missouri River, before revealing
the spreading city of cement and steel. We had an 8:00 p.m. date
with the National Symphony Orchestra. During my last year living in Center, North Dakota was selected for one of the symphony's
residencies. For nearly two weeks, the orchestra would give workshops, breakout performances, and large symphonic concerts across
the state. No musicians came to our small coal-mining town, but
Mom had gotten us tickets for this, as the *Bismarck Tribune* said,
once-in-a-lifetime-event.

When we arrived at the Bismarck Civic Center, a large, cavernous building that typically hosted the Class B basketball state
championships, monster truck rallies, and rock and country music
concerts, I noticed a large black curtain divided it in half. There
weren't plans for the ten-thousand-person arena to sell out.

Mom and I shuffled along and settled into our seats. We sat,
pulled out our programs, and smiled at each other. There were
names of composers I didn't know—Dvorak, Peter Schickele, and
Brent Michael Davids. When my eyes roamed around the program,
I noticed that unlike Dvorak or the one composer I had heard of,
Tchaikovsky (because Mrs. Harrison, my elementary-school music
teacher, had played his *1812 Overture* for us in third grade), both
Schickele and Davids were alive. I had thought all classical music
composers were dead men with white hair. I realized, then, that

beyond the wheat fields and short stubble grass of Center, other ways of living in the world—beyond coal mining, ranching, or working at a power plant—existed.

A violinist stood, nodded his head, and the haunting sound of an oboe cried out into the civic center. The strings began to swirl into tune. I turned my head and listened closely. Mom glanced over at me. And then out burst Leonard Slatkin, the conductor of the National Symphony Orchestra. Applause rang out from the audience. The elfin Mr. Slatkin, dressed in tails, stepped up onto his podium, bowed to us, turned, flicked out his baton, and snapped his arms through the air.

There was a crash of cymbals. I gripped the arms of my seat and leaned forward. This was Dvorak, his *Carnival Overture*. The strings blazed into a bright tempest as a *ba-dum* banged out from the timpani. Tufts of Slatkin's hair floated through the air like silver silk. I smiled at Mom as my head quickly jolted back and forth, my hands gripping the arms harder, desperate to hold on to the world.

THE SUMMER OUR HOUSE was for sale in Center, my parents let me fly by myself for the first time. We drove four hundred miles to Minneapolis so that I could take a direct flight to visit Tanya and her husband, Mike, who had been her high-school sweetheart, for a couple of weeks.

In Seattle, I saw silver salmon flung across Pike Place Market, ate my first pain au chocolat, and wiped dripping juice from my chin after biting into softball-sized peaches. Before my visit, the only skyscraper I had ever seen up close was the twenty-one-story state capitol building in Bismarck.

Here, I stared down at my feet as we walked around downtown. There was so much shiny steel and glass. My eyes felt as if they were burning.

One day, my sister took me to the bank where she worked. I met Luke and Stefan. Luke and Stefan didn't have grease on their hands like the men back home. My sister told me that Luke and Stefan got manicures. Stefan's beard was groomed. Luke even plucked his eyebrows.

The men I knew prided themselves on having beards that looked like tumbleweeds, eyebrows that looked like caterpillars.

When we got back outside and into my sister's Mustang, I asked her why the men back home didn't take care of themselves like Luke and Stefan.

My sister sighed. "Because they don't care how they look, Taylor. And because they're not gay."

# 22.

We believe that Levi should not change around other men because he's attracted to them. Just like straight men shouldn't change in the women's locker room. If you believe Levi should change in the women's locker room, sign your name below.

THIS WAS THE MESSAGE, on a lined piece of notebook paper, tacked to a clipboard, which circulated in the boys' locker room during my sophomore year of high school in Bismarck.

Levi, a boy in my gym class, wore sequined jeans, long beaded necklaces, bright shirts, and a zebra-patterned fedora. The makeup unnerved the football players, confirming, for them, that Levi was gay, that he must find them attractive, and that he wanted to have sex with them. The foundation on Levi's face was bedrock to his identity. Some days, Levi wore lip gloss.

When the girls heard about the petition making the rounds in the boys' locker room, they jeered. The boys, they said, needed to get the fuck over themselves. The faces of the boys, large, hulking football players and wrestlers, fired red. The girls, in booming voices, said they'd *love* to have Levi change with them.

When the petition made its way to me in the onion-scented locker room, I looked at the names on the list and committed them to memory. I quietly passed the petition along but didn't sign it.

These were the days when I snuck into our basement, turned on the big-screen television, and watched *Will and Grace* and *Queer Eye for the Straight Guy*.

I'd sit close to the television, the volume barely on to avoid detection, and watch the parade of gay characters. I'd see real-life gay men dress and advise straight men—worlds so far away from what I knew. Whenever I heard one of my parents rumble closer to the stairs, I switched stations—maybe to a baseball game or NBC—and slowly turned up the volume.

WHEN LEVI SASHAYED in the art deco marble and brass hallways of Bismarck High School, the boys stared. He smirked.

I envied his fierce independence and his confidence. Being coy was his ace in the hole. The jocks smoldered with hatred.

I was trying to fit into a new school—a high school where my class was larger than my entire hometown. I wanted to be me, in the way I thought Levi was being himself. But something about me rankled boys, agitated them—or at least it had in Center. I learned out of necessity to stay quiet. In Bismarck, I found my friends in band class, or selected them by their high grades in Mrs. Lord-Olson's English class—that's how I found my friend Paul.

———

To RIP UP PRAIRIE GRASS, a person must grip the blade as close to the ground as possible, heave back and forth, wait for the soil to loosen, and then give one final yank. It does not happen quickly, may take several attempts, and can draw blood from hands.

Even when successful, part of the root remains underground, hidden, left behind. It refuses to leave home.

TALL AND LEAN, Paul played tennis and was part of a friend group of three boys and four girls. He started to invite me to hang out with his group of friends. We played Twister or Catch Phrase, a word game where a person tries to describe the clue on the electronic screen without saying the first letter of the clue, using a word that rhymes with the clue, or the number of syllables the clue has.

When I'd see Paul in class on Mondays, I'd thank him for letting me hang out with his friends.

"They're your friends, too, silly," he'd say to me, smiling.

Had I really had friends before, though? In Center, birthday parties felt like placeholders for something else, some filler for a future life I couldn't yet see.

Now, in Bismarck, there was a group in my life, friends who started to ask me if I wanted to go to a movie or see a play at the local college. My world suddenly felt wider—like there was room for me.

IT TOOK THREE DAYS for the Bismarck High School principal, a portly man with a halo of white hair, to put the kibosh on the petition to have Levi change in the girls' locker room.

————

My new group of friends included a tall blond boy named Drew.
Drew played tuba in band with me and was a lineman on the foot-
ball team. When he guffawed, everyone went silent, then laughed at
Drew's laugh.

Throughout high school, Drew and I were on student council, split the "good guy" vote for homecoming king, and screamed
together while riding roller coasters on our band trip to Los Angeles.

In high school both Drew and I dated women.


By the end of sophomore year, Levi transferred high schools. I felt
like a blade of prairie grass again, swaying singularly in the breeze.

# 23.

I T WAS A BOOK that shifted my imagination during my junior year of high school. In Ms. Montgomery's AP English 11 class we read George Orwell's *1984*. Our summer assignment had been to read Orwell's dystopian novel on our own and create a study guide for our classmates for the first day of class. I didn't think I could do it. Not only did I not get why the clocks struck thirteen, I felt dense— Orwell proved to be something more than a challenge for me. His writing felt at the time, under the George W. Bush administration, too real and too close to home, like the innocent veil of my childhood was peeling away and the weight of responsibility—of reading the news and following politics—was now upon me.

In AP English 11 we spent weeks on Orwell. Ms. Montgomery had us investigate the Patriot Act, enacted shortly after 9/11. We dissected commercials to watch for patterns of propaganda. We learned about countries where certain books were outlawed. I got a chill in class because I started to see connections to the United States government.

Ms. Montgomery was relentless. Tall, with full cheeks and

cropped chestnut hair, she challenged us: "What page is that on? Where'd you get that idea? Are you just saying what you hear at home? Beachey, do you agree with Taylor? Paul, challenge Taylor. Is that the best you can remember from that passage?" Class felt like a gladiatorial match. It wasn't so much daunting as thrilling.

As the semester rolled on, I spent more time on English than other homework. When we read Miller's *The Crucible*, we researched modern-day witch hunts. When we read Remarque's *All Quiet on the Western Front*, we self-selected between two sides to debate one sentence that is a stand-alone paragraph at the end of the book: "He stood up."

"Did he or didn't he commit suicide?" asked Ms. Montgomery. "Pick your side."

For two days we debated like the British House of Lords. We pointed. "How could you think that?" We yelled. "That's absurd!" We rooted our arguments and persuasions in the text.

On the second day, Erin Weller switched sides. "Traitor!" shouted her boyfriend, Kurt. The debate reached a fevered pitch when Kurt accused another classmate of using a liar's technique.

"All right, all right, let's cool down," said Ms. Montgomery.

This was not the world of Center, of hard bodies hitting one another on the football field or of driving for a layup. Unlike Center, this was a world where I sensed my teachers' politics were different from my parents', where the world felt a little bit more open, like there were options.

DURING THE SPRING semester my brain exploded. We spent most of the term on two men: Ralph Waldo Emerson and Henry David Thoreau. Some shock wave hit my body: these men got me. Transcendentalism became the closest thing to a religious experience I had had up until this point in my life—*simplify, simplify, simplify?* Check. *Different drummer?* Oh yeah. Seeing some *lives of quiet desperation?* Uh-huh.

At times in class, Aaron Frenette, whom we all called Fernie, or Baby Fern, undid me: he would lean back in his chair, wrap his hands behind his head, and flex his biceps. I would flush, tell him to *Stop it*, try not to giggle, but turn bright, like a cherry tomato.

LATE IN MY JUNIOR YEAR Ms. Montgomery was recognized with the National Education Association Foundation's highest honor, the Award for Teaching Excellence. Harvard called and offered her a spot in a PhD program.

"I think I want to stay in the classroom," she told us one day.

"But, Ms. Montgomery, it's *Harvard*!" we said.

That year was Ms. Montgomery's last teaching at Bismarck High School. She left for Harvard.

Senior year I felt her absence when walking past her old room.

WHEN I WAS A SENIOR, I had Mrs. Pole, but, as talented as she was, I missed Ms. Montgomery. I missed nature writing. I missed finding stories I could fit into, written by men who felt what I seemed to feel whenever I was out in nature.

We read *Hamlet* and recast scenes from the play, acting them out in front of our classmates. My group did *The Real World: Elsinore Castle*, after *The Real World*, the MTV reality show where a group of strangers lived together; I dressed as a goth version of Hamlet and dyed my hair black.

We read *Jude the Obscure* and compared Little Father Time to Pearl Prynne in *The Scarlet Letter* from Ms. Montgomery's class and laughed about how they'd be a perfect match with all their brooding and angst.

I realized then that having Ms. Montgomery as my English teacher was the first time I ever wanted time to slow down, when I was opened to a new world, when it felt like it was possible for me to be me. I found a type of security in books, which revealed that there were more stories, more ways of living, in the world.

By the end of high school, I was voted Nicest Senior Guy and Most Likely to Be President in the senior class awards. I was Bilbo Baggins in the school play of *The Hobbit* and first chair in the jazz band. When it came time to apply for colleges, I only looked at out-of-state schools. I needed to leave the prairie I grew up on. I needed to find more boys like Levi, men like Luke and Stefan. I needed to be transplanted to someplace else, to feel rooted, secure. I needed a new community.

Years later, I saw Drew post an engagement announcement on social media. We had lost touch, but when I looked at Drew's announcement, I stopped scrolling.

Drew was engaged to a man.

I wrote to Drew, asking him why we never came out to each other in high school. All those band rehearsals, student council meetings, movie parties—we never whispered, never gave any hint, that we were keeping up appearances.

When he wrote back, Drew mentioned how religious his family was. But when he wrote *Because I like to be liked*, goose bumps ran up my neck.

I thought back to being on the homecoming court with Drew, his hands on his head as the homecoming king crown hovered back and forth, my eyes darting in his direction, waiting for the crown to land on one of our heads. I knew he wanted it. I wanted it, too. I wanted to prove that in two short years in my new school, I had made myself the most popular boy there. I *needed* it to be a popularity contest—because many people voting for me would then be confirmation that I was liked, was accepted, that maybe I was even safe.

In Center, the small town swallowed by the prairie, it wasn't my harassers who hurt me the most. It was the silent classmates—whether they knew it or not—the ones who didn't stand up for me, the ones who had no words. It's impossible to be safe at home when no one gives you a sense of security.

I kept thinking how validating it would be to be crowned in Bismarck.

But that didn't happen. The crown landed on the quarterback's head.

Drew rolled his eyes.

I clenched my jaw and slowly clapped.


At the end of Drew's email was a final sentence:

*And because of Levi.*

Levi, before he left the school, was testing the soil. He showed us it wasn't safe to be gay at Bismarck High, that everything Drew and I loved or wanted would be taken away if we were found out. Drew dated a sassy, fierce flautist and, for two weeks, I dated a high-kicking member of the Demonette dance team. We needed cover, some sign of protection so rumors didn't circulate about why we weren't dating anyone—I was always busy studying, or busy working after school at JCPenney, or busy, busy, busy. Weren't we horny, just like the other boys? We were, but anytime I dated a girl, it lasted, at most, only two weeks. Guilt welled inside of me. All I wanted to do was hold their hands, to style their hair, and to watch *Rent* with them, singing along.

I remember once kissing another girl on my doorstep at home. I knew my father could see us. I wanted him to see. I needed insurance that I was safe. That if I performed kissing someone of the opposite sex, my parents would stop wondering why it took me so long to date. That any other questions might be quelled by my pretending to be straight.

Whenever I told the girls I wanted to stop seeing them, they cried. One made me take her to an elementary-school playground because the garage door opened as I broke the news to her. She couldn't bear to have her parents see her like this. We sat on swings as she wept. I kicked at the gravel. I didn't want to hurt her—or to hurt any of them.

In my imagination I can still see Levi—his high cheekbones and sharp, angular jaw. In the picture of him in my mind his fedora is pulled down, close to his eyebrows, one of which is raised *just so*. He has a furtive gaze. He knows something, something we both knew all along: I am gay.

*I am gay*—the shortest, most life-changing sentence a person can say. But it wasn't really being seen by someone else that confirmed my gayness, it was my self-knowledge. The knowledge that it wasn't my hobbies or preferences that made me gay, but something deeper inside of me, something beyond my control, like my red hair or being diabetic. Being gay, I realized then, was as rooted inside of me, as bedrock to my being me, as the prairie that had shaped my imagination. But at that time, in high school, with Levi being made an example of, I also knew something else: to survive home, I had to leave.

# 24.

Two weeks after I graduated high school, I lobbed my thumb off like a knob of butter. I was working on an assembly line at Bobcat, where Dad worked. I was building rollers and idlers—metal widgets that went into Bobcat's skid-steer loaders—to help pay for college.

In two months, I would be off to St. Olaf College in Minnesota to be a music major, starting on the long track, or so I believed, to become the symphony conductor I always dreamed of being.

But on that warm June day, at around 4:00 p.m., I daydreamed and pushed the button to lower the press, which squeezed the metal pieces together.

My left thumb was over the hole where the press ground down. Three thousand pounds of pressure per square inch.

I didn't even feel it.

When I pulled my hand away, there was a hole on the thumb of my glove. The fabric was clipped away clean. Bright blood shined on the sleek steel.

I gripped my thumb, held it above my heart, and sped to the nurse's station.

------

WHEN MY SUPERVISOR saw me hurry away from my press, he yelled.

I opened my hand.

Blood shot at him.

Color leeched from his face.


WHEN I KICKED OPEN the door to the nurse's station, she told me that it was nearly time for her to be done for the day.

I moved into the small office, sat on a chair, my hair damp under my hat, and told her she needed to call 911.

"What?" she asked.

She looked at my hand and began to scream.

In even tones, I kept telling her to call 911.

She didn't.

Eventually, I grabbed her blue silk blouse with my good hand, pulled her close as blood speckled the tiled floor, and said, "You need to stay calm, so I stay calm. Call 911."

She nodded.


IN THE BACK of the ambulance, I cracked jokes as the nurses tried to find a vein for an IV. I told them I had tough skin. They feigned laughter.

Sweat pooled at my temples. I closed my eyes, focused on breathing. I didn't know where the missing hunk of my thumb was, having guessed I left it, crushed, at my workstation.

There was a fleeting thought that maybe someone went back and got it.

———

IN THE EMERGENCY ROOM, a white sheet blocked my left side.

I closed my eyes again and focused my breath. My hand and forearm were numb.

A minute passed and a booming voice broke into the room. Beside my bed stood a large salt-and-pepper-haired doctor.

He told me that his name was Dr. Erickson and that, lucky for me, he was in the hospital when the ambulance brought me in. He was, he stated proudly, the hand specialist in the region.

"Will we be able to reattach my thumb?" I asked.

He lowered his head and sighed.

"No."

I turned away from him for a minute.

"What can you do then?"

"You're lucky you didn't hit a knuckle with the press," he said. "We won't have to amputate your entire thumb. You'll only lose the first digit."

I swallowed hard.

"What I'm going to do, Taylor, is fold your skin over the wound, tuck it into place, and reshape what I can so that it still looks like a thumb. You'll never have a nail grow there again."


WHEN THE DOCTOR stepped out for a minute, I heard the surgical team behind the white sheet. Eventually, a wheeled chair squeaked against the shiny floor.

"Here we go," Dr. Erickson said.

Then there was a tug on my hand.

I do not remember what they used, if there was a grinding sound, or if I asked and the surgeon told me he was using a scalpel.

I remember the tugging, which seemed to be constant. My skin folded over and tucked into itself, stitched in place.

THROUGH THE EMERGENCY ROOM window, I saw my dad. He was talking to a nurse, who pointed over at me. He couldn't come in, but he turned toward the glass.

I imagined that that must have been what it was like when I was a butter bean newborn, my dad looking at, as he said to one of my uncles, his "whopper" of a son. Dad cooing, scratching his fingers against the glass, all those years ago, trying to get me to look at him, counting all ten toes and fingers.

I wonder what it was like when he first held me, his son who would inherit his own red hair, his deep gravelly voice, his love of baseball. How perfect I must have seemed to him, his own image in so many ways, reflected.

BUT NOW, in that emergency room, my father was looking at his eighteen-year-old maimed son. The son who was clumsy enough to cut off a chunk of his thumb, the finger that makes us human, that allows us to grip, to tie our shoes with ease, to curl under and continue scales on the piano, to give a thumbs-up, signaling everything's A-okay.

That small, crucial part of me was now gone. I was no longer his perfect son.

Deformed, I lay there and looked at him.

———

I REMEMBER HIS ONCE telling my mother that he didn't want me to work at Bobcat, that it was too risky.

I RESTED MY HEAD on the pillow and looked at him.

He stepped toward the glass and tears pooled in his eyes.

I feigned a smile and took steady breaths with each tug on what was left of my thumb. I wondered what it looked like, my new nub, what it felt like to fold skin over exposed bone and muscle, to try to give some appearance that I was just like everyone else, to be resculpted in the rest of humanity's image.

DAD STOOD THERE. What else was there for a father to do?

My eyes didn't break from his, and he let his tears slide down his cheeks. His eyes reddened.

"I love you," he mouthed through the glass to me.

I closed my eyes, gently nodded, and opened them.

I stared at my father.

"I love you, too."

# SPROUT

# 1.

COLLEGE TRANSFORMED the landscape of my mind. I started reading Kafka, Paul Tillich, and Kierkegaard (after all, I was at a college with the second-largest collection of Kierkegaard materials outside of Copenhagen). Among the novelists I consumed were Eudora Welty, Salman Rushdie, and Barbara Kingsolver. Sometimes it felt like my head was filled with applesauce.

And there were gay men. Men who shook their hips, whose faces could shift as quickly as Play-Doh, who dressed as geishas—*gay*-shas (forgive me)—for Halloween. Men who, I thought, were more comfortable with themselves, and others who were, I thought at the time, too gay for me. Men who weren't the model for the type of man I was, the type of Marlboro man I was trying to become.

I was a Brorby. I came from the prairie. I hunted and fished. I had killed things. I liked tackling and roughhousing with my friends. I liked trying to feel tough. I didn't need to look tough, but I wanted people to know I wasn't a pushover.

———

IN EIGHTH GRADE my social studies and physical education teacher, Mr. Fass, a Vietnam War veteran who had had my own parents as students, called me Muhammad Brorby, after Muhammad Ali. My parents had both been all-state athletes, and my sister—who, a decade earlier than me, also had the pleasure of having Mr. Fass—played volleyball and basketball. I was naturally athletic, so Mr. Fass liked me.

One day, during a lesson on the American Civil War, Mr. Fass belted to the class. "You had to be tough as nails to fight. Tough like Jim Brorby, Taylor's dad." My face flushed. "I mean, Jim Brorby was in school before we had wrestling. He would've been a good wrestler. He would've liked to hurt people and not get in trouble for it."

Dad, my dad, the Harley-Davidson biker, the man with a Hulk Hogan handlebar mustache, the man whom I had seen cry only at his mother's funeral. The man who once, while adjusting some shutters on the second story of our house, when I was about twelve, fell from a small stool. I was outside at the time and saw the stool start to jolt. Dad's body did a slight lean forward and then catapulted backward. He fell like a watermelon from the sky. His shoulder glanced and broke a large, coral-colored flowerpot before he smacked the ground. A large gush of wind bleated from his body. His eyes bulged like a carp on the riverbank, fighting for air. He didn't break his back, and we took him to the emergency room, forty miles away, in our own car. He refused to have an ambulance called.

The next day he went back to work.


ALTHOUGH MY COLLEGE might not have been as diverse as other places, compared with Bismarck, North Dakota, it seemed cosmopolitan—students from around the world, students from inner-city Minneapolis, students from suburbia. In some ways, I felt like the token frontiersmen: Davy Crockett from North Dakota.

In a humanities seminar during my sophomore year, I remember going through a unit on literature inspired by biblical imagery; the professor lectured on how "the devil is a snare." He then asked if any of us had set a snare before.

I had, but I didn't raise my hand.

While he attempted to educate us on how a snare not only is set, but how it works, I began to shift in my seat. He had it wrong. At the end of his talk, my hand shot up.

"Professor," I said deferentially, "that's not correct." I proceeded to share how I had set snares with my cousin Shane in childhood, how I had helped him kill squirrels and rabbits. The room fell silent and tense as classmates—friends—turned in their chairs to look at me, the little ginger in the back, who had the temerity to correct our professor. Once finished, the professor looked at me from the lectern, a Pop-Tart in one hand, his cellphone in the other. I felt like an ass. Throughout college there were points, like this one, where I revealed too much of where I came from.

But, more often, I had professors who were tender, particularly tender male professors. Gentler, they seemed like the counterweight to my father—less Harley-Davidson, less authoritarian, less prone to raising their voice, modeling a certain type of commitment to the life of the mind and the life of engagement.

Jonathan Hill, whom I had as a first-year writing professor, and who would become my adviser, was the first man who unraveled my staid notion of masculinity. A Brit, Jonathan was educated at Keble College, Oxford, receiving both a bachelor's and a master's degree.

He and his wife, Barbara, spent a year in Dublin, then Sweden, before Jonathan took a one-year position at St. Olaf. As he so often put it, "I came for a year and stayed for a lifetime."

IN FIRST-YEAR WRITING Jonathan assigned books I had read before in high school—*To Kill a Mockingbird*, *Lord of the Flies*, *Beloved*, *The Great Gatsby*. This should be easy, I thought. And then we got to *Lord of the Flies*, a book I had read with Mrs. Lord-Olson my sophomore year of high school. Except, I realized, I hadn't really read it.

Jonathan pulled off his glasses, rubbed his shiny head, which was ringed with a halo of gray hair, and began to read from page 44. Poised, Jonathan knew, perhaps due to the authority of his British accent, he had us gripped.

"Smoke was rising here and there among the creepers that festooned the dead or dying trees."

Did I even know what the word "festooned" meant?

"One patch touched a tree trunk and scrambled up like a bright squirrel. The smoke increased, sifted, rolled outwards. The squirrel leapt on the wings of the wind and clung to another standing tree, eating downwards. Beneath the dark canopy of leaves and smoke the fire laid hold on the forest and began to gnaw. Acres of black and yellow smoke rolled steadily toward the sea. . . ."

My pulse quickened. Jonathan laid it on thick—leaned onto the table, his shoulders up to his ears.

"The heart of flame leapt nimbly across the gap between the trees and then went swinging and flaring along the whole row of them. Beneath the capering boys a quarter of a mile square of forest was savage with smoke and flame. The separate noises of the fire merged into a drum-roll that seemed to shake the mountain."

One paragraph and we all remained silent, rapt, as Jonathan picked up his glasses, which resumed their perch upon his nose. We took a communal breath and began discussion.

I had missed the music of the language, the rhythm of the sentences, when I first read *Lord of the Flies* in Mrs. Lord-Olson's class. But now, that music—how language could be used to not only tell a story, but to build imagery and tension through sound and syntax— adhered to my brain.

For the first few weeks of the semester, Jonathan allowed us to choose whether we wanted to submit creative or academic essays for class. We read a novel a week—always novels—and submitted a four- to six-page piece of writing as well. I always chose creative essays.

One that I submitted to Jonathan recounted a fly-fishing trip to Montana. When describing the moment a fly flits through the air, as it prepares to land on the water, I wrote that the fly "floated like a ballerina in Tchaikovsky's *Swan Lake*." The following week, while visiting Jonathan in his office to go over my essay, I sat next to his desk in a low, wooden leather chair. Jonathan, glasses off again, deciphered the hieroglyphics of his own writing.

"Now, Taylor, I appreciate what you're doing here in this moment. The focus, the clarity. I can see it."

Whenever Jonathan spoke, I was entranced. He used language like no one else I had met—was it *only* because of his British accent?

"But this is too much," he said. I nodded along as he spoke. "You need not be *that* specific. Tell us that the fly is like a ballerina—

nothing more. You need not specify a composer, much less a particular work. It's idiosyncratic."

I thought I knew what he meant, but not really. Why couldn't my brain work like his? No one in my family read books—at least nothing outside of Mary Higgins Clark or Stephen King. I couldn't call up a family member and discuss William Shakespeare, much less William Golding. There was a thread to my family that felt like it was fraying with each passing week. Certain parts of me that had to stay silent, locked up in a little box—parts that I didn't share.

# 2.

O N A COLD NIGHT, during junior year of college, I went to
Pearl's, a dive bar in the small downtown next to the Can-
non River. At night, out on the overhang, the town of Northfield
glowed—warm yellow from lamps reflected off the gray river, a few
cars illuminated the ice on the streets into a stream of light. As I
stood outside on the patio, the gurgle of the water helped conversation flow. After standing outside for a few minutes, I went back in to
get another rail gin and tonic.

I pushed through a sea of warm, sweaty bodies, nodding and
saying hello to friends. It was karaoke night, and someone was singing "Don't Stop Believing" by Journey. Someone always seemed to
sing to Journey on karaoke night.

When I made it to the bar, I wedged between two barstools,
placed my right foot up on the brass rail, and leaned onto the long
mahogany bar. I waited to flag down the bartender. My friend Leslie
sidled up next to me.

Leslie and I had first met while touring Olaf as prospective students our senior year of high school. Bashful, we both said we were interested in other schools.

"I'm certainly going to Wellesley," said Leslie.

"Who would go here?" I said. "I'm going to Middlebury."

The truth is, I wanted to go to Middlebury College, an idyllic school in the Green Mountains of Vermont. All the college guides said it was a mini-Ivy. But in 2006 Middlebury cost $40,000 a year, and St. Olaf was $35,000. I did the math and knew that St. Olaf would be $20,000 less over four years. No one had ever told me how financial aid worked. As the first in my family to go to college, I thought the sticker price was *the* price of admission. The next fall, as first-years, Leslie and I were in a sociology class together at St. Olaf.

"Hello, Taylor!" shouted Leslie as she pulled up to the bar. She gave me a hug.

"Hello, Lezzle-Dezzle," I said, smiling.

Leslie let out a laugh. When she smiled, her eyes disappeared. Her blond hair swung back, barely brushing her shoulders.

"What are you drinking?" I asked over the din of Pearl's.

"Oh, I don't know. What are you having?"

"I'm having a gin and tonic. Let me get one for you." I slammed my hand down on the bar to get the attention of the bartender, who was flirting with a classmate.

"What can I get you, bud?" asked the bartender.

"Two g-and-ts, please."

"Sounds good," he said, turning around to grab a bottle of Seagram's.

Leslie and I waited, and I rubbed my foot along the brass rail. I looked down.

"How are you, Taylor?" asked Leslie.

"Oh, I'm good. I've got class at eight a.m. tomorrow."

"God, that sucks."

"Tell me about it."

I kept rubbing my foot back and forth. The bartender was taking his time.

"Hey, Lez," I said. Leslie looked over at me. "Can I tell you something?"

"Of course you can. What's up?"

I breathed in and out, felt it rising in my throat. It was coming. I couldn't stop it. Leslie looked at me.

"Taylor?"

I looked down at the floor and said it.

"Leslie, I like boys."

"Haha," she cackled. "So do I!"

Our drinks arrived. Leslie leaned over and kissed me on the lips. "That's *so* great!"

"Lucky man," said the bartender.

"Thanks," I said. "Put these on my tab."

Leslie gave me a hug, and we turned and headed back into the crowd. She held my hand and a wave of relief washed over me. *That wasn't so hard.* There was a bit of a sigh in my body. I breathed easier. She was the first person I told; this was the first time I said it out loud to anyone. *It wasn't so scary*, I thought.

It was public: I am gay.

THE PREVIOUS YEAR the *New York Times* arts section highlighted a young, Peruvian tenor named Juan Diego Flórez. At thirty-five, he was the first person since Pavarotti to get an encore at the Metropolitan Opera, and the first person since the 1930s to have done the same at Milan's La Scala, the grande dame of world opera houses. In the *Times* article Flórez looked enticing—young, lithe, with dark eyes and dark curly hair. Frankly, he was sexy.

He was starring in Donizetti's comic opera *La Fille du Régiment*, known in English as *The Daughter of the Regiment.* I went to Jonathan Hill's office to tell him about my new discovery. Florez was known for his rendition of a particular aria, "Ah! Mes Amis," the four-minute mile of the tenor's repertoire: there are nine high Cs, a feat even most of the greatest tenors can never pull off.

"Taylor, come back on Friday. I have something I think you'll enjoy," said Jonathan.

By this point, I had been to Jonathan's house for lunches and suppers—homemade chicken noodle soup, tomato soup with Thai basil and a splash of black truffle oil, pork tenderloin with hoisin-sherry sauce—all of which Barbara, a formidable chef, prepared.

On Friday I rapped on Jonathan's office door.

"Taylor, hello—yes, let's stop down at the hall and then go upstairs."

We walked down the hall together. Jonathan opened a hallway closet and retrieved a record player—yes, a record player.

"Let's go," he said in a voice so low no one else would hear.

We made our way to a cavernous room in the English department. The lights were off, but faint afternoon light trickled into the room through the alcoves of leaded windows.

"Let's go toward the back of the room," whispered Jonathan.

He set down the record player on a large seminar table in front of a stone fireplace. Jonathan unspooled the cord and plugged the player into the wall.

"I'll be right back," he said, whisking away into the hall.

I folded my hands. I didn't have a clue what Jonathan had in store, but I couldn't wait.

"Yes, here we go," he said as he returned. He pulled out a dark vinyl from an album cover. "You'll enjoy this."

Through the warm crackling of the record, an orchestra began to play. It was "Ah! Mes Amis"—but whose voice? Jonathan and I leaned back in the caramel-colored captain's chairs and listened.

I watched a smile form on his face. His eyes were closed. And there we were, my teacher and I, doing something we never did in English class: listening to music. Music—it was a passion of his and Barbara's, our lunches and dinners often flooded with conversation about Beethoven's quartets, Brahms, and Schoenberg.

WHEN THE THE LAST HIGH C crescendoed and the music finished, Jonathan emerged from a transfixed state. "Ah," he said, as if savoring wine.

"Who was that, professor?" I asked.

"That was a young Luciano Pavarotti. Barbara and I saw him before he was a superstar. 1972. But of course he was always a superstar. Look at this, Taylor," said Jonathan. He showed me the record sleeve. It was yellow, with a picture of the young Pavarotti. In strong, thick ink, the tenor's signature was splayed across the cover. "When we saw him, we brought this along and thrust it toward him so he could autograph it."

"Incredible," I said.

"Well, there we are," said Jonathan as he packed up the record player.

A moment, that's all it was, but transformation can happen in a moment shared together.


I ACCOMPANIED the St. Olaf Choir as a CD seller my junior and senior years. In my senior year, the choir toured the East Coast, notably singing in Carnegie Hall. On our free day in Manhattan, I called to get rush tickets for the Met: Flórez was reprising his role in *La Fille du Régiment*. Few people wanted to attend, choosing other places to sight-see, but my friend Kirsten agreed to join me.

Being with her always reminded me of the book line where we first met. At the time—the first semester of college—I was so very homesick. It was so bad, in fact, that I'd call both my mother and sister each day, and the very sound of their voices reduced me to sobs. Then I'd crack a Diet Coke and weep next to my mini-fridge.

In the line that day, I turned to Kirsten, books piled to her chin, and asked, "Are you ready for this to hurt?" We both giggled nervously and walked back to our first-year dorm together. From then on, I was friends with Kirsten, stopping by her room regularly, making friends with her friends. We shared a love of dancing—bumping and grinding, twirling, dropping it like it's hot. Our favorite dance of the year, Drag Ball, meant drag queens and bass-thumping music. Men and women dressed in drag—even my straight male friends, who were, let's face it, hideous as women, joined in. I'd have faux butterfly tattoos on my shoulder, sea green eye shadow, channeling my inner diva. Kirsten would pencil on a goatee and wear a basketball jersey and baggy shorts, an off-kilter baseball cap on her head.

Now we were in New York City, going to see a star of the stage, the heartthrob Peruvian with the world-renowned voice. When we got to Lincoln Center, we entered the large lobby, where two massive Chagall tapestries hang, collected our rush tickets, and stood at the back of the hall. When the curtains pulled back and the audience began to clap, we held our breath as the lights lowered.

The opera began and soon it was time for that signature nine-high-C aria. Kirsten, unfamiliar with the opera, didn't know when the aria was coming. On the way to Lincoln Center, I had informed her, over and over and over again, how incredible this aria was—and when the time came, I looked over at her, and poked her in the thigh: it was go time.

There was electricity in the audience as Flórez roamed about the stage. When the violins buoyed, he stood and faced the audience. There was one, there were two, there were three high Cs. Kirsten looked at me, a smile across her face. He went and went and went. When "Ah! Mes Amis" finished, we erupted with the requisite *Bravos!* and whistles, too.

SINCE CARNEGIE HALL took over the CD sales for the St. Olaf Choir, the next day was another free day for me. I decided to go to the Museum of Modern Art to see Jackson Pollock's paintings.

Wandering through the white-walled corridors, I eventually came around a corner and there it was: *One: Number 31, 1950,* that large splattering of white and black across tan-colored canvas. Like a magnet, it pulled me in, engulfed me, devoured me.

A family quickly left the room when I entered. I was alone with the painting. I sat on a small black leather bench and studied Pollock's lines. I had never taken an art history or art appreciation class, but there was something primal Pollock did for me—was it chaos or order or spontaneity? I didn't know. But I knew I liked it, that I couldn't look away.

After a while a man came into the room. About five feet ten, trim, with a contoured blue blazer, white oxford shirt, its three top buttons unfastened, a curly tuft of brown hair around his head, dark, mahogany eyes.

He sat down at the opposite end of the bench. I looked over at him and we smiled. After a few minutes, he rose and walked in front of *One: Number 31, 1950*, temporarily blocking my view. His pants were tight, and I stared at the outline of his ass. When he reached the end of the painting, kitty-corner from me, he looked over his shoulder and smirked. I turned red and looked away. He crossed in front of me and sat back down on the bench, this time straight as a two-by-four, content, smiling, and looking ahead at the painting, his hands folded in his lap.

I wasn't nearly as well dressed as he was, with a large peacoat over a camel-colored oxford shirt, black slacks, and a black, blue, and gold scarf. I had not come to the museum to try to radiate sex appeal.

Regardless, I sat up, breathed in, and rose. I walked in front of *One: Number 31, 1950* puffed up like a goddam peacock. When I crossed in front of him and reached the end of the painting I, like him, looked over my shoulder. He smiled.

He rose, came over to me, grabbed my hand, and whispered, "Follow me."

Somehow, we found a single-person bathroom. When we got in, he locked the door and smiled.

At this point, I had taken to carrying a condom in my billfold. I don't know why—I wanted to have sex, but, like any repressed gay man from the prairie, I was too shy to find it on my college campus. I didn't dare tell my partner I had never done *it* before. It was time for me to put my book learning about how to have gay sex to use.

Then we started in.

WHEN WE FINISHED, I said, "Thank you." We washed up and left the bathroom—separately, of course. Suddenly, what Jackson Pollock was doing in all those paintings struck me on a different level.

# 3.

IN EIGHTH GRADE, I took second place in state wrestling. Or that's what I told new friends in college. There was something about the close contact, about using my body to push and heave and pull against other boys, that appealed to me. But everyone on the team—including Matt (my future brother-in-law's younger brother), Robert (a boy three years older than me), and my neighbor Mark—seemed to have a chip on their shoulders: they all seemed to scowl more than smile, and seemed to enjoy their newfound skills in overpowering people. Some boys on the wrestling team seemed to relish the ability to beat up smaller children. I had no need to beat up anyone. What I needed was a narrative to help change what I thought people perceived me to be.

In neighboring Minnesota, when I was at St. Olaf College, I began to test out my new made-up narrative. I gave credit to my father. Five hundred miles from home, I told my college friends that my father had pressured me to be in the sport, which, to my memory, he never did—but since he looked like Hulk Hogan, everyone believed me. Of course, he'd want his son in wrestling, they thought. And since I have a small frame, one that when I crouch has a low center of gravity, people believed me even more: I looked like I could've been a wrestler. I concocted the story of taking second place because taking first seemed like sheer bragging—plus, second place had a better punch line: I told people that I knew I could've taken first when I was on top of my (imaginary) opponent if I just whispered "I'm gay" in his ear. They would laugh. The joke seemed to work. They believed that I could've been a wrestler.

Throughout elementary and middle school, I played basketball. I practiced layups and free throw shots, played shirts versus skins, ran up and down the court to work on my stamina. But chasing a ball made me feel like a dog, and watching other teammates' eyes widen and stare at my belly so they could anticipate where I would cut on the court made me giggle.

Football didn't appeal to me. My father had knee surgery just before I entered seventh grade, the year I was eligible to join the team, and he kept saying it was because of the sport that he needed the operation. It didn't help that when I slipped a football helmet on my head, I started to hyperventilate and panic because my vision was so limited by the hard plastic. Whenever I went to a football game, I thought the players looked like great heaving rhinoceroses as they slammed their bodies into one another, and someone inevitably got carried off the field.

Instead of wrestling, I joined the speech team in seventh grade. Mrs. Harrison, the frizzy-haired, full-bodied woman who had also been my music teacher, was our coach. I was the only boy on the team.

It was obvious I was not part of the community of boys, not part of their camaraderie. I wasn't wrapped up in the world of the people I lived around. I wasn't part of a team, really—or the right kind of team, at least. I was relegated to an activity where my winning or losing was solely based on my individual ability.

But I was good at it.

EACH MONDAY OUR small school would have announcements— reports from the sports teams, upcoming events, and who took what place in speech competitions. I began to dread Mondays because, on Saturdays, I would inevitably place in those competitions. It began with seventh and sixth places, then I slowly notched up, qualifying for the state competition in categories from Humorous Interpretation and Humorous Duo to Dramatic Duo and Poetry. And then the mocking would come. I had become a sissy, a faggot, a *girl*—because only girls, I was reminded by other boys, were on the speech team. My parents would gleam with pride when I'd bring home a shiny trophy each weekend, but I would bite my nails knowing I'd be harassed at school. With each Monday, I felt more and more uprooted: each week I felt a taste of glory, while the boys in my class, who had inevitably lost their football and basketball games, snarled with envy.

BUT THE TRUTH is I did wrestle in college, in a way. My first year at St. Olaf College I was in a saxophone quartet with a boy named Chris. I was a music major, and he was a chemistry major. With our two other new friends, Emily and Alex, we squared off and played arrangements of Bach's *Brandenburg Concertos* or Fauré's *Pavane*. In high school, I had friends who loved music, but I was always first chair in wind ensemble and jazz band. Now, I struggled to keep up with Emily, Alex, and Chris. They were better than me, their fingers more dexterous.

After practice, Chris and I would make arrangements to play racquetball. We'd hurry back to our dorm rooms, change, and meet at the campus gym to check out rackets. We'd wallop the bright blue ball against the high walls, off the ceiling, trying to place it *just so*— right in the pocket, in the corner, close to the floor, which would kill the spin on the ball, making it impossible for our opponent to get there in time.

We played weekly throughout college, learned the intricacy of the rules and each other's moves—Chris knew my left backhand was weak; I knew if I smacked the ball hard enough off the back wall, Chris wouldn't sprint fast enough to reach it before it bounced twice. I'd get a point. We'd sweat and huff, sometimes we'd laugh and murmur *Nice shot*.

It was a competition, but in many ways it wasn't. There was something intimate about running around a room, trying to get better, but there was also a type of joy in having an opponent who was close in skill to you, someone you knew you could beat on your best days, but you prayed that each day you played was your best day. Chris and I would often go into tiebreakers.

I CAN'T REMEMBER the year of college when it happened, but one day after we called it quits on the court, I put Chris in a headlock to give him a noogie—or maybe he put me in a headlock. Sweaty, we gripped each other and rocked back and forth. I asked him if he wanted to go to the wrestling room just down the hall so we wouldn't get hurt on the hard wooden floors of the racquetball court.

He agreed.

We opened the door to the wrestling room, slipped off our shoes, wiped our sweaty brows with the back of our forearms, and walked across the soft mats to the far circle. We squared up, raised our arms in front of our faces, and shot at each other—sometimes we locked up right away, other times we shot at each other's knees or belly.

I picked him up and tried to slam him, to put him on his stomach, to get on top of him to . . . well, to what? I'm not quite sure.

We tried to pin each other, but it seems that we were more interested in rolling around, in putting each other in holds, of sometimes making the other person tap out, or come close to tapping out and whisper in his ear, *Ya done?*

It was a different type of struggle, one that brought me closer to Chris, both physically and emotionally. From then on, we still loved to play racquetball, but there was always the assumption that wrestling matches would follow. There was no second appendage, no racquet; it was just our bodies, our hands, our sheer weight on the other person, trying to keep him down.

Sometimes we'd go for evening walks through the prairie that circled around the college and Chris would tell me what he learned in chemistry. By this point in our friendship, I had switched to an English major and raved about Lord Byron and the poetry of E. E. Cummings. We'd find some patch of grass in the darkness and roll around together. Or we'd get into it in our dorm rooms, the space cramped, the floor hard, our sweat pooling in the stagnant air. Wrestling was now a type of bond, the kind of camaraderie the other boys had had in high school. There was some urge in me that each time Chris and I were together, we had to get physical. I didn't fully know what it was, but I experienced it as a type of overwhelming surge in my body—to put him in headlocks, to see if I could escape his holds.

No matter where, while we tossed around, I kept my ears open. I would sometimes turn my head slightly to see if I caught the subtle sound of someone coming—conversation flowing across the fields, the squeak of a shoe just beyond the dorm room door. I didn't want to be caught; I wanted this to stay between Chris and me. Wrestling with him tapped something in me, something I hadn't felt before.

I ALSO WRESTLED with other guys in college—former jocks more muscular than me. There was a deep satisfaction about pinning a guy who was stronger, someone who spent time lifting weights and building muscle; there was a self-knowledge that I knew how to use my body in ways a friend didn't—that, if we got close, I could put them on their back, smile overtop them. A self-satisfaction that confirmed I could outmaneuver them. Sure, they could put more weight on a rack than I could, but they couldn't pin me, make me tap out. There was pride in that for me, a boy who struggled with a type of inferiority complex about how small he was.

One of those other guys I wrestled with was named Tom. He was a few inches taller than my five-foot-six-inch frame, weighed about twenty pounds more than me, and had run cross-country and played soccer in high school. Tom was so fit he had veins like rivulets flowing across his biceps.

Tom would throw his hands up in front of his face, then snap them behind my sweaty neck, and we'd push against each other, his hot breath making my nose scrunch.

One day, during our sophomore year, the door to the wrestling room opened. The college wrestling coach walked in. He was a small, wiry Iranian man.

I immediately let go of Tom. My face flushed.

"No, no, keep going," said the coach. "I want to see how you two work."

Neither Tom nor I was ever on a wrestling team. Neither one of us had been taught to wrestle by a coach.

We refocused. I looked at Tom with a slight frown (Tom whispered to me that it was going to be okay), and we went at each other.

The coach would stop us, ask me to do a move—to repeat it, to try it faster. He never asked Tom to do a move.

Tom became a type of wrestling dummy for me to grab, to trip, to toss down on the crimson wrestling mat. It made me feel confident that I could outmaneuver men stronger, physically bigger, than me. That I knew something of the world of aggression and how to use momentum, how to leverage my small body against an opponent, not only gave me an outlet for any aggression stewing inside me, but it also gave me a private type of confidence that allowed me to not be so afraid of straight men. In wrestling, it seemed, I found I could hold my own.

"You should come to our practice tomorrow at five," the coach said to me. "You're a natural."

I closed my eyes, swallowed, nodded, and thanked him for the invitation.

"You're serious that you've not been coached before?" he asked.

I shook my head and told him no.

Afterward, as we put our shoes on, Tom smiled at me.

"Oh, look at you. You could be on the wrestling team, Mr. Tough Guy."

I pushed him as we sat on the floor and tied our laces. We smiled at each other.

BUT I NEVER WENT to that wrestling practice because some type of embarrassment bubbled inside me. I had been spotted by a third party practicing my private pleasure with a close friend, and I wanted to keep wrestling a secret—my own worry over my homosexuality and the homoeroticism of wrestling kept me in check. I wanted to hold in that I found struggling against other men pleasurable, that I enjoyed being close to other men, that there was something inside me that wrestling disabused me of: that I was weak, easy to overpower. The act of wrestling men stronger than me, and realizing that I could beat them (I naturally knew moves my friends didn't) reinforced that I, at heart, wasn't a powerless little gay boy, that I could, if I wanted, hold my own against strong men. I knew how to press their elbows against their ribs so that they'd rip their arms up into the air to make me stop hurting them—I could then shoot into the hole they made, pick them up, and slam them down. The move was called a duck under.

I felt something else wrestling with Chris, something I didn't feel with Tom or other guys, and as college progressed, Chris and I spent more time together—or I pressured him to spend more time with me.

I was friends with his many girlfriends—but I was friends with them so that they liked me, which would mean they'd say nice things about me to Chris, which was my ulterior motive.

Over time, something else was added to Chris's and my friendship, something I had never done with another man—we started to cuddle. We'd lie down on the futon in my dorm room: Chris would be the big spoon and I'd push myself back into him, the two of us curled together like a pair of question marks.

I don't remember when it first happened. I don't even remember how it happened. The origin moment has faded from my memory, but it feels like it was always there, like we had always cuddled.

But we hadn't, and we wouldn't.

BY SENIOR YEAR, Chris and I lived in the same suite, with a common room with eight other men. We'd stay up late, play *Super Smash Bros.* or *Mario Kart* together on the N64. I'd eventually poke him in the rib when he'd start to fade, my signal that it was time to wrestle, and he'd jump on top of me. We'd roll around as quietly as possible. I prayed none of our suitemates heard us.

When my roommate would spend the night in his girlfriend's room, I'd ask Chris to spend the night with me. I'd fold down the futon, throw a blanket or two and a few pillows onto it, and we'd settle in.

I knew Chris was straight, but I couldn't tell why he'd submit to cuddling with me. Sometimes, as we were lying there, I'd ask him why we were doing this—why we were spooning, why we were sleeping next to each other.

"Because it feels good," he'd say.

"It doesn't bother you that I'm gay?" I'd ask.

"Of course not."

I'd silently smile and press against him. I liked how he'd slip one of his legs between mine, how we fit tightly into each other. I liked when he wrapped his arm around my chest and held me.

---

THERE WAS A MORNING, though, where we were discovered. Early one Saturday, loud banging on my door snapped me awake.

"Taylor, is Chris in there?"

It was Chris's girlfriend.

I shook Chris awake.

"Tara's here," I whispered sharply, my eyes wide.

Groggy, Chris woke up. "Shit," he mumbled.

He put on his shirt, ambled over to the door, and slipped out.

I heard Tara's voice say how she had tried to call him multiple times last night, how she was worried about him, how she had texted him. Why was he in my room so early in the morning? she asked.

I sat up on the futon and hunched over, shirtless, looking at the floor. This was it. We were found out—though, what exactly were we found out about?

Chris was straight, I was gay. We liked to wrestle, and we enjoyed sleeping next to each other. Chris confirmed over and over that we just liked to cuddle. That was it, nothing more.

I always thought Chris's girlfriend, Tara, was a lesbian. Because she had a strong body, played softball, and seemed emotionally stifled and reserved, I projected stereotypes that she must be queer. And that made me think—or hope—that Chris might be gay. Maybe they were both keeping up a front, I thought.

It's illogical, of course, yet at the time my love for my friend went into a realm beyond friendship. I grew up on a repressed plain where bonding happened in coal mines, fixing fences, or at the bars. Getting into fights was a more permissible way of showing emotion.

Wrestling now had become something else between Chris and me. It became more fraught.

AFTER COLLEGE, Chris and I both lived in the Twin Cities. He was in graduate school for chemistry, I for writing. There wasn't a wrestling room anymore. Instead, late at night, we'd wrestle on the hardwood floor of my duplex. I hoped we wouldn't wake my two housemates. Our wrestling began to happen so late at night that I'd always ask Chris to spend the night. Usually, he would.

By now, in our midtwenties, I knew I loved Chris, but I couldn't say it. I didn't want to lose his friendship, but my inability to express what I was feeling—channeled through increasingly tense wrestling matches—pushed Chris away.

So did my drinking.

I'd go out to gay clubs on the weekends and on weeknights. I loved the two-for-one nights of glasses filled with cheap gin and a squirt of tonic—how they fired down my throat, temporarily burning away the pain I was feeling inside.

I danced on top of cubes, watched men perform in a shower at the Saloon, and listened to drag queens lip-sync to Cher, Britney Spears, or Madonna at the Gay Nineties.

My gin-infused world was something I knew, coming from a long line of alcoholics: my great-great-grandfather drank himself to death; my great-grandfather drank heavily into his nineties and went blind; my uncle, a diabetic like me, drank until he died after his second divorce; and when my paternal grandmother's siblings came back to town every summer, we locked the doors because, after drinking, they got violent.

Now, in the Twin Cities, I couldn't cope with my overwhelming love for Chris. I'd slowly and drunkenly drive the East River Parkway home to my duplex. I traced the meandering Mississippi River in a drunken haze, passing underneath a canopy of oaks and maples. I'd focus on the curb and the dotted lines. I told myself to take it slow, that if I went slow, I'd be safe.

But sometimes I raced onto the highway, gunned my small Dodge Stratus, barreled toward . . . toward what? I didn't want to die, not really, not yet. But I wanted love. And I wanted that love to be between Chris and me. Drinking was a way of dealing with my love for him.

CHRIS'S AND MY FRIENDSHIP came to a crashing halt on the night of my twenty-fifth birthday party. Friends in St. Paul hosted; I made cheese platters and charcuterie boards, taking those to their home along with cold bottles of champagne.

As the night went on, I began to wobble. I began to swish. My housemate James thanked the hosts, gripped my shoulders, slipped me out the door and into his car, and drove me home.

Two other friends were waiting for us as I stumbled into our living room, ripped my jacket off, and flung it against the wall. James's eyes widened as I passed Molly and Sarah, a pair of sisters.

"Play something on the piano," I stammered at James.

He began to play Bach when I returned from the kitchen with a gin and tonic. I plopped down onto the bench with James, looked at Molly and Sarah, and asked, "You want to know what Bach sounds like?" I started singing along to the melody. "This is what Bach sounds like with a dick in your mouth."

No one laughed. I didn't even laugh. I folded over onto my thighs, the gin and tonic in my outstretched hand.

I pushed up from the piano bench and stumbled into the kitchen, pulled out a half-empty gallon jug of milk, went into the dining room, which connected to the living room, and hurled it across the rooms. It skidded across the floor and stopped by Sarah's feet.

I remember Chris eventually arrived. James mentioned that I was his problem; Molly and Sarah left for home.

"Okay, big guy," Chris said as he wrapped my arm over his shoulder to help me to bed.

And then I woke up and it was morning. Chris was no longer there.

And Chris didn't call me back for days, for weeks. He didn't answer my texts. I felt he was ghosting me.

WHAT I EVENTUALLY learned from an angry voice message from Chris was that when he got me into my room that night, I went limp and fell on top of him on the bed, fully clothed.

And then I humped him.

Repeatedly.

I was told I didn't kiss him; I didn't even say anything. That, after a minute, I just rolled off him and passed out. Chris took off my shoes, placed a light blanket over me, and left.

That was the last time I saw him for years.

I CREATED THE WRESTLING narrative, I suppose, as an attempt to make myself seem exotic. In adulthood, with a move every few years,

I had the opportunity to reinvent myself, which usually meant embellishing the boring real facts of my life: that I was a homosexual who loved listening to NPR, going to the orchestra, fly-fishing, researching fossil-fuel extraction, reading, singing Disney songs, and going out dancing. What no one expected—because it was an outright lie that I was skilled at making everyone believe—was that I was once a wrestler. The narrative fit into people's perceptions of North Dakota: why of course I was on the wrestling team—what else was there to do? Wrestling, unlike polo or riding, is a lower-class sport, and yet there was a type of appeal for everyone—or at least so I thought— because it was hard-bodied boys in skintight singlets. Women sighed while thinking of muscular high-school wrestlers; men groaned, regretting they weren't one. Though no one admits it publicly, it's not the violence and power we're attracted to in wrestling—it's how much skin shows between two men hunched so close together.

I *wanted* to be a wrestler. So, I made up that I was.

But the imaginary story I told revealed a deeper story about myself: I wanted to be straight. Because only straight boys, I thought, were on the wrestling team. I wanted to fit in: it would have been so much easier to be straight when everything—every coyote, every pheasant, every person—struggled. I wanted to struggle a little bit less, and telling my made-up story allowed me to believe that, if only I had been brave enough to join the wrestling team, I would've found a way to fit into my small world. My lie became a way to continually beat myself up, the realization that if only I could have conformed and been what my town wanted me to be, I would have not been bullied, and I would not have fought to get out and go to college.

Another reason I wanted to be on the wrestling team was that I wanted my body to change. I wanted some insurance that I wouldn't be bullied, that I would learn how to get stronger, how to hold my own, how to pump iron and get a body like my neighbor Mark. I liked the team's little singlets, imagined wearing the skintight outfit, hoisting the straps over my shoulders and letting them snap against my skin before entering the circle and spinning and flipping against an opponent. I wanted to be on the wrestling team because it was hand to hand, close quarters, in your face. It was an individual sport, one where you tested your mettle against someone else.

But I didn't crave wrestling to hurt anyone, to outright overpower them. I think I wanted to wrestle because there are so few opportunities for boys and young men to be close to each other. You don't hug other boys in middle school. You don't place your hand on their shoulders as a sign of affection. You punch them. You push them into lockers and smile. You test them through sheer brute force. But some part of my brain thought wrestling could exist on a higher plane— like, if you had the right teammates, they would find grappling to be a type of affection, not a kind that led to sex, but one that just acknowledged you were given permission to be close to another person of the same sex. That you were in some type of struggle together, that, as teammates, you were trying to make each other better.

Since the prairie is a place of vulnerability, both physically and existentially, where humans and animals must be resilient to survive its harsh conditions, I think I wanted to bring some fragment of home with me when I left for college. I wanted some story that I had dreamed up, one rooted to a type of physical prowess necessary for survival. Nothing, after all, survives on the prairie by being tender.

So, I fled.

But deep inside me was a yearning for home, for a way to return. For me, home is a place constructed by the beauty of milky buttes, of the bright song of the western meadowlark, of the elusive bobcat slink-ing through the river bottoms. Home, for me, is land. As I've so often said after leaving North Dakota, "I love the land, not the people."

And perhaps that's where this self-aggrandizing myth originated. I wanted a story of me battling against the bullies, rather than playing music through tears when I skipped study hall. I wanted new friends to believe that I was more complicated than what I perceived as my clichéd gay narrative of the little boy who liked the arts.

I wanted to rewrite my narrative to imagine there was a way that, if only I had been brave enough when I was small to stick my neck out and join the wrestling team, I would have liked living in my small town, at least on some level.

I wanted to find a story where a little gay boy could fit into the world he came from, rather than running to find a way to escape the prairie of his childhood.

A FEW YEARS LATER, Chris and I met at Everest on Grand, a favorite Nepali restaurant of mine while I lived in the Twin Cities. Over momos and chicken palak I shuffled and apologized to Chris. Now, in my late twenties, I admitted that I had been in love with him throughout college and graduate school. I didn't dare say it during those years because I was afraid of losing our friendship, which I had done by pressuring him to wrestle with me and by growing jealous of his relationships with women.

Chris nodded, said he knew, but that in hindsight he, too, was getting something from our wrestling matches, our nights cuddling together on futons and in beds—not love, not in the way all those years earlier I wanted to love him, but something like comfort. Yes, something like that.

My shoulders relaxed. We smiled and ate our meal.

# 4.

IN MY FOUR YEARS at college, I tried to hide the fact that I came from western North Dakota. I tried to lose my Midwestern accent, use polysyllabic words, and read the "great books." Like lignite coal, I smoldered into something else—and, I hoped, the change was to something bright and luminescent. North Dakota was not a place to write about. A benighted place with backward people, North Dakota, as I was told by the wider culture and college classmates, was empty, void of culture, of history, of meaning.

But Jim disabused me of that notion.

THE FIRST CLASS I took with Jim Farrell was Environmental History. I was briefly a history major, so I expected to encounter primary sources, arcane reading, and a plethora of footnotes. Jim, instead, gave us an essay that appeared in *Minnesota Monthly*, about one woman's examination of shoes, particularly her great-grandmother's shoes from nineteenth-century prairie life in the still young state of Minnesota.

The essay read well. It was infused with historical detail and meticulously researched—but no footnotes, no endnotes. What was the point of this? It wasn't what I was used to reading as "history." I had drunk the Kool-Aid of academe: researched writing should be dry and stuffy, and it should not read well—it should be a difficult task to decipher what any author was saying.

"This—this article—is how you might consider writing history," Jim said. "Don't you want to keep reading? Isn't it engaging? It's fun."

And it was. It was a casual writing style I wasn't encouraged to use in my other history classes. This woman wrote "I" statements: "I noticed my grandmother's shoes," "I felt a connection to her." *We*, those of us who took college seriously, weren't supposed to "notice" or "feel" in our academic papers for other classes. The text *showed*, the author *stated*—and there was no room for "me," for "I" statements in academic writing.

JIM'S METHOD OF TEACHING was Socratic. Instead of "professing" his expertise, he asked questions that created conversation. "What did you think about this? Did you notice something unique in the reading? How do you feel about that?"

One day in Environmental History, after reading about big-box-store consumer waste, I was on fire for social justice.

"Why the fuck do people shop at Wal-Mart?" I bellowed naïvely. My classmates chortled.

And Jim, in his quiet, wry way, made it into an educational moment.

"Why did you all laugh when Taylor said 'fuck'? Is it because you don't think we should swear in college classrooms? Where do we think we should be able to say the word 'fuck'? Why don't you laugh when I say 'fuck'?"

"Fuck," in this instance, became one of Jim's notable "dense facts." This was an idea Jim infused throughout his classes: everyday items represented more than just what they appeared to be—a bumper sticker is not just a bumper sticker, it is a social moniker. We believe the sticker is an individualized expression of ourselves—and bumper stickers are not only on car bumpers, but also on computers, reusable water bottles, guitar cases, or doors.

Pulling back the everyday to reveal patterns, social constructs, and problems, not only with bumper stickers, but with food waste, with consumerism, with education, and with how we treat the natural world, was what, according to Jim, education was for.

For several years, Jim hosted *Dr. America*, a short radio program on WCAL, the college radio station. Dr. America—Jim's alter ego—oversaw the (wholly imaginary) American Studies Museum, where, for five minutes each week, he pulled out one of his curiosities—the Nike swoosh, the Mall of America, the saying "shit happens," or the high heel—and peeled it apart, layer by layer, to reveal the cultural work inside the object. These musings were the basis of the second class I took from Jim: Introduction to American Studies.

In Intro to American Studies, we read Barbara Kingsolver's *Animal Dreams* (Jim was the only non-English teacher I studied with in college who used novels, poetry, and essays to teach another field). We studied billboards, watched commercials, and debated Martin Luther King Jr.'s "Letter from Birmingham Jail."

We kept a journal, too, something we had done in Environmental History. I noticed questions we used as prompts on the syllabus:

"Why am I here? What's education for? What are my goals in education? Why am I in this class? What are my goals for this class?"

Why was I there? Because it was an introductory class, sounded interesting, fulfilled a requirement, and would be, or so I thought, an easy A.

What's education for? To get a good-paying job. After all, that's what Mom and Dad often reminded me it was for.

What were my goals for education? To skate through with a decent GPA to get that good-paying job, maybe as a lawyer, or even a doctor.

Why was I in this class? Because I liked Jim.

What were my goals for this class? To not fail. To get an A. To do the work, but not all the reading.

I looked down the list of how the semester was organized and wondered how Jim's brain thought up this stuff: "Why We Brush Our Teeth and Other American Studies Questions"; "The Truth About Stories"; "The Stories About Truth"; "The Truth About Commercial Stories"; "TV Stories"; "The F-Word and American Culture"; "Stories of Race"; "Stories of Color and Blindness"; "Stories of Citizenship"; "Toy Stories"; "American Dreams, American Stories."

We read *The Truth About Stories: A Native Narrative*, by the Canadian writer Thomas King. In it, he wrote, "There is a story I know. It's about the earth and how it floats in space on the back of a turtle. The truth about stories is that's all we are."

And I thought of the stories of my life—of hunting with Dad and Uncle Greg, the smell of gunpowder in the air after shooting at pheasant, pheasant we'd later throw in the Crockpot and slather with cream of mushroom soup. And I thought about the stories of my great-uncles, Uncle Frank and Uncle Pete, two men I never met, but about whom my Grandpa Hatzenbihler told such vivid stories that I'd swear they just walked out of the room.

Somewhere in me I knew what Thomas King meant, for it is stories that helped orient my life. Stories were bedrock. Stories—stories of others going to college—led me here, to St. Olaf. And now, too, I was creating a new story in my family: the ability to go to college. I went to professors' office hours frequently because I craved their stories: How the hell did they wind up here? What is this thing called graduate school? Could that be part of my story? Can you really make a life reading and writing and still pay the bills?

TOWARD THE END of the semester, we each had to pick an item that symbolized American culture, write a one-page essay that dug into the cultural work and assumptions of that item, and be prepared to present the item and our essay as a part of the American Studies Museum, which was open to the rest of the campus for viewing the final two weeks of the term.

My classmates chose a basketball, a bottle of water, a baseball hat, a shopping bag, lipstick. I chose the bumper sticker that says "Shit happens."

When Jim handed back the first draft of my essay, I flipped to the end and read C.

I went to Jim's office, which was up a steep, narrow flight of stairs. I got winded each time I climbed the stairs to see him. A line of students waited outside his office.

After an hour, I was next.

"Come in, Taylor."

I entered Jim's windowless office. I found it odd—the guy who was known around campus for speaking about building design, about being outside, was tucked away in a cream-colored office with faux wood-paneled bookshelves. His office had no natural light, no windows, no fresh air.

"Jim, I noticed I got a C on this essay, and I'm not sure why."

I waited for him to say it was because it wasn't very good, that I wasn't a good writer, that I probably shouldn't even be in college.

"It's because you haven't written shit into your essay."

"I'm sorry?" I asked, believing I misheard him.

"Aren't you writing about a bumper sticker that says 'Shit happens'? Don't you think, then, that you need to write about shit?"

"But that's not what the bumper sticker's getting at. 'Shit happens' is a euphemism for the bad stuff that happens in our everyday life."

"And don't you think how we treat shit is part of the bad stuff that happens in our everyday life?"

Dressed in one of the too-large sweaters he favored—this one maroon with some holes in the elbow—Jim rocked in his chair, legs crossed, his top leg pumping up and down.

"I'm not sure I follow," I said.

"I bet you do. You know that when you flush the toilet each morning your shit goes someplace. And you know that that shit and water must be treated—probably with a lot of chemicals, right? And you know that, somehow, once it's broken down, it reenters the water system."

"I do," I said, but I didn't really—partly because I had never really thought about it until this conversation with Jim.

"You need to do more research on what we do with shit once we flush it down the toilet because, you're right, the bumper sticker is a euphemism. But I think you can drill down on what the sticker is literally saying: Shit happens. And it happens every day and, as you just proved, we rarely think and talk about it."

A mountain of books sat behind him, and I thought, *Has he really read all those books?* Around campus I'd heard he was trying to write a book about how every facet of college life affects the natural world.

"Thanks for the help, Jim. See you next class."

I was still frustrated—a damn C. When I called Mom to talk about school, her rejoinder was "Try harder."


IN THE SPRING of my senior year, I registered for Campus Ecology, my last class with Jim. It was an environmental studies course that asked us to look at our place—the college campus and surrounding prairie—and delve into the environmental and socially constructed world and work of college. We toured the campus power plant, met with the facilities director, read Wendell Berry (the author of *The Unsettling of America*), and graffitied the campus with annotations about the environmental implications of—excuse me—taking a shit, eating without a cafeteria tray, or turning down the heat. The class asked us to wake up to moral responsibility and our everyday actions.

We kept a journal about a spot outside—our "plot"—documenting the plants, the animals (human and otherwise) and the happenings. We were supposed to notice and articulate how the plot changed over the course of the semester. We were to pay attention.

We read a book called *Earth in Mind*. The author, David Orr, had come to St. Olaf my sophomore year and lectured about meeting with potential 2008 presidential candidates and shifting their views on environmental issues. Tall, with deep blue eyes and a band of hair circling his shiny head, David spoke with a slight drawl. He talked to us about the warming trends in the atmosphere and about the "precautionary principle," a metric that asks stakeholders to consider environmental impacts multiple generations into the future when making decisions, challenging us, as college students, to lead the charge in making environmental issues *the* issues in that upcoming election. But I hadn't read Orr until now.

When I did start reading *Earth in Mind* for class, I stopped on page 11: "Fifth, there is a myth that the purpose of education is to give students the means for upward mobility and success."

*Isn't that what an education is for?* I wrote in pencil in my copy.

> The plain fact is that the planet does not need more successful people. But it does desperately need more peacemakers, healers, restorers, storytellers, and lovers of every kind. It needs people who live well in their places. It needs people of moral courage willing to join the fight to make the world habitable and humane. And these qualities have little to do with success as our culture has defined it.

There was something there, something that pulled at the silky part of me: the world desperately needed more "storytellers, and lovers of every kind." It needed "people who live well in their places."

I loved the landscape of western North Dakota. I knew the stories of Lewis and Clark. I knew stories of picking juneberries in July with Grandpa and Grandma Hatzenbihler. I knew stories of catching emerald-colored walleye and tadpoles in backwater pools.

But it was the final sentence in this passage that stung me: "And these qualities have little to do with success as our culture has defined it." I wondered if "success" might be a construct. My parents had spent the entirety of their lives working jobs they hated—might it be possible for me to find a job I loved? Might there be other qualities to work—pleasure, challenge, effort, enjoyment, good colleagues—beyond the pay scale?

And I thought about how Mom and Dad would talk about the houses on Fox Island, the wealthy part of Bismarck on the Missouri River: how the housing development was filled with doctors and lawyers, "successful" people; or how big someone's yard was (even better if they had *acres* of land around their house); or how people could retire before sixty (those people were "successful" by my parents' standards).

I put a "Q" next to this passage in *Earth in Mind* to save it for use in a future paper. Something in that paragraph snagged me.

However, it was another writer whose work I read in Campus Ecology, not an academic, who helped me fall in love with my home on the prairie.

By the time I read Paul Gruchow, during my senior year of college, he had been dead six years, having taken his own life near Lake Superior. Gruchow was a man without a college degree who, I later found out, had taught at St. Olaf College. In Jim's class we read *Grass Roots: The Universe of Home*, published when Gruchow taught in Northfield. It is a collection of essays with magical names, such as "The Transfiguration of Bread," "Snails Have Faces," and "Naming What We Love." We weren't assigned the entire collection, but it was the essays that Jim left off the syllabus that changed the nature of my thinking.

One night I pulled my copy of *Grass Roots* from my briefcase.

Earlier in the semester, I had accidentally spilled coffee along the bottom of the book. The pages, slathered sepia, had now congealed. They crinkled as I turned them. I looked over the table of contents and turned to the essay "What the Prairie Teaches Us":

> The prairie, although plain, inspires awe. It teaches us that gran-deur can be wide as well as tall.
>
> Young prairie plants put down deep roots first; only when these have been established do the plants invest much energy in growth above ground. They teach us that the work that matters doesn't always show.

*The work that matters doesn't always show.*

Jim was the only professor on campus whose classes gave me permission to express my values. In English classes I argued about what the text said, in philosophy I got a headache, in mathematics I learned about Babylonian "widgets." While all of these created a patchwork of curiosity in my liberal arts mind, Jim was the only truly interdisciplinary teacher I encountered. Jim continued to ask his students confounding questions: "What is a *real* education?" "What are our expressed values (those we say with our mouths) compared to our operative values (those we express with the rest of our bodies)?" "What is the good life?" "Is college life part of the supposed 'real world'?" Jim taught us that the work that matters might very well be the work of understanding why it is we do what we do and how we might reenvision the world.

Gruchow's brief essay continued, and I noticed each paragraph began with a declarative sentence. As if he were laying bricks, Gruchow builds a wall of assertion, something to defend the prairie, my home bioregion: "The prairie is community," "The prairie is patient," "The prairie grows richer as it ages," "The prairie is tolerant," "The prairie turns adversity to advantage," "The prairie is cosmopolitan," "The prairie is bountifully utilitarian."

There's something I came to trust in Gruchow's voice, something that unearthed the particular of place—like listening to someone who has spent a lifetime paying attention. *If he can do it*, I wondered, *could I? Could I learn all of this from looking at grass?*

THE OAKS AND MAPLES began to bud out as April rolled around during my final semester. While walking across the quad, I went to an Adirondack chair, set my bag down, pulled out my phone, and sat down. I could hear wind chimes ring. Classmates sunned themselves on blankets, the first nice day of the year. I called my sister, Tanya.

"Hey, what's up?" she asked.

"Do you have a few minutes to talk?"

I asked her how her husband, Mike, was; what Logan and Noah, my nephews, were up to.

I glanced around. No one was that close to me, and the couple who was nearest, snuggled up to each other on their blanket.

"Sheba Queen, can I tell you something?"

"What's up, Nerdbomber?"

I looked up. The tops of the trees swayed in the midday breeze; a smear of white trailed an airplane high above me.

"I'm gay."

There was a pause. I looked around to see if anyone heard me.

"Aren't you surprised?" I asked.

And then she laughed.

"C'mon, Taylor. No, I'm not surprised."

"Really?"

"Really."

"Why not?"

"Nerdbomber, everyone knows you're gay as soon as you open your mouth."

We busted out laughing.

"Plus, you *loved* wearing Mom's high heels. And do I need to tell you how often you watched *Mary Poppins* or twirled in aprons that Grandma Brorby made for you?"

"Okay, I get it. But I don't think we should tell Mom and Dad—do you?" I asked.

"No, I think let's keep this to ourselves for a while."

We kept talking as if nothing happened because, in a way, nothing did—my world changed, but my world didn't change. It was as if I told my sister that I liked pistachio ice cream instead of rocky road. I sank into my chair as Tanya and I chatted away. I watched the couple on the blanket and breathed a sigh of relief.

# 5.

THE EVANGELICAL LUTHERAN CHURCH in America, the church
of my childhood, approved the ordination of openly gay clergy
in 2009. Before this, people like me couldn't come out of the closet
to openly serve as pastors.

I didn't want to be a pastor, but somehow that same year, my
senior year at St. Olaf, I was in the process of applying to seminaries
and theological schools. I had a short list: Harvard, Yale, Princeton, and the University of Chicago. I knew this was ambitious, but
I wanted a big city, a better chance for me to be me, a place far away
from the childhood prairie.

For some reason, my plan was to get ordained, serve as a pastor
for three years—even though church-basement potlucks made my
stomach churn—and then hightail it out of the parish to get a PhD
and become a professor: being a pastor, should teaching fail, would
be a safe fallback plan. Pastors read, wrote, and were with people at
pivotal moments in their lives. It would be good enough—and there
was job security: the church needed pastors without white hair.

I needed options, multiple safety nets. No one in my family had finished college, much less gone on to graduate school. For the second time, I was stepping onto a new and unfamiliar path. No one in my family could help me or give me advice. I needed some sense of stability.

In childhood, my family went to church only on Easter Day and to the candlelit Christmas Eve service. We didn't pray before meals, and I didn't pray before going to sleep. I did have to go through confirmation classes, where we memorized the books of the New Testament by doing hand motions.

The reason I was raised in the Lutheran church was that my mother, when she was nineteen, got pregnant; Dad was twenty. Instead of placing her child with Catholic Charities for adoption, as others in her family had done, my mom walked down the aisle of my father's Lutheran church, a billowing white bump growing beneath her wedding gown.

The Catholic church wouldn't marry my parents.

My sister arrived three months later. It would be ten years before my parents had their second and last child.


As I've mentioned, I called my mother and sister every day during my first semester of college. I couldn't do it, I told them. College was too hard. I didn't know how to study. I didn't know how to write college papers. I cried in the shower so my eyes wouldn't burn red and make my roommate worry about me. I found study nooks in the library where my tears quietly slid down my cheeks. I was thankful my roommate's and my beds were bunked so that I could turn toward the wall as my pillow became damp.

I ping-ponged between them, my mom and sister. As soon as

I felt stable and hung up with one of them, a great wave of sadness would wash over me. I'd be on the phone, dialing the other's number.

Desperate, my mother told me to go visit the college pastor. "That's what he's there for," she said.

When I knocked on the pastor's office, a giant figure emerged. When he asked if he could help me, I blurted out that I needed someone to talk to.

"I've never been this far away from home," I said. "I don't know how to study. I don't want to be a music major anymore. I can't do *this*," I said as my arms flailed around me.

Pastor Benson looked at me, opened his private office, gestured for me to come in, and closed the door behind us. He asked me if I had any friends. I knew one junior boy at the college, a guy from back home, but he already had friends, I said. I told Pastor Benson that three of my best friends from high school went to school at the University of Minnesota.

"Why don't you go up there for the weekend?" he asked.

I protested, said it was because I didn't have a car. That I was supposed to be *here*, studying, learning how to be a college student.

"There's a shuttle that you can take up to the Mall of America. You can hop on the light rail, ride it to the Twins stadium near downtown, close to the U's campus. Your friends can meet you there. If you can't figure that out, I'll drive you to your friends and pick you up myself."

That weekend, I saw my friends from high school. I choked backed tears and counted the minutes until I would have to take the light rail back to the Mall of America on Sunday, and then the lonely forty-five-minute shuttle ride out of the Twin Cities, back to Northfield. I didn't want to leave my friends. I wanted comfort, some semblance of stability in the new rockiness of my college life, a life far away from home.

I started seeing Pastor Benson every two weeks. When I looked at his bookshelves, I noticed he had more novels than religious texts. He told me he had been an English major in college.

AT ST. OLAF COLLEGE, there was daily chapel. Classes stopped for twenty minutes as a dusting of students, faculty, and staff drifted throughout the pews of Boe Chapel, a large limestone, gothic building anchoring the campus.

Eventually, I began to go to chapel. I listened to professors talk about social justice, about how the Bible promises an abundance of life, not a life of abundance. I heard Ezra Pound and E. E. Cummings quoted as often as St. John or Jesus Christ. I started to read the whacked-out stories of the Old Testament—staffs slithering into snakes, being down in the dank hot belly of a fish for days, God being wild inside the whirlwind while stumping Job with ecological questions.

By then, I was an English major. I knew I wanted to hang out with Satan in Hell in *Paradise Lost*. I read the underpinnings of religious thinking in Marilynne Robinson's writing and Dostoyevsky's *Brothers Karamazov*. Religion, particularly Christian thinking, infused the writing I read in my English classes. I laughed at Flannery O'Connor's short stories. I felt the heartbreak in Toni Morrison's sentences in *Sula* and the indignation of racism in James Baldwin's prophetic essays. It seemed everything I read related to everything else and each work, in turn, related back to me—or at least to what I was feeling.

Yet, I never prayed in private, thought of God as some active force in my life. Sure, I recited the Apostle's Creed, and I prayed when directed to in daily chapel or during Sunday worship services—but I thought of those more as ritual, meditations, a way of entering a spiritual space of connection with other people. This cerebral form of religion connected back to my book learning, the music of sentences. All this learning frayed the thread that bound me back to my family.

My mother's family are devoted Roman Catholics—rosaries, confession, saints. I remember one of my mom's sisters once coming inside our lake house after a fire, telling me that studies showed that when priests prayed over the bread, it was later found to have bone fragments in it—it became the literal body of Christ.

At twelve, I listened patiently before getting more marshmallows for the fire.

She said nothing of the wine becoming actual blood. Church wine never tasted metallic to me.

Later, when she and Mom visited me in college, I remember that she would not go up to receive communion from Pastor Benson. She could receive communion only from a Catholic priest, she told me, and Pastor Benson was a Lutheran pastor.

With Mom's family, it felt like I was back in the sixteenth century, still locked in the religious battles of the Reformation.

In hindsight, I'm not fully sure why I applied for seminary—I knew I wanted to teach, not preach. I liked the idea of shaping a classroom into a safe place to explore complicated thoughts and emotions.

Walking into a parish felt like navigating a political minefield.

But the gravity of being the first to finish college weighed on me: I had to prove that I made something of myself. Parish ministry was stable. It was needed in the small towns where I came from. I figured, if anything, some parish in western Nebraska would need a pastor.

But I also loved Pastor Benson's care, his attentive ear. I watched joy wash across his face whenever a college student chose to be baptized. I loved memorizing hymns, their ancient melodies connecting me across time and space to friends and people long dead. And reading. I wanted a profession where reading was bedrock, where I had time for contemplation, where I could call upon my learning to help others in their time of need.

# 6.

AFTER COLLEGE GRADUATION the days all blurred together. Suddenly, it was already August, and Logan, my older nephew, was turning five. I washed up after my shift at a food supply warehouse and headed over to my sister and brother-in-law's, who had moved to Bismarck from Seattle three years earlier, for cake and ice cream.

It was a family event—my parents, Mike's mother and aunts, my Aunt Shelia and her partner, Al, and me. A cake, lit with five candles, rushed by me. My sister took it toward Logan, whose face beamed.

The Pfliger Sisters (what everyone calls Mike's aunts and mother) launched into a harmonized version of "Happy Birthday."

Logan blew out the candles and smoke swirled into the air.

My sister, round with the twin boys she was expecting, grabbed the cake to take back to Mike for him to slice in the kitchen. I followed her.

As Mike cut frosted red, blue, and white pieces of cake, I loaded them on plastic-coated paper plates to hand to Tanya.

"Did your aunt Raylene call you?" Mike asked me.

"No."

I gave him a puzzled look.

My mom's younger sister, Aunt Raylene, and I were close, but with five children of her own, we never talked on the phone.

Tanya returned to get two more pieces of cake.

"You didn't tell Taylor Raylene called?" Mike asked Tanya.

Tanya shot Mike a glare. My stomach turned. I looked at Tanya.

"What'd she want?" I asked.

Mike continued to load cake on the plates as I handed them to Tanya.

Silence.

Frustrated, I grabbed a plate and went into the living room.

"How's summer going, Taylor?" asked Mike's mom, Charlene.

"Oh, it's fine. It's good to work at the food supply warehouse. I've got to save money before moving east," I said.

"Yes," said Mike's aunt, Claudia, who had been my sixth-grade teacher in Center. She taught me about the Romans, the Greeks, and the Beatles. She exposed me to history and the world beyond the wheat fields in my backyard. "We hear you're going to Princeton Seminary! Can you believe it? Little Taylor Brorby from Center, North Dakota, going to Princeton!"

The Sisters squealed.

"You must be so proud, Jim and Denise," said Judy, another aunt, with a glittering smile.

"Yup," Dad said in a clipped, gruff voice.


THE TIME PASSED and the sun sank toward the horizon.

"Well, I have to go. Nearly nine," I said. "Have to work early in the morning."

The Sisters each gave me a hug and I bent down to hug and kiss my nephews.

"See you at home," said Dad.

AT HOME, I TOOK OFF my socks and threw them in the laundry room. I flexed my feet, which had a few broken and callused blisters from my steel-toed boots. I stood against the kitchen counter for balance and massaged a foot at a time.

The phone rang.

I stretched my arms and back as the garage door rumbled open.

The caller ID read VETTEL. I knew it was Aunt Raylene.

I ripped the phone from the wall and went down the stairs to meet Mom at the door.

"I'm going to bed; Aunt Raylene is calling. Good night; love you." I handed her the phone.

I entered my room, turned my nightstand light on, stripped to my underwear, and got into bed. I grabbed Annie Dillard's *The Writing Life* from my desk and pretended to read. I leaned my head to the side. Mom's voice reverberated down the hallway.

I looked around my room. My five-pound-ten-ounce bass, two ounces heavier than the one my dad had mounted, glowed on the wall. Above my closet was a long strip of paper with BRORBY painted in Floridian sea life from a family trip to the Keys, and in front of me was my sister's cross-stitch of freshwater fish—walleye, catfish, bluegill—framed on the wall.

Suddenly, Mom went silent.

I pretended to read.

I heard the phone beep and a whisper. "Jim."

I curled my toes and pulled my comforter up over my belly.

What was that call about? I wondered. Why were there whispers in the house, why was Aunt Raylene calling everyone, but not calling me?

Muffled footsteps came down the hallway, and a sharp knock rapped on my door.

"Come in," I said softly. I cleared my throat. "Come in," I said again.

Mom opened the door, and they both stood in the doorway. Mom adjusted her glasses and stepped into my room. I put down Annie Dillard. Mom moved and sat on the edge of my bed as Dad leaned against the doorframe, arms crossed. The comforter stretched tight against me.

Her voice quaked a bit. "Taylor, I just got off the phone with Raylene, and she's worried you might be gay."

*Lie*, I thought. *They don't know. You haven't told them. Just say you're not. You only have a month left with them. Just do it—say you're straight. You don't even have a boyfriend. Tell them later, when you're far away, when you've found someone for life.*

"Why does she think that?"

"She said you've posted some articles online about gay clergy getting ordained. Are you? Are you gay, Taylor?"

Time stopped. Or maybe it roiled. Heat climbed up my throat and I couldn't stop it. This was the moment I feared—feeling trapped, at home, on the prairie. I had heard—read—the stories of gay children disowned by their families. It was my own fear: I knew my parents loved me, but I worried their love only extended so far.

"Yes. Yes, I'm gay," I said.

Mom's eyes widened. For the next wash of time, I talked about the mistranslated passages in the Bible, how I had known I liked boys since I was fourteen. Mom cut in.

"But we don't know any gay people."

I breathed in.

"You lived with one for eighteen years."

It's as if she had a stomach pain—she didn't wince, but it was as if she almost folded into herself. Or did her head do an ever so subtle twitch? I couldn't tell.

I rambled, tried to focus. In the back of my head was the worry over pedophilia associated with male homosexuality.

"But you don't have to worry about me with the nephews."

Silence.

Mom looked away.

Now my eyes widened. Heat again as my voice raised.

"*You'd worry about me with my nephews?*"

I smoldered out. We stopped talking. Dad turned and left the room. My bed shifted as Mom got up.

Silence again.

I turned out my light and couldn't hear their voices. It was clear outside my window. The moon was a bright pearl against a gray curtain of night.

THE NEXT MORNING, I had to be to work at 5:30 a.m. I left in the cool morning air before the sun rose. Dew glistened on dark grass.

I listened to NPR as I drove the still silent streets of Bismarck. My back and shoulders ached, like I just had come from a massage.

In the U.S. Foods parking lot I sent out a text: *Came out last night. Seemed to go all right. No drama, Thank God.* I pressed send and sent the text to my sister and friends from college.

I brought my phone with me as I entered the large steel warehouse.

"Brorby, get on the forklift," hollered my boss, Ron.

The food was already in, and it promised to be a long day.

"Fucking more shipments than we can handle," yelled T.W., a small, round, balding man. Sometimes T.W. brought a steel bat into work and whacked his, and others', forklifts.

We zoomed and whipped throughout the day, unloading ice cream, raspberries, liquid smoke, and coffee flavoring.

I switched to the highman to load food on the shelves. Two thousand pounds of mozzarella in fifty-pound boxes. Three thousand pounds of cheddar. Two hundred gallons of ranch dressing. My back burned.


"WRAP IT UP, BOYS," yelled Ron close to six p.m. No one talked as we left work, knowing we had less than twelve hours before we'd be back at it.

I checked my phone—texts of support from everyone. I started the car and drove home. I pulled in, slammed the car door, and walked into the entryway.


THE HOUSE WAS QUIET. I sat down my lunch pail and unlaced my oil-stained steel-toed boots. Sore, I used the smooth banister to climb the stairs.

Mom was in the kitchen and Dad was sitting on the left side of the table, which was odd since he normally sat at the head. *Wheel of Fortune* wasn't on, and, for some reason, I knew to not even say hello.

Dad looked out the sliding glass doors as I sat down at the head of the table, between my parents.

Mom brought a plate of steaming corn on the cob to the table.

I grabbed a cob and a pork chop. I cut the cob and corn. In chunks, it toppled onto my plate. I began cutting my pork chop into cubes, trimming the fat, which I knew Dad would later eat off my plate.

Dad cleared his throat.

"I've got one thing to say."

I kept cutting. I couldn't look at him.

"It's not okay for you to be this way."

"Okay," I said. *Just clear your plate, then you can leave. Focus on eating. Just eat and leave,* I said to myself.

Goose bumps rolled across my back.

"Now I don't read much," said Dad, more confidently, "but in the Bible I know it says God created man and woman and He said, 'Be together.'"

"I don't think it quite says that," I said, timidly.

"It's that liberal college and all those liberal ideas it put into your head," said Mom.

*Don't raise your voice. Just eat—and don't raise your voice.*

"I don't think being gay is liberal or conservative," I said. I quickly crammed bites of my food into my mouth.

"Where are you going to live? People get killed over this."

"Where, Dad? Where do people get killed for being gay?"

"In Wyoming. Some guy got killed over it in Wyoming."

"His name is Matthew Shepard. I don't live in Wyoming. I don't go to unsafe places."

My corn and pork got smaller.

"How about those guys from college, are they gay? Any of them your boyfriends—Chris, C.W.?" asked Mom.

"No, they're just friends."

My throat dried. My eyes blurred. My voice got smaller.

"I'm done eating."

I scraped my food in the garbage and put my plate in the sink.

I LEFT. The August heat hit me as I trudged the mile to my sister's house. I slapped away the tears that flowed down my cheeks. At one point, my knees buckled. I'd been slamming my feet hard against the ground as I walked. I couldn't yell, couldn't scream. I was in public and needed to keep it together.

WHEN I GOT TO Tanya's house, I walked through the open garage door, past strewn Frisbees and bikes and bats, and pounded on the door. It opened.

Logan stood there.

"Uncle Taylor, why are you crying?"

I crouched and looked him in the eyes. I grabbed his T-shirt to bring him close, and I looked him up and down.

"Oh, buddy, sometimes people say some things that make us sad."

"Why, Uncle Taylor?"

"I don't know, buddy, I don't know."

"But why, Uncle Taylor. Uncle Taylor . . ."

"Everything okay?" said Tanya from up the stairs.

I stood up and looked at her. "Supper didn't go so well," I said, holding my face in my hands.

"Mike, watch the boys," yelled Tanya, who waddled down the stairs.

We got in her van as Tanya drove us south and out of Bismarck.

"What happened, Taylor?"

"I don't know. I thought it went okay last night. I came home and they teamed up on me."

We got to General Sibley, a campground south of town and pulled into the parking lot next to some cottonwood trees.

For the next three hours I cried. Tanya cried. We screamed. We blew our noses.

Eventually, it got dark and we left the campground.

"Do you want to stay with us?"

"I have work tomorrow. I'll go home and go right to bed."

Tanya pulled into Mom and Dad's driveway. The house was dark, except for the entryway light.

"It looks like they've gone to sleep," she said. "Call whenever. I'll come get you. Come over tomorrow. I love you."


I OPENED THE DOOR to a quiet house, took off my shoes, went to the bathroom and showered. My tears seemed unending.

I dried off, went into my room, and gently closed the door.


AFTER WORK THE NEXT DAY, I came home and there was a note in Mom's handwriting.

Went to Sturgis for the bike rally. See you next week.

I cried out into the quiet house.

# 7.

FOR THE NEXT three weeks my father lived at our house on Lake Sakakawea; Mom and I avoided each other in Bismarck. I kept going to work at U.S. Foods and, on some days while I loaded Kool-Aid packets, liquid smoke, and rolls of paper towels onto the shelves, I cried. I tried to cry whenever I worked in the freezer or refrigerator. I figured the cold air would make it less apparent that I wept. My coworkers could tell something was up, but when a few asked me about it, I shrugged it off, said it's private, and, to my surprise, they didn't heckle me or ask any further questions.

Each night I came home and quarantined myself in the basement; Mom stayed upstairs.

I came up for leftovers from supper well after she ate. She stayed in her and Dad's room in the evenings.


TOWARD THE END of August, she scheduled a family therapy session with a Catholic counselor. She could only get a time during the early afternoon, so I asked for time off from work. Tanya joined us.

The day came and I tossed my lunch pail into the car and drove to the west side of Bismarck. The counselor rented an office space on the other side of the street from Lowe's, Best Buy, and Texas Roadhouse. It was small. The office reminded me of being in a home design show from the 1990s, which was how the counselor dressed—a floral-patterned shirt, business slacks. I could smell her hairspray and was inclined to not like her as I didn't think I should have had to be there. It was my parents who were the ones that needed counseling, not me.

TANYA AND I sat on a leather couch on one side of the room and my parents sat on the other. Dad had chew in his lower lip and crossed his arms. Mom sat nearest to the counselor. Tanya and I leaned back in the couch.

"So, Denise, you scheduled this because you and Jim recently found out Taylor is a homosexual."

"No, they didn't 'find out,'" I said. "I was outed by my aunt."

Everyone but Tanya turned and looked at me.

"I just want to make sure we get the facts straight."

"So, your sister told you that Taylor was gay?" she asked Mom. The counselor had one of those lilting voices that sounded like it's always on the verge of crying.

"She said she was 'worried' I might be gay," I said.

"All right," said the counselor. She looked at me and smiled. "Now, Jim or Denise, was this a surprise to you?"

Dad sat there stiff as Stonewall Jackson.

"I mean, it was," began Mom. "We never thought of him that way. He was just Taylor. I mean, he didn't really date, or if he did, we didn't hear about it. I mean, I guess we should have known, looking back."

"Can you say more about that? What do you mean 'you should have known'?" asked the counselor.

"It's just that Taylor wasn't like the other little boys around him. He didn't really want to do sports," said Mom.

"What concerns you about Taylor being gay?" The counselor leaned in and rested her elbow on her knee.

Mom looked up at the ceiling.

I stared directly at her.

"That he won't have a normal life. That he won't have children. That being this way will make his life harder. I mean, he couldn't even tell us this. That hurts."

"I couldn't tell you this because I knew *this* was how you'd react," I said.

"Do you worry that Taylor might go to Hell for being gay?" asked the counselor.

Dad didn't speak. I can't remember what Mom said because I was too focused on the question.

Mom cried. Dad just stared out the window.

"It's just that our children never had to hear no. We gave them whatever they wanted," said Mom.

I looked over at Tanya.

"When Taylor wanted piano lessons, we bought a piano and put him in lessons. When he needed a saxophone, we bought him a new one. They never had to hear no," Mom said as she tried to wipe away her tears.

"I'm sorry," I said as I sat up and looked over at the counselor, "But I thought we were here to discuss my being gay, not what my parents did or didn't buy me."

"This is what your mom wants to talk about right now," said the counselor. She smiled and nodded at me. "So, we're going to go there right now, okay?" The counselor placed a hand on my mom's shoulder as she wept.

I sat back in the couch and crossed my arms just like Dad. Two Brorby men, both pissed, who now refused to talk.

In that moment, I thought back to the night I lost my thumb in the accident at Bobcat. That night, four years earlier, back at home after the surgery, while lying on our green cloth couch, I pressed my face into soft pillows. They absorbed my tears. I cried out, gulping for air like a fish out of water, my left thumb bandaged. The octave key for my saxophone.

The thumb was now shorter. I wouldn't know until weeks later, when the bandages were removed, how much shorter. Short enough that it could no longer rest on the octave key, which meant it slowed my technique, which meant we would have to scour the country for an instrument repairman to rebuild my saxophone.

I would eventually give up saxophone, and music, after my first semester of college. The pain of my diminished technique, the trauma pulsing through my body whenever the nub of my thumb missed the octave key, was too much for me.

"It'll be all right," Mom had tried to reassure me, the night of my accident.

"But what about music?" I had cried into the pillows.

Our living room went silent.

When I rolled over, peeled off the pillows and wiped my face, my mother looked at me and said, "Remember—you agreed to work there. It paid well. You should've been more careful."

———

THE THERAPY SESSION eventually ended.

"Now, I want you all to stand up and give each other a hug," said the counselor with a smile.

Dad snorted.

"There's no way I'm giving fucking hugs," I said as I grabbed my lunch pail and walked toward the door. "Have a good day," I smiled at the counselor. "I'll call you later," I said to Tanya.

"Feel free to come over for dinner," she said as I walked out the door.

I LEFT THE BUILDING and hit the early afternoon August heat. The pavement wiggled in front of me. I made my way to my car, hopped in, turned on the ignition, and drove away from the counselor's office.

On the way back over to U.S. Foods, I pulled in to a photography shop's parking lot. I parked the car and turned off the engine; my chin pushed down toward my chest. The parking lot lines blurred. I couldn't read the shop's signage. I looked left and right and began to cry.

That twine that connected me to my parents now felt so thin. How was I going to do this? I was leaving for the East Coast in ten days. I knew no one there.

I stepped out of my car, found a half-drunk bottle of water in the backseat, opened it, and splashed a bit of water on my face. My eyes were bloodshot when I looked in the side mirror. I rubbed my hands up and down my face and my stomach slowly stopped jolting. My tears, for a moment, stopped.

I opened the car door, got inside, started the engine, and drove back to work. The twine still held on to something, but I didn't quite know what.

EARLIER THAT SUMMER I had begun the "call" process for the Lutheran church. The Evangelical Lutheran Church in America (ELCA), the largest and most liberal group of American Lutherans, had revised its position on ordaining gay people the previous year. In the past, though the church would ordain homosexuals, they would have to remain celibate.

My synod, the Western North Dakota Synod, was perhaps one of the most conservative regional organizations of ECLA congregations in the country. Throughout the summer, before meeting with my Candidacy Committee, I had expressed my concern to the synod's director, Beth, over my being a homosexual.

The Candidacy Committee in the ELCA serves as a type of sounding board for the candidate seeking ordination. The committee asks questions of the candidate and supports them in their journey throughout seminary. The ELCA believes that not only must the candidate have a call from God to serve in ministry, but that that call must also be confirmed by people apart from the candidate.

Beth, a bright, quick-witted, compassionate woman, affirmed that the committee would be supportive and that, at the end of my meeting with them, she would ask me whether there was anything else I would like to share in case *it* didn't come up.

"There's no way the committee can block you from seeking ordination, Taylor, since the ELCA now affirms the ordination of gay people."

I breathed a sigh of relief. I never imagined myself in front of a congregation, but it was 2010, another year of the Great Recession, and I worried about job security. Dad had been laid off the year before, when the coal mine where he worked closed. I wanted the security that was supposed to come with a college degree, but I also wanted the expansiveness of a liberal arts education to continue. I chose seminary, perhaps insatiably, so I could study more languages, history, philosophy, and literature. I wanted to understand people's values and where they came from. It wasn't so much that I believed in God. It was that I didn't know what it was I wanted to do for a job. But I knew that being a student was a job I could do well.

WHEN THE DAY CAME for me to see my Candidacy Committee, we met in an elementary-school classroom in Bismarck. The committee was made up of two men and three women, one of whom, Sarah Heindrich, was a professor of Old Testament at Luther Seminary in St. Paul, Minnesota.

Over the course of the two hours of questioning, it felt like I was testifying at a Senate hearing.

I was asked how I first felt a call.

"Well," I said, "it's not like I woke up one night and the moon came in through the window and my hair stood up on end and I heard the voice of God say, 'Taylor, my son, you must be a preacher.'"

We all laughed.

"My sense of call comes from the academic tradition of our faith—I mean, Martin Luther had a doctorate, and I believe in serious study, and serious questioning, of our religious texts. I believe the church needs rigorous, curious preachers."

Then other questions came—my relationship to the church, how I interacted with people of multiple generations, and so on.

As our time wound down, we hadn't approached the church's stance on gay ordination.

I eyed Beth.

"Well, I think that nearly does it," she said. "Taylor, is there anything else you believe your committee should know before we move along in the candidacy process?"

I took a breath. "Yes."

And I looked down at the tiled floor flecked with brown. It felt like forever before I raised my head.

"I believe it is important for my committee to know that I am a gay man."

Before I finished my sentence, Dr. Heindrich slammed her palm down on the table and did a vigorous fist pump. She stood up and pointed to me.

"I've been waiting for you for thirty years."

I was stock-still before laughs echoed around the room. I sank into my seat and felt relieved.

After Beth and I left the room, I hugged her.

"Thank you for making that easy for me," I said.

"You knocked it out of the park, Taylor," she replied.

# 8.

WEEKS LATER, the sun was setting by the time I landed in Newark. I gathered my suitcases from baggage claim, purchased a ticket, and boarded the train.

A woman who had been a year ahead of me at St. Olaf promised to meet me at the Dinky stop. The Dinky connected the town of Princeton to the main rail line that passed between Philadelphia and New York City a few miles to the southeast. But I hadn't purchased the additional ticket for the Dinky spur train, thinking my train ticket was good for my entire route.

"I should let you walk the three miles from this stop to Princeton," huffed the middle-aged conductor. "When we get to Princeton, you damn well better purchase the ticket. No freeloaders ride *my* Dinky."

I nodded my head and looked out the darkened window. As we screeched toward Princeton, black leaves were backlit by telephone poles. I rested my head against the cold glass and practiced my breathing. I was so far from home, but home was now always on my mind.

———

WHEN I MET KATIE and told her about the conductor, she just shook her head, took my carry-on bag, and threaded her arm through mine as we began to walk from the train station into Princeton. We started to chat.

"How far is it to—"

"Hey, you! Did you already forget what I told you?"

Katie and I stopped, turned around. Katie smiled at the conductor, adjusting her coral trench coat.

"Sir, we're with the seminary, and this is one of our special guests."

"I don't care who he is, he's—"

"Sir!" Katie narrowed her eyes. "Have a good night."

We turned around and began to walk away. Katie squeezed my arm tightly and we giggled.


WHEN WE GOT to campus, Katie showed me to my room in Brown Hall, a two-hundred-year-old colonial building complete with cupola and columns.

"I'm having my boyfriend bring over a pillow and a blanket for you," she said as we stood outside of my dorm room. "He'll have a key to help us get into your room since it's too late to go to the housing office."

Once in my room and settled, I turned on the lamp on my desk, opened my suitcases and began to place my clothes in the chest of drawers. Outside my window, the seminary's campus was lit. I could see a few people walking under the lamplight near the chapel. I had done it: I had made it to Princeton from a trailer house in coal country.

THE NEXT MORNING, I went to the seminary post office to retrieve three large plastic totes I had mailed from Bismarck. When I arrived and said my name, a wiry old woman behind the plexiglass window raised her eyebrows and pointed behind me. There were my totes.

"You'll need a dolly," she said. Suddenly the small door next to her Plexiglas window opened. "Here you go; bring it back when you're done."

I lugged the dolly up the stone steps and out of the post office, set it up, locked it in place, and went back to retrieve my totes.

As I wheeled across campus, people smiled at me, introduced themselves, asked me where I was from. "North Dakota?" they'd say. "I've never met anyone from North Dakota." I'd smile, tell them there weren't many of us from there, and that I was glad to be the first North Dakotan they'd met.

The leaves were still lush and green, lolling in the early morning light. The sun hit the white colonial chapel at just the right angle that I needed to shield my eyes when I passed it.

WHILE I WAS UNLOADING my totes, someone knocked on my door.

A tall and gangly guy entered, introduced himself, and shook my hand. "A few of us are going to go for a walk in a bit. Albert Einstein's house is just down the block, and we thought it'd be fun to get to know the area. You're a first-year, yes?"

I nodded, thanked him, and said that I'd join them another time.

He smiled and said he'd see me around.

I closed my door again and kept unloading my totes. I pulled out my sheets and made my bed. I hung up my winter coat and found the pictures I had wrapped in its pockets. I placed a photo of Tanya and me, set in a small silver heart-shaped frame, on the bookshelf over my desk. It was a picture I knew well: I, at seven, rested on Tanya's left shoulder. My front teeth were missing. We both had wide smiles. My dimples showed, my typical childhood buzz cut flared against the dark background. Tanya wore lipstick and her pearly teeth glimmered in the shot. Her luscious red hair was curled and *just* touched her shoulders.

Tears streamed down my cheeks and dripped onto my desk. I sat down and began to sniffle. I then choked back sobs and bent over in my chair, holding my face in my hands as my shoulders heaved.

THE FIRST WEEK of classes passed in a fog. I couldn't remember the name of any saints in my church history class. There were people called preceptors, doctoral students who would teach special breakout sessions to help us understand the material covered in large lectures. I couldn't focus on Hegel in my philosophy class or manage to understand what we were covering in Greek. It felt like I was being pulled underwater, that no matter how much I tried to lock the trauma of the prior month in a box and shove it deep in the closet of my mind, it'd rip open.

One evening, while perusing Princeton University's art collection, I sat in front of a lithograph called *In the Spring, 1941*, by Grant Wood. A sturdy man in overalls, hands at his hips, smiled out from the lithograph, rendered in graphite, toward me. He was laying posts to build a fence. A few sheep were grazing in the background near a barn.

I stared at the man, who reminded me of a young Grandpa Hatzenbihler, which then reminded me of shelterbelts, of farming, and of Oliver County. Before I knew it, I stood up and rushed away from the drawing; a few people turned and looked at me. I heard murmurings as I rushed by, a hand up near my eye, catching my tears.

I passed through the glass doors of the museum and out into the night. I walked over to an oak tree and sat in the dark, out of the lamplight, and again held my head in my hands. I sniffled, hocked a loogie, and cleared my throat. I wiped my eyes.

I tried to shake the memories of back home. After all, I was here, at Princeton Seminary, where I heard I would be able to take classes at the university from people like Joyce Carol Oates, Toni Morrison, and John McPhee. I wanted to teach, but my upbringing taught me to have some type of insurance. I wanted this, to be here, I told myself. I wanted to make my family proud, though now I didn't know if they ever would be, if they would ever forgive me for my being gay.


A FEW DAYS LATER, on a Saturday, I quietly practiced Ancient Greek in my dorm room. There were puffy clouds outside my window as some seminarians snapped a Frisbee across the quad.

"Alpha-beta-gamma-delta-epsilon," I murmured to the tune of "Mama's Little Baby Loves Shortenin'." "Zeta-eta-theta-iota-kappa-lambda." I even threw in a slight clap and bobbled my head from side to side. "Mu-nu-xi-omicron-pi-rho—" And then I stopped. I began again. But again, I stopped after "rho." I got up, stretched my arms, looked out my window, and sang to myself. It wouldn't come. I couldn't break through to sigma. I couldn't finish the alphabet.

I sat down on my bed and began again. And again. And again. I was like a broken spoke on a wheel—I could get only so far before jamming up. I refused to open my book. It was only twenty-four letters. I tightened my fists. I pounded on my thighs slowly, like I was practicing a fingering for piano. But I couldn't get it.

I picked up my phone, found Pastor Benson's home phone number in the white pages online, and called him. His wife, Carol, answered. When I told her who was calling, she said she'd go get Bruce.

I barely spat out the words before I fell into sobs. I told Pastor Benson what had happened the prior month, how I couldn't keep track of my studies, how I was failing to get a grip.

"There is nothing to get a grip about, Taylor," he said. "You're hurting, you're in pain. It's okay to cry and be upset right now."

I continued to cry. I told him I didn't know what to do. I was at *Princeton*, for god's sake.

"Taylor, it is okay to not be there." There was a pause. "You could take a leave, come back later, once things have settled down. You don't have to do this right now."

I continued to cry on the phone.

At the end, Pastor Benson made me promise to call him and tell him what my plan was once I had time to think about it.

When we hung up, I walked over to my window. The Frisbee was still flying across the quad. I wiped my nose with the back of my hand. In the distance, people laughed. I stood there for a minute, or an hour, turned back toward my closet, opened the doors where I had stacked my three plastic totes, began to fold my winter jacket, and filled each bin. I went over to my desk, pulled out three sheets of white paper, uncapped a black Sharpie, and wrote my home address in Bismarck on each piece of paper. I laid them atop the totes' lids, pulled a roll of tape from my desk drawer and secured the labels to the lids.

I was going home.

# 9.

BISMARCK ALWAYS SEEMED gray that fall. I didn't know what to do. After moving back to Bismarck, I became almost immediately desperate to get out, but I didn't know how.

Eventually, I went back to my former high school, walked through its gray hallways and into the marbled foyer where the principals' offices were. I asked the secretary if I could see Mrs. Hill, the kindly assistant principal, a petite woman whose hair was dyed red, who drove a red Cadillac and, often, wore red. I told her that I planned to apply to master's in education programs and that I wanted to student-teach at Bismarck High School.

"It's difficult to get you into the classroom when you're not affiliated with a college, Taylor, but let me see what I can do," she said.

A FEW DAYS LATER it worked—I was in. From September to the end of November, I taught three classes. For AP and sophomore English, I was at the side of my former teacher Mrs. Lord-Olson, discussing the green light in Fitzgerald's *The Great Gatsby* or how

Brutus was just having a bad day in Shakespeare's *Julius Caesar*. Basic English 12 was team-taught with the Special Education Department and Mrs. Sukauskas; it was a class where, among other things, we each drew our own version of the "monstrous hell-bride" who is Grendel's mother in *Beowulf*. In Literary Magazine, I helped Dr. Warner teach students about meter and rhythm in their poetry and prose.

Every Monday through Friday after school, I walked two blocks from Bismarck High to the public library, and stayed there until it closed. I told my parents that I had so much grading to do that being in the library would help me focus.

The truth was, I didn't really have any grading. I went to the library and roved the internet for jobs in Minneapolis, or other graduate programs to apply to. I spoke with job counselors from St. Olaf about which schools I should apply to for a master's in education— anything to get me out of Bismarck, to recover from the shell shock of being outed.

At nine o'clock, I'd gather my bag and notebooks, maybe check out a book on Handel or Brahms from the library, walk back to the high school parking lot, hop in my red Dodge Stratus, and slowly drive home along the oak- and elm-lined streets.

There, I'd park my car, shut off the headlights, and take a deep breath. I'd open the car door, gather my things, pop the key in the side garage door, and slowly slip into the house.

Mom and Dad were always already in their bedroom. The din of the television in their room carried down the hallway.

They were generous in wanting to feed me well. On the stove would be leftover pork chops, lasagna, or baked chicken. I'd quietly remove a plate, open the silverware drawer, spoon some food out of its container, and slink downstairs, where I'd eat in silence. We rarely saw one another.

By the time I rose in the morning, Mom already had left for work. I quickly showered, made a lunch for the day, snagged my book bag, and shot out the door before Dad woke up. If it was too early for me to go to the high school, I spent some time in Starbucks, waiting for my coffee.

Every other Friday, after teaching, I got in my car and sped toward Minneapolis. I tried to explain to my friends there what I was going through: why I was no longer at Princeton, what I was doing living back in my parents' basement, how I was going to get out.

Most Saturdays and Sundays I wandered the large rooms of the Minneapolis Institute of Art. I'd sit and look at Van Gogh's olive trees, painted in those thick, luscious brushstrokes against a backdrop of a lemony, pulsating sun, or Monet's grain stack, which seemed as if it had been rendered with a feather dipped in soft pastel pinks and browns.

I'd sit for hours, gazing off in the distance, somewhere beyond the paintings I was in front of, and surging with worry about how I was going to survive. My parents weren't being abusive, but I didn't give them much chance for conversation. Avoidance was my solution to the issue; distance was a way for me to feel safe.

On the weekends I was in Bismarck, I drove south from our house, toward the University of Mary. Designed by the celebrated Bauhaus architect Marcel Breuer, the university is perched on a large bluff high above a bend in the Missouri River. There, I'd drive to the university library, park my car, and wander into the CD collection. I'd grab a few recordings of the Brahms symphonies by Herbert von Karajan and the Berlin Philharmonic or Beethoven's symphonies with Carlos Kleiber and the Bavarian State Orchestra, and then plop down at a carrel with a multidisc CD player. I'd pop a CD out of its case, set it in the slot, and the player would suck it in. I'd put on my headphones, press play, close my eyes, and try to escape to a different world.

Sometimes at the library, I'd leave my carrel and dawdle over to the large glass windows. I'd sit down there, mesmerized at the changing light over the Missouri River Valley. The cottonwood trees, now apricot, were slowly beginning to fall; the bones of the trees were set in sharper relief. The Missouri River pressed south; the slopes on the western line of the horizon gleamed gold when the sun struck just right. The view was an ever-changing canvas of color and texture, something that, though shifting, helped me feel rooted to the reality that, somehow, I was going to get out of my parents' basement.

ONE NIGHT, after I got home from the Bismarck library, Dad was sitting at the darkened kitchen table waiting for me. I jumped when I came into the kitchen.

He looked at me.

"How are you affording all this?" he asked.

"All what?"

"Going to the Twin Cities and stuff like that—your gas, the meals, whatever it is you do down there."

I adjusted my bag on my shoulder.

"I have some money in my savings account."

"Well," he said, "you're certainly not making any money student teaching. Are you leeching off your friends?"

I looked at him.

"You are, aren't you?"

"I'm not, Dad. I'm barely spending any money."

He leaned across the table.

"And what are you going to do when it runs out? When are you going to get a real job?"

I turned, shuffled out of the kitchen and down the stairs, flicked off the entryway light, and disappeared into the basement.

LATE ONE NIGHT, Kari Lie, a Norwegian professor I'd had in college, who lived in Minneapolis, shot me a message on Facebook.

"Hey, I see you dropped out of seminary—what's up?"

I told her about my saga, how I was back living at home. How I was miserable.

"You should come live with me. I have a basement area and a nice, blow-up mattress. I need a house sitter in January anyway when I'm on vacation in the Caribbean. How about when you're done with student teaching you move in?"

I couldn't believe it. I agreed, right then, and thanked Kari. I felt a bit lighter as I began to make plans to leave Bismarck—finally, a way to escape.

ON MY LAST DAY of student teaching each class threw me a surprise party. I received a tie, autographed with each student's name, from Mrs. Lord-Olson and drawings from Mrs. Sukauskas's class. Dr. Warner's Literary Magazine was the last class period of the day.

Two female students. Amanda and Dania, went up front and

SPROUT 173

stood behind a podium. The whiteboard, streaked with blue and red and green markers glistened behind them.

"Mr. Brorby, we have something for you," said Amanda.

Music began to play. Some students started to sway in their desks. I couldn't place the tune, but it sounded familiar.

Eventually, Amanda and Dania began singing original lyrics to the tune of "Lucy in the Sky with Diamonds." I closed my watery eyes to listen. They were singing about me.

When it came to the chorus, the entire class of twenty turned in their seats, looked at me, and belted: "Mr. Taylor Brorby is awesome! Mr. Taylor Brorby is awesome!"

I let out a crackling laugh, held my hand over my mouth, and tears flowed down my cheeks. Students pounded on their desks, "Mr.-Taylor-Brorby-is-awesome!"

At the end of the song, the students pulled out cans of silly string and sprayed me. Goopy ropes of pink and green hung off my shoulders. Amanda raced toward me and placed a crown atop my head.

I held my face in my hands, smiled, and thanked them. That's all there was to do. They didn't know how they kept me going those few months, how they took a bit of the gloom away, how coming into my former high school with my book bag gave me a few hours away from the pain that worked its way out from my stomach, up my side, into my shoulders.

But now it was over, the vast expanse of what-to-do-next was on the horizon of my life. I was moving to Minneapolis, but then what . . . what was there for an English major to do during the height of a recession? Where would I find stability beyond the bloodlines of family?

In that moment, between the tears and laughs and silly string, I stood before my students and felt fleeting joy replace the tension. I could breathe. I could breathe.


THE NEXT MORNING was gray and foggy. I didn't waste any time and filled my Dodge Stratus with clothes and as many books as possible. With each load my shoulders relaxed, and yet my chest was still heavy. I was again leaving home, worried that this would be the yin and yang of my life.

When I finished loading the car, I stepped into the bathroom to shower. I turned on the water to cover up opening a side drawer in the vanity. In it were large bottles of Tylenol, Advil, and Excedrin. They glowed in the bright light. I took each bottle from the drawer and shook them gently. There were enough pills. I lined up the pills like little soldiers on the counter and then walked over and sat down on the toilet lid. I told myself that I could take them, that I could then get in my car and by the time they'd kick in, I'd be zooming down I-94. It'd be a fog. It'd be a blur. It'd all be over quickly.

And then I heard my parents' door creak open.

For some reason I told myself I couldn't do it while they were awake—that, somehow, even if I stashed the bottles, they'd find them, that they'd then call the state troopers or that they, themselves, would fly down the interstate in their GMC pickup and catch me. That I'd then be locked up in some psychiatric institution and would have to enter some rehabilitation program.

Somewhere, deep inside me, I knew my parents still loved me, even if they couldn't accept having a gay son.

I didn't contemplate taking the bottles with me and stopping at some rest stop along the interstate, sitting in my warm car on a cold day near the prairie pothole region of east-central North Dakota, taking pill by individual pill while watching Canada geese and trumpeter swans bob along in the small lakes of that mirrored landscape. I didn't, when it came down to it, want to be a headline:

LOCAL MAN OVERDOSES AT REST STOP.
FAMILY MOURNS MAN'S SUICIDE.

I didn't want to die, but I didn't know how to live in this new tension with my parents. I wanted to be alive in the bright beautiful world that now was tinged with pain—like a sliver in the supple part of my hand, something I couldn't remove, couldn't pull out, something that wouldn't leave, or leave me alone.

I slowly put each bottle in the drawer, closed it, stripped out of my clothes, showered, dried, and dressed. Then I crept out of the front door and drove away.

# 10.

MY SHOULDERS CAME UP to my ears as I stepped out of my car under a clear, moonlit Minnesota Christmas night. I wrapped my scarf around my neck as I tromped through the bright snow to press the doorbell. My old English professor, Jonathan Hill, and his wife, Barbara, came into view in the breezeway, and opened the door.

"Merry Christmas," they said, welcoming me into their warm house.

It was my first Christmas without family.

LIFE WAS UPSIDE DOWN.

I'd been living in Minneapolis in Professor Lie's house for a month. I slept on her air mattress in the basement, the space heater blasting, while I applied to temp agencies for work. I rarely called my parents, and when I did, there was anger in my mother's voice as well as in my own. I felt that things were now insoluble.

Just a few years before, while I was adjusting to being away at college, we'd talked on the phone every day.

Until college, I had been away from my parents only three times. Twice to diabetic camp, when I was six and seven, where I met other chronically ill children. The other time was the two-week vacation to stay with Tanya and Mike in Seattle.

But now, phone calls home made me depressed. They weren't comforting. I wanted my parents, but my mother's once warm voice was now icy. She didn't berate me for being gay—she would dig deeper, cut me in more slant ways. "I can't believe you won't come home for Christmas," she'd say. I'd make up some excuse, like I didn't have enough money (which was true), or that I had some job (I didn't) that was making me work right before and right after Christmas Day.

Won't. *You won't come home.* Her words were true. I wouldn't come home. Couldn't. There was a knee-jerk reaction inside of me to get in my old Stratus, gun it out of Minnesota and across the high plains of North Dakota, and go home for the holidays. But there was something deeper, something more primal—a feeling that home was no longer safe. It had now become a tenuous place, a place where my presence made everyone go silent.

When I escaped to Kari's basement in Minneapolis, I can now see that I was depressed—I lay on the air mattress for most of the day, the gentle buzz of the space heater warming my back. Other than that, it felt like all sensation had left my body. Color was muted. Food tasted bland. On my side for hours, gripping a pillow, I'd stare at the wall. Some days I was too numb to cry.


BUT NOW, at Jonathan and Barbara's, the smell of caramelized brussels sprouts, savory roast beef, garlic cream-laden mashed potatoes filled the house.

Their niece, Madeline, was visiting from London. A sleek, fashionable woman ten years older than me, Madeline was a vocalist. And as Barbara finished the final touches on Christmas dinner, Jonathan, Madeline, and I sat down to discuss music.

Madeline's group was rehearsing William Byrd, Thomas Tallis, and Claudio Monteverdi. These were names I had never heard of until high school, when I started checking out classical music CDs from the local libraries in Bismarck. I was raised on Led Zeppelin, Garth Brooks, and Shania Twain. At fourteen, Dad and I went to the Alerus Center in Grand Forks for a joint AC/DC and Aerosmith concert. We rocked and jammed as, even in the nosebleed section, I could see the crater that was Steven Tyler's mouth. I looked over to Dad and we both smiled.

As I listened to Jonathan and Madeline compare the virtues of Monteverdi and Tallis, my mind drifted five hundred miles back home, across the snow-covered tallgrass prairie, the tabletop-flat Red River Valley, the sleek, mirrored prairie potholes, all the way to the cold, thin, liminal place of my imagination: the Missouri River, this time of year looking as if it were dolloped with whipped cream. I was there. I could see it. But I wasn't—and I couldn't.

Home was, and is, for me, a sensation—thinner air, dust on the skin, dryness, eroded hills and buttes, a sheer amount of weather whirling across the canvas of sky. It's overwhelming. It can knock you out. Home, inevitably, always reminded me of how small I am.

But I now felt small in another way, a way that provoked pity. I don't remember if I had told Jonathan and Barbara exactly what was going on—if I had emailed them with vague phrases like *Can't go home for Christmas* or *Things aren't so good with my parents*. I had certainly told them I was back in the area when they knew I was supposed to be out east, studying the Bible.

My mind remained around my parents' oak table. Cousins, aunts, and uncles, no doubt rolling dice, playing cards, laughter from a group of relatives with cream-heavy bodies whose bloodline to me now felt thin. My nephews—five, two, and twin newborns—learning the hard reality: Uncle Taylor doesn't come back for Christmas.

But it's not just Christmas. It's Thanksgiving, birthdays, the Fourth of July.

In childhood, the Fourth of July was spent at our lake house. Cousins wailed as they flew across the wake of our boat as Dad madly whipped them in circles, the tube, weighed with flailing children, skipping higher and higher. S'mores—gooey and warm—spread across our cheeks as our faces glowed by flickering fires. Firecrackers snapped throughout the evening before the big batteries of fireworks blazed the sky green, purple, and orange.

To this date, I still have not spent a holiday with my twin nephews.

There is no way to escape this pain. The birthday season begins with two nephews in August, the twins in September, my mother's in October, mine in November, Thanksgiving, Dad's birthday in early December, then Christmas, New Year's, my sister's birthday in January. Each year is a six-month gauntlet of memories that could have been, times when I've thought—even for just a moment—of getting in the car and showing up with presents. Then I remember: my presence is not welcomed by all.


AFTER OUR CHRISTMAS DINNER of beef, sprouts, potatoes, and other steaming side dishes, Barbara went into the kitchen and Jonathan smirked at Madeline and me.

Barbara hurried back with a dark mound of what looked like a cake.

"What is that?" I asked.

"Christmas pudding," said Barbara, "and here's the cream to go with it. But don't begin just yet."

Jonathan's smirk widened into a smile.

Barbara returned with a steaming steel pot.

"Jonny, would you do the honors?" asked Barbara, handing him a pack of matches.

Madeline and I exchanged bemused glances.

Pouring out of the pot and across the pudding was warmed brandy. Barbara circled the pudding and, when the last drop hit the pudding, said, "Now, Jonny."

"A flambé," clapped Madeline as a blue flame tore around the pudding.

"But wait," said Jonathan, who passed around British crackers. "And these, too." He passed each of us a paper crown to wear as Barbara rolled her eyes. "Now cross hands," said Jonathan, "and hold tight, and—pull!"

We yanked. Our crackers exploded.

In that moment I was there, in southeastern Minnesota. I heard the crackle of paper. I smiled and laughed, smelled the warm pudding. I was there, and I was so far away from home.

AFTER A FEW WEEKS of searching for work and living in Kari's basement, I stumbled into a master's program in liberal studies, starting in January, at Hamline University in St. Paul. The routine of class, of homework, of having to say *something*—anything, some type of obligation—distracted me, if only a little, from the chasm I felt growing between me and my parents.

In February, I moved to South Minneapolis to house-sit for another St. Olaf professor; he and his wife were away for the semester in Estonia on a Fulbright. Even though I was in a master's program, I kept applying to seminary programs out east and in Chicago. I couldn't accept the fact that I had dropped out of Princeton and wasn't on the original plan I had envisioned for myself: master of divinity, ordination. I had planned to go to a prestigious seminary followed by a prestigious PhD, because prestige is what separates those who leave home from those who stay, or so I thought at the time. I wanted my parents to be able to say, "Oh, our son, he's at Princeton—and then of course he'll go onto Harvard for his PhD." I wanted them to still be proud of me, as they had been after my jazz band concerts in high school, or when I was voted Nicest Senior Guy in my high school graduating class. I wanted to check all the right boxes: college, master's, doctorate. I wanted to transcend what I perceived to be the limitations of the small coal country town I grew up in and then teach in some hallowed halls of knowledge, where people talked about visiting the latest Rothko exhibit at the Museum of Modern Art or about an upcoming trip to Austria to hear the Vienna Philharmonic. The intellectual world I craved existed somewhere well beyond the periphery of the prairie where I was planted, the prairie I paradoxically still yearned for, a place for me to feel rooted, still, and call home.

THE GRADUATE CLASSES helped get me out of my head for a while, but, eventually, I began to slide backward. After hemming and hawing I decided, for the first time, to go to counseling. I couldn't keep asking my friends to deal with the miasma of my life. The church

I went to in South Minneapolis—warm, welcoming, what we all called the "party" church—could get me only so far. I needed help, and though I believed I could just "push through it," I made an appointment with a counselor at Hamline.

When I called my mother to tell her I got into another Ivy League seminary, she responded by saying, "I don't know why anyone would want to go there."

In my next session, my therapist told me I needed to stop communicating with my parents because they weren't supportive.

But my parents had been supportive in the past. During high school, whenever they'd return from parent-teacher conferences, my stomach flipped when I asked them how the conversations with my teachers went. They'd stay silent as they'd climb the stairs in our split-level house.

"We can barely fit our head through the door we're so proud," Mom would burst out.

"They all love you, buddy," Dad would affirm.

And my father, a graveyard shift welder, wept at my college graduation. It was one of the few times I saw him wear a tie. He wiped his eyes. "I'm so proud of you, Taylor," he said.

Earlier, at the start of my senior year of college, my parents had made the one-thousand-mile roundtrip to hear me give a three-minute opening convocation speech as student body president. I can remember the band playing "Fanfare and Grand March," a determined tune written for band and organ written by Timothy Mahr. The cymbals and trumpets echoed off the vaulted ceiling of Boe Chapel. And as I processed, there they were, Mom and Dad, all the way from Bismarck, their eyes pooled with tears as I smiled and walked by on the way to give my remarks.

My parents, it's so clear to me, did everything they could for me, yet they could not in any way prepare themselves for who I really was.

IN THE FALL OF 2011, at Hamline, I took a class called The Essay, a required course in my program, but one I was hesitant to take as horrific images of the academic essays I wrote in college came to mind.

We began reading pieces like William Hazlitt's "On the Pleasure of Hating," which made me laugh out loud as Hazlitt sounded like some fashionista giving a model a dressing-down; or Zora Neale Hurston's "How It Feels to Be Colored Me," which rocked my mind, or Nancy Mairs's "On Being a Cripple," which echoed my own struggle with diabetes and the burden of having a disabled body in a world that isn't designed for bodies of different abilities.

These essays were different from the academic essays I wrote in college. *These* essays jolted me awake, pushed me into a personal realm with these authors; *these* essays helped me believe that *I* might have something to say, that *I* might want to be a writer.

And yet, each fall I was at Hamline I continued to apply for seminary programs and kept getting in. I never left again for seminary, though; I'd always choose to stay in my program at Hamline. I couldn't leave, for some reason. I finally had a community in my church in Minneapolis; old friends from St. Olaf lived in the Twin Cities. I felt stable. I felt settled, even if my relationship with my parents was on shifty soil.

———

MOM AND DAD rarely called me, nor I them. I'd open my phone, scroll down my list of contacts, and look at Mom's name on my screen. My thumb would hover over the call button. I'd then set the phone down, cup my face in my hands, shake my head back and forth, and practice taking long, slow, deep breaths.

When I did talk to Mom, there'd be crackling silence. Cautiously, I'd ask how they were. "Fine," she'd reply. "And you?" I'd start to tell her about classes at Hamline, or how I was working on my writing, how I thought I could maybe work at being a writer. But that part of the conversation never lasted too long—my mother had to go, had some errand to do, had some place she'd rather be than talking to me. I can now see it must have been too much, her boy continuing with life, struggling along in the one place, school, where he ever felt safe and secure.

And over time I stopped calling, almost completely. Sometimes I'd send a text, but even that felt too difficult. The weight of messaging Mom—the person I'd call when I was homesick in college, the woman who cried at graduation—was too much. Her short texts, her short words, now felt like barbs hurled from home. I wanted to apologize—but for what I did not know.

# 11.

FROM THE SACRISTY I heard the din of church members, family, and friends of the grooms entering the sand-colored Christ Church Lutheran in Minneapolis's Longfellow neighborhood.

I hung my blazer in the closet as I grabbed a white robe. Kristine, my pastor, entered—more light always seemed to fill the small sacristy whenever she was around.

"I *love* your shoes," I said, catching a glimpse of her bright yellow flats.

"Oh, thank you, Taylor," she said, as she sashayed back and forth.

I called us the A-Team whenever we led worship together, whenever I was scheduled to be assisting minister, the person who holds the worship book, announces the prayers, and models perfect behavior for the congregation.

That day, though, I knew I had to be on—the gays were there. It was my and Christ Church Lutheran's first gay wedding.

Kevin and Will, the two grooms, invited the entire congregation. It was a traditional Scandinavian wedding—no attendants, only Kevin and Will, Kristine and me, in front of everyone. Two wooden chairs for the couple were placed off-center in the chancel.

All eyes were on us.

While going over the order of the wedding the night before, Will's mother, a poised and coiffed eighty-year-old, sat in the second row of pews. When the moment came in the rehearsal for the grooms to say "I do," Will's mother shouted, "Now you boys say it loud enough so everyone can hear!" Will, in his forties, was reduced to a blushing four-year-old.

We all laughed.

On the wedding day, organ music resonated throughout the church—a midcentury modern building, the last project designed by the famous Finnish architect Eliel Saarinen. Known as the Church of Light, Christ Church Lutheran's simple, asymmetrical design gleamed with sunshine.

In the months after dropping out of seminary, while searching for secure footing once I'd moved to Minnesota, I'd started attending weekly worship at Christ Church, whose small congregation embraced me.

Kevin and Will were two of the first people who welcomed me, greeting me at the door with warm smiles during the tumult of recovering from . . . from what, exactly? Feeling abandoned? Ashamed? Like there was no place for a gay son in my family? I had called aunts and uncles on the phone. They had cried to me, the weight of their Catholic upbringing making them believe I was to spend an eternity burning in Hell.

I fastened the collar of my robe, which made me feel like I was locked in a sauna. I removed a long cincture that would girdle my waist from the closet and looked at Kristine.

"I always feel like cattle whenever I wrap this rope around me," I said.

THAT FIRST FALL and winter away from home, Kristine's sermons had kept me grounded.

Kristine wove poetry from Ezra Pound and from Jack Gilbert (a poet I hadn't heard of) into her sermons. And, each week, she reminded us that we were loved, that God was with us in the light and in the darkness. There were times, sitting in my pew behind Howard and Erla, a quick-witted, white-haired couple who had been married for sixty years, when I looked down, when it seemed as if Kristine were speaking only to me, reaching out toward a young man who wondered why he was gay, why—if there was a God—God would make him this way.

Kristine, in her weekly sermon, let me know that I was loved.

"TAYLOR, WE BETTER go downstairs and get to the narthex. The processional is getting close," Kristine smiled.

"You look great, Kristine."

"Thank you." And we hugged each other. Our robes billowed behind us as we flitted down the stairs.

When we walked into the narthex, Kevin and Will were there, suited and staring into a filled sanctuary. They bit their lower lips.

The organ swelled as we took our places toward the back of the processional—a line of Will's family members. Some of Kevin's family, I learned the night before, had not been supportive of him.

I opened the worship book.

As we processed, the church filled with song.

*Let us build a house where love can dwell and all can safely live,*
*A place where saints and children tell, how hearts learn to forgive.*

The entire congregation was there. My vision blurred as I caught the eyes of friends, their eyes also puddling with tears.

THIS WAS 2011, and two men could not yet legally marry in the state of Minnesota. Weeks earlier, Kevin and Will had driven to Decorah, Iowa, where same-sex marriage was already legal, and tied the knot in a small ceremony. But on this day, we gathered in Minneapolis to sing the happiness of their love, to share in their commitment, to pledge to them our loyalty in their happy union.

WILL'S FAMILY FLOWED into their pew as the couple and Kristine and I continued up to the chancel, where the grooms soon stood in front of their chairs, a small table between them.

When the hymn ended, I sat in my chair as Kristine warmly welcomed all who were gathered, telling us that there would be a Scandinavian feast of salmon, cheeses, meatballs, and good beer and wine waiting for everyone after the wedding.

I spotted Howard, who winked at me, and Erla, who gently lifted her hand and waved at me, in their pew.

"This is a day to celebrate," said Kristine. "And we here at Christ Church know how to party. Please sit back and relax as we celebrate this union between two men who are so dear to us here at Christ Church Lutheran. Welcome, everyone."

As various friends and family read from scripture and as we stood and sang hymns, I snuck a glance every now and then at Kevin and Will. They held hands, sometimes sang, and sometimes held back tears.

And then it came, the time for the two to be wed.

Kristine and I walked from the side to the center of the chancel, where the couple, still holding hands, joined us.

I cracked open the worship book as my eyes went back and forth between Kristine and Kevin and Will.

When the vows came, my breath quickened.

"Will, repeat after me," said Kristine. "'I take you, Kevin, to be my husband from this day forward.'"

I felt a surge of heat under my collar, the pooling of tears in my eyes. A man had publicly said he would take another man as his husband. I was there—*right there*—and one of the first to hear him say it.

It was the gift Kevin and Will gave to me: to be so close, so present to the beginning of their marriage.

"Now, Kevin, repeat after me."

There was a stillness in the nave, as if we all were watching a miracle unfold.

"Taylor, will you please hand me the rings?" asked Kristine.

"Now, Will, repeat after me: 'Kevin, I give you this ring as a sign of my love and faithfulness.'"

Will slipped the glinting band around Kevin's finger. Their eyes were only on each other.

"Kevin, please repeat after me: 'Will, I give you this ring as a sign of my love and faithfulness.'"

I looked at Will's mother, who held her hand against her pearls, lifted a handkerchief, and dabbed her eyes.

At that moment I thought of my own mother—what it would be like for her to be here now, what it would be like if she were at my own wedding, if I were to get married. I shook my head quickly, looked back at Kevin and Will, and smiled.

Kristine stepped back, lifted her hands above her head, and looked at the entire assembly. "Kevin and Will, by their promises before God and in the presence of this assembly, have joined themselves to one another as husbands. Those whom God has joined together let no one separate."

An eruption of amens and thanks be to Gods rang around the church as Kevin and Will kissed.

We clapped and whistled, and, for a moment, it seemed that all was well, that everything was now possible for me: I had a model before me of two men getting married, in front of an entire church filled with supportive people. I began to think that perhaps my life was beginning to change, that the clasps of the straitjacket of pain was loosening its hold.

# 12.

THE SNOW SLOUGHED off the railings of Lake Street Bridge as I wrapped my hands around the steel. Goose bumps crawled up my arms. I shook my head and climbed on. I used a neighboring lamp for support so I wouldn't slip. I heaved higher up each railing.

A hand gripped the back of my jacket, yanking me down from my perch on the rails of this bridge between Minneapolis and St. Paul. I could hear small ice sheets in the Mississippi grind against one another that January night, sometime after two in the morning. The snow fluffed away from my body as I landed, hard, on the cold pavement. Like Clarence Odbody, the angel in *It's a Wonderful Life*, who rescues George Bailey, the bicyclist who stopped me from killing myself extended his gloved hand and asked me where I lived. Just up the road, I told him. We began to crunch through the snow, under amber light, the streets muffled, the snow still falling in large clumps.

For three years I had struggled to speak to my parents. Life would be easier in exile from the dry buttes of the prairie. Here, I was in a verdant landscape where enough water fell, where people were more open-minded about my being gay.

That night, however, I'd been determined to end it all—to put out the coal burning beneath my breastbone, the lump of pain I tried to keep hidden.

BUT THIS NIGHT the weight of my exile, the weight of knowing that if only I were straight, they'd still love me, was too much.

Earlier, after my housemates had gone to sleep, I put on my peacoat, gloves, and hat and walked along the Mississippi River while the snow floated like butterflies in the black night. There was a numbness in me, some stoic resolve. This, what I was about to do, would silence my pain, would put a stop to the nights of banging out hymns on the piano, escaping my emotions by lifting weights in the gym, grinding against men on dance cubes at the gay clubs in downtown Minneapolis—all those attempts to live in my body instead of my mind. I would fall the sixty or so feet and smack into the cold, black river—it would knock me unconscious, the weight of my wet coat, gloves, and snow boots would pull me under. My lungs would fill with water. It would all be quiet, would all end quietly.

I looked at the glistening skyscrapers upstream, in downtown Minneapolis, as I walked along the Lake Street Bridge. No cars drove by; the neighborhood businesses were dark.

Four bridges upstream, in 1972, John Berryman, a major "confessional" poet, had jumped and waved to university students before he shot down and disappeared into the churning Mississippi.

There would be no witnesses, no second thoughts, for my suicide. It was time.

I couldn't cry anymore on the phone to my sister.

Long, lingering silences crackled across the telephone when I called my mother, if she answered at all.

I no longer spoke with my dad.

A YEAR BEFORE, I'd been published for the first time. I wrote a commentary about being outed for Minnesota Public Radio and meditated on the shortest, most life-changing phrase: I am gay.

Stupidly, once it was published, I emailed the piece to my mother. I thought, in some corner of my mind, that the piece would show her my pain, that it would serve as a type of signal flare shot into the sky, a desperate plea, a message that I needed help—that I needed their love, and that their renewed love would prevent any further ideations of suicide.

But this was not to be.

Later that year my parents came to visit me in Minneapolis. During our meals we only heard our scraping silverware. When a smiling young waiter came up to us and asked the table how we were doing, one of us would sharply blurt, "Fine." We'd hide behind our menus, quickly give the waiter our order, and then pass the time by sipping our beer or water, avoid one another's eyes, while waiting for our food to arrive.

During one supper, I offered my father a taste of an IPA, my favorite kind of beer. As the suds foamed across his mustache, his face crinkled. "Too much flavor," he said.

When I took them to my favorite spot for brunch the next day, the Birchwood, a small farm-to-table restaurant nestled between neighborhood houses, my father couldn't find anything on the menu to eat. I suggested basic eggs and toast and coffee. He replied that they didn't have the *right* eggs or toast or coffee.

My parents spent the rest of the day shopping while I sulked in my duplex, alone.

The Sunday of their visit was Mother's Day. Robin fledglings chirped; the oaks' leaves had begun to whistle in the wind. I invited my parents to my church before we would go to a special brunch. I had made a reservation weeks earlier. I wanted Mother's Day to be a type of new beginning, a reconciliation like Paul wrote in his second letter to the Corinthians. If God forgave me my trespasses, maybe I could find a way to forgive my parents theirs. And I thought they would want to reconcile, too, to come back together, to find a path toward healing—after all, they had made a four-hundred-mile drive from North Dakota to spend the weekend with me.

That morning, I was assisting minister, and after the first hymn, during the announcements, the pastor mentioned that I had an op-ed in the local paper.

During the passing of the peace, I made my way into the sanctuary to hug and shake the hands of my friends. My white robe billowed behind me.

When I shot over to my parents, my dad stared straight ahead. My mother pulled me in and could only sharply whisper, "What did you write this time?"


AFTER THE CHURCH SERVICE, I couldn't find my parents, and I ran out to their car with a glass vase filled with flowers for my mom.

They stood beside their shining silver Buick.

"Aren't we going to brunch?" I asked, feigning a smile.

Dad guffawed and opened the door to the driver's seat and got in.

My eyes widened. I looked over at Mom, dressed in a sleeveless, ankle-length cotton dress.

"We have to get on the road to get home," she said. "It's going to be a long drive."

I looked at the ground and blinked hard before looking back up at her.

"I got these for you," I said, holding out a bouquet of tiger lilies and white daisies.

"Why?"

I leaned back slightly. "Because it's Mother's Day."

Mom opened the passenger door, got in, and shut it. No hug. No goodbye.

They drove off.

I still held the vase of flowers.

AFTER THE BICYCLIST dropped me off at my duplex and watched me close the door, I heard him peel down the snowy street as I whacked my boots clean of snow.

I walked into my duplex, removed my peacoat, hat and gloves, and took off my shirt as I passed through the living room and dining room and into the short hallway toward my bedroom. I opened and quietly closed the door, finished undressing, and fell onto my bed. The sweat from the night soaked into my sheets. I sat up, leaned my elbows on my knees, held my head in my hands, and felt an electric numbness spark across my feet. I didn't cry, but I looked out my window, past the hedgerow toward the warm lamplight beneath the towering oak trees, and watched the snow continue to fall in the still, cold night.

In May 2013, sweat pooled at my temples as I lifted my arms up and out of my black graduation robe and tried to adjust my mortarboard. The newly budded leaves hung limp on the branches, and I flapped my arms like a pelican to try to get a breeze under my polyester robe. We began the procession from the gym to the front of the blond-bricked Old Main at Hamline University. I had made it through graduate school.

As we walked by the shiny silver bleachers, I heard Grandpa Brorby and his second wife, Jean, call my name. I looked at them, smiled, and waved. Grandpa smiled and snapped a picture.

"We'll see you afterward!" shouted Jean.

I smiled again, nodding, and Grandpa put his two pinkies in his mouth. A sharp whistle shot at me. I shook my head as Grandpa grinned at me.

A few weeks before, when I'd texted Mom to see whether she and Dad would like to come for my graduation with my master's in liberal studies, she responded, "I don't think we'll have time."

The Tuesday before my graduation, I sat on the cold marble floors of the Minnesota State Capitol. Together with friends from Christ Church Lutheran, I marched around the lobby, singing songs in support of same-sex marriage. In late February HF 1054, officially titled "Marriage Between Two Persons Provided for, and Exemptions and Protections Based in Religious Associations Provided For," was introduced in the Minnesota legislature to legalize same-sex marriage. Days before we went to the Capitol, it had made it through the

House. Now, this day, it was up to the Senate to pass it and move it along to the governor's desk, and Governor Mark Dayton had promised he would sign it into law.

That morning, when I entered the towering rotunda, whose cobalt dome was ringed by renditions of Timidity and Minerva advising the American Genius in Edward Simmons's murals *The Civilization of the Northwest*, a wave of chants washed over me: "Now is the time, this is the year!" Activists on both sides, those waving rainbow flags and those shaking pink signs with black silhouettes of a man plus a woman equals a baby, were crying out.

I stood in the midmorning light and took deep breaths as I read signs that read DON'T ERASE MOMS AND DADS and GIVE LOVE A CHANCE. There were men and women holding rainbow Mardi Gras beads and small children clutching rosaries.

Throughout the day I walked around the levels of the rotunda, smiling at some people, looking away from others. I found a quiet spot near a portrait of Minnesota's thirty-fifth governor, Albert Quie. I pulled a sandwich out from my backpack and sat down on the floor. Would it happen today? Would Minnesota become the second Midwestern state, after Iowa, to legalize same-sex marriage?

I watched videographers and news reporters record reels in the quiet recesses of the Capitol. College students snapped selfies with their arms wrapped around each other. I quietly chomped on my salami sandwich when two women sat down next to me.

"Mind if we join you?" asked one of them, a woman with cropped gray hair and glasses.

I shook my head, my mouth full of sandwich. I swallowed quickly.

"Not at all. Please. I could use some company. I'm Taylor."

"I'm Anne, and this is my wife, Joan."

"It's great to meet you, Taylor," said Joan, a tall woman with shoulder-length silver hair.

When the pair sat down, Anne leaned over toward me as she pulled out a bag of almonds.

"Now, are you with us or against us?" she asked in a light, disarming tone.

"Oh, I'm with you," I said earnestly. "I'm gay."

"Thank fucking god," smiled Joan. "With all these religious nut-jobs, and these poor children holding those damn pink signs about Moms and Dads, we get worried whenever we see a solitary man."

"You don't have anything to worry about with me," I laughed. "I sashayed out of the womb."

Anne and Joan laughed.


THROUGHOUT THE DAY, the three of us told one another our coming-out stories and talked about how things stood—or didn't—with family members and what the legalization of same-sex marriage would mean to us. Joan and Anne laughed easily; they leaned in and listened when I spoke.

"What do you think, Joan? Should we adopt Taylor?" asked Anne. "He's certainly cute with all that red hair."

I blushed.

"Do you want to get up and make a round?" I asked the pair. "I'm getting kind of stiff."

"Oh no, we're fine," said Joan. "If you want, you can leave your backpack here and we'll watch it. What do you think, Anne, let's camp out here for the rest of the day—"

"Look what she did there," burst in Anne. "*Camp!*"

The three of us laughed.

I shook my head.

"I'll be back in a few minutes, you two," I said and began to roam around the rotunda.

In the late afternoon, more people had gathered inside the Capitol. Pastors with long rainbow stoles walked the corridors, priests clutched their rosaries as they prayed with their flock. A man on the second floor of the rotunda strummed a guitar and sang, "Give love a chance."

For a minute, I stopped, closed my eyes, and listened. The Capitol sounded like a cete of crying badgers.


WHEN I RETURNED, Joan was resting her head on Anne's shoulder. Both women had their eyes closed. They rose and fell like a gentle wave as they breathed together. Then, suddenly, people started to gather near the west corridor steps. I snagged a college student.

"What's going on?" I asked.

"We think they've decided," he said, walking away.

I turned to Joan and Anne, crouched, and rubbed Anne's shoulder. She shook herself awake.

"Hi, Anne, I just heard that they think they might be making an announcement. They think the Senate has decided."

Anne jolted. Joan's head bounced off her wife's shoulder.

"What the hell was that about?" Joan moaned, her eyes still closed.

"Honey," said Anne, "it's time. They've decided. It's time to get up."

I gripped Anne by the hand, said, "One, two, three," and helped hoist her to her feet. Joan gathered their bags and, when she was ready, I helped her up, too.

We made our way to the stone steps and waited.

Suddenly, a page burst high into view atop the steps. He cupped his hands and shouted.

"It's passed!" he cried. "It goes to the governor tomorrow!"

What I remember is tears. I remember hugs. I remember rainbow flags streaming around the corridors. I remember, in that moment, feeling that the world had changed.

THAT SATURDAY, I was the first in the long ceremony to graduate, and when I walked across the stage, I felt a little taller: I had done it. I received my master's degree, another first in my family.

I could hear Grandpa and Jean yell when my name was called. I waved to them.

AT THE GRADUATION RECEPTION, I introduced Grandpa and Jean to my thesis adviser, Patricia, a small woman with cropped chestnut hair and walnut-colored eyes. When she smiled, her eyes shimmered, and her white Chiclet teeth shined. Pat had advised me in writing about whether the canon of Western literature encouraged consumerism. I looked at the mead hall in *Beowulf*, the celebrations of feasts in the Book of Psalms, the opulent English gardens in *Emma*, the glittering glamor of Gatsby's life in West Egg. My conclusion? Of course, literature encouraged us all to be good little consumers—I had learned that years earlier from Jim Farrell.

Pat stepped back after shaking Grandpa and Jean's hands. "Are you Taylor's parents?" she asked.

I looked down, feigned a smile, and kicked at the grass.

"Oh, no." Grandpa laughed. "We're his grandparents."

"You must all be so proud," said Patricia.

I looked up at Patricia, who smiled at my grandpa and Jean.

"You bet we're proud," said Grandpa, wrapping his arm around my shoulder. We smiled, the two smallest Vikings in the Brorby family, and gripped each other tight.

I hadn't told him—not yet—that the grandson he was proud of also had a secret.

# 13.

O n Veterans Day, when I was twenty-six, I sat with my mother's father, my eighty-eight-year-old Grandpa Hatzenbihler, in Denny's on the south side of Bismarck, near the civic center and Kirkwood Mall. I had brought my great-aunt Frances, my grandpa's sister-in-law, along as backup. I planned to tell him I was gay.

We sat at a table surrounded by booths filled with Vietnam War veterans, Korean War veterans, and a wraithlike gaggle of World War II veterans—heroes all, but many of them now using canes or gripping walkers.

Aunt Frances—who was a combination of Betty White's charm and Maggie Smith's sharp tongue—looked ladylike on the outside, but she could cut you down if she had to. She ordered toast and sausage, I ordered a ham and cheese omelet, and Grandpa ordered his favorite pumpkin pancakes, timely for the season.

I brought Aunt Frances as backup because her granddaughter was gay, was married to a woman at the time, and had twins. My grandfather, Aunt Frances had told me, adored Bethany, my cousin, and her wife, whom he nicknamed Spike because of Adrianne's gelled, spiked hair.

When I'd phoned her to ask whether she would come to lunch with Grandpa and me, she said, delightedly, "I wouldn't miss it."

When our food arrived, I told Grandpa I had something to say. Aunt Frances, uncharacteristically, kept her head down and remained quiet.

I turned to the man who, when I was a child, threaded worms on my hook to help me catch crappies. The man who taught me to waltz, who came to each of my jazz concerts in high school and rocked in the bleachers while I wailed on my saxophone. The man who, my mother later told me, wept the day he asked for help loading a trailer and my twelve-year-old hand was pinned under the weight of attempting to slide the trailer onto the hitch.

In childhood card games among Grandpa, Grandma, and me, he would feed me cards, helping me win in cribbage. Grandma Hatzenbihler, who believed children shouldn't be helped if they were to play adult games, scowled.

My grandpa, who helped me build playing card forts, testing their strength by turning on a rotating fan, me cranking the knob, the wind blasting against the clubs, spades, diamonds, and hearts.

He built great paper airplanes, turned on the ceiling fan, and let me hurl the planes into the blades. The planes shot like rockets around the room as Grandpa and I yipped and hollered.

Sometimes he strapped ski goggles to his face, leaned back in our old La-Z-Boy loveseat as I rolled between obstacles like an American Gladiator as he shot Nerf darts at me.

When I close my eyes, I can still see him lowering those tall branches of juneberries to me in the dank coulees of Oliver County. There was a muffled ring as, berry by berry, he and I filled our Bridgeman ice cream pails with the purple fruit, which Grandma would later bake into pies or kuchens. Grandpa and I would drop the berries atop a mound of vanilla ice cream, stained purple from the juice.

Now, I held his skillet-sized hand while Aunt Frances sawed away at her pork sausage. I cleared my throat.

I looked directly into his warm eyes. "Grandpa, I date men," I said and paused. "Grandpa, I'm gay."

He pulled his hand away, cut his pumpkin pancakes. I heard Aunt Frances's cheap knife scrape her ceramic platter.

"Taylor, the priests say it's against our religion, but screw what the priests say—you're *my* grandson."

I sighed. My eyes watered. I stole a glance at Aunt Frances, who smiled.

She sniffled.

I wiped my face.

Grandpa bellowed, "Try these pumpkin pancakes, they're fabulous."


I GAVE AUNT FRANCES my arm as we stepped out into the blustery November day.

"Hold on to your hair—or what's left of it," chuckled Grandpa as the wind whipped flurries around the parking lot.

Aunt Frances clenched my forearm. When we got to Grandpa's white van, she patted it and whispered, before hopping up into her seat, "The Lord was with us today, Taylor."

———

WHEN I DROPPED Grandpa off at his tidy, two-bedroom apartment in Bismarck, I walked him to the door. In the rock bed along the sidewalk to the door was a stone sign: WELCOME TO GRANDPA'S HOUSE. I could hear he had left the television on. He turned, this man I spent more days with in childhood than anyone else, his cream-filled belly now smaller than I remembered it as a child. His arms opened, as they always did, and, for a minute, I swear I ran to him as I remember doing at the old house in Center—me bursting through the door from the garage, where Grandpa kept live minnows and brewed chokecherry wine, into the bun-scented warmth of the kitchen, his great *ho-ho-ho's* booming as I ran and threw myself into his arms.

I threw myself into his arms again. My head rested on his shoulder. I turned my head, trying desperately not to let my voice crack, and whispered, "I love you."

"Ho-ho-ho," he boomed, as always. "I love you, too. I love you, too."

A FEW DAYS LATER, I came out to Grandpa Brorby, my father's dad, over the phone. He now lived in Michigan, and I hadn't seen him since he and his wife, Jean, came to my master's graduation in St. Paul.

I didn't know when I next would see them, so I'd decided it was finally time to tell him.

I called him from behind a pair of Dumpsters in Bismarck. If he rejected me, I wanted to be hidden, someplace where no one could pass by and see me crying.

I'd tried to call him the day before, but Jean answered the phone.

Jean updated me on her latest hobby—making rugs out of old plastic bags—and how guitar lessons at church were going. She told me that Grandpa wasn't home, but that I could try him later.

"There's something important I have to tell him, Jean," I said.

After a brief silence I blurted out that I was gay.

Jean asked me if she could talk to Grandpa first. I told her she could. She said that I should call back the next day, that he would be home then. She'd make sure of it. I hung up the phone and sighed.

So, there I was behind the Dumpsters for the second day in a row. I took a few deep breaths and called my grandpa.

"Hello, young fella," came the booming, silvery voice I had always known.

"Hi, Grandpa," I said.

"Now, Taylor, Jean told me what you're going to tell me, but I have one thing to say before you say anything. . . ."

I caught my breath. My eyes watered as I looked down at the ground.

"You are my grandson and that's all I know. I love you because you're you."

Of course, I cried. I said, "Oh, Grandpa" over and over again. The man who sang in our small-town musicals, who made me a small oak box where I kept the lump of coal and the 1896 Morgan silver dollar he gave me when I was eight, who used Brylcreem to part his hair *just so*, came through, transcended what I thought—had experienced— men of the American West were capable of—loving gay people.

To GROW UP as a gay boy on the prairie is to live in a type of peril. For me, it always felt like I was swallowing the burning coal of who

I was—if I conformed to my small town's expectations of hating school and playing football or developed a love of *killing* (not hunting), then I could be accepted. But I had grandpas who taught me to love dancing, and Grandpa Brorby loved sawing and sanding and shaping cedar chests, entertainment centers, and cornered shelves with wooden bows. He loved creating beautiful things.

Whenever I walked down the street to my grandparents' house, Grandpa Brorby was in his woodworking shed. Grandma would give me a pair of bright orange earplugs so I could say hi to him before coming inside to have lunch with her.

I can still smell my grandpa's woodshop: planks of cedar floated overhead on rafters, an occasional piece of maple or cherry propped against the back wall, a small iron stove warmed the room.

Grandpa would wave, smile his wide smile, and turn off the band saw. He would hold up his pointer finger, turn around and, inevitably, pull a Tootsie Roll out of his pocket. He did this for everyone— he even had two Tootsie Rolls painted on his golf cart. To me, he was Grandpa; to everyone else he was the Tootsie Roll Man.

THREE YEARS AFTER I came out to him, while visiting his home in Michigan, Grandpa Brorby took me to his basement workshop. He cut small crosses out of his favorite myrtle wood. I remember his planks of myrtle wood from my childhood in Center—how he'd keep them hidden, using them only for his most precious, small projects.

Now, here in Michigan nearly twenty-five years later, his supply had dwindled. When I asked why he loved myrtle wood, he told me how easy it was to use, how forgiving—that when you put varnish on top of it, it shines like glass. He showed me how steady the wood stayed in place as he maneuvered around the words and phrases he carved in his small crosses: JESUS; I AM THE WAY, THE TRUTH, AND THE LIFE. He bit his lower lip while carving the standalone "t" in truth, the "ruth" becoming one, singular movement.

"The truth of the matter is, Taylor, cutting out 'truth' is fucking hard," he snorted.


IN THAT MOMENT I thought about both my grandpas, men of the Greatest Generation—Grandpa Hatzenbihler the farmer and Grandpa Brorby the coal miner. When I told them the truth, I was nervous, but it wasn't hard: I didn't have to cut the truth out. I just had to share it. And in those moments—in those small, quiet moments in Denny's and over the phone—my grandpas told me their truth: they loved me.

# SHOOT

# 1.

MEDORA, NORTH DAKOTA, is the gayest town in the West. Cowboys with prairie-hardened thighs amble down Main Street, their bright buckles glint in the noonday light; freshly pulled saltwater taffy shines in the candy store; lovers, a feathered boa wrapped around their shoulders and dressed in fishnet stockings or buckskin, pose for sepia-toned old-time photographs; near the entrance to Theodore Roosevelt National Park is the North Dakota Cowboy Hall of Fame—all those men wrapped in chaps grit their teeth for the camera, a pad of tobacco tucked into their lower lips. All that barbed wire; all that sage perfuming the layered bentonite bluffs of southwestern North Dakota's badlands.

Across the railroad tracks and over the Little Missouri River is the Chateau de Mores, the historic home of the Marquis de Morès, a French entrepreneur and aristocrat who built this town (named for his wife, Medora von Hoffmann) in the 1880s to use it as a hub for the newly made refrigerated railroad cars bound with cattle for the Chicago markets.

It was a bust.

But in the town's first few years, the marquis built a twenty-eight-room chateau—considered rustic by aristocratic standards—at a time when most people in what was then the Dakota Territory lived in sod houses or tar-paper shacks.

Uphill from the chateau is the Medora cemetery, where there are gravestones for William W. "Six-Shooter Slim" Kunkel; French Baby; Baby from Hotel; "Farmer" Young—Cowboy Who Owned Two Acres of Land; William Riley Luffcey—his gravestone reads "Killed in an argument on June 26, 1883. Marquis de Mores had purchased land for his cattle, then closed old hunting trails. A dispute ensued. The Marquis was tried and acquitted three times. Many years later another man confessed to the killing. His identity has never been disclosed due to his family's wishes." There's also a grave for The Man the Bank Fell On—meaning, a riverbank fell and killed a man no one knew.

Farther uphill, past the cemetery, is the crown jewel of the region, the Medora Musical, whose high-kicking cowboys twirl and yip as they sing across a star-spangled musical revue—Theodore Roosevelt, his storming of San Juan Hill; the founding of Medora; Harold Schafer, the philanthropist who helped rebuild Medora as a type of company town, and the man who originally made his fortune by creating Mr. Bubble; horses; shootouts; damsels in distress.

One of my first memories is of the Medora Musical. At four, I remember sitting in the open-air Burning Hills Amphitheatre, watching black pigs hop along on their hind hooves. Later in the show—as with every show I've seen there since—children were asked to come onstage as a bright-toothed blond woman, clad in a cowgirl hat and fringed shirt, wailed away on "You're a Grand Old Flag."

Each year, the musical hosts ask veterans to stand as they sing the Armed Forces Medley. At the end of the show, by which time you're spinning inside a whirlwind of red, white, and blue, Theodore Roosevelt appears in a spotlight, riding his trusty steed, in some type of phantasmagoria from yesteryear.

It is here, in this tourist town of a little over one hundred year-round residents that, at the age of twenty-six, I had my first summer fling.

# 2.

A T THE HEIGHT of the Bakken oil boom, in 2014, I took a
job with a North Dakota nonprofit to interview landowners
impacted by the oil development transforming the region into what
was then the second-largest oil play on the continent. Throughout
May and into August, I was tasked to get seventy-five interviews
that would help the nonprofit build a case against the fossil-fuel
industry—its mismanagement of wells, its pipeline spills, its harm to
local agriculture. I was based in Dickinson, in the southern tip of the
boom region, renting a basement room from a professor. This town
contained nearly 16,000 people when I left for college in 2006—
now it hovered somewhere near 40,000. There were more bars, more
hotels, more grocery stores, and a newly built YMCA complete with
indoor waterslides.

Of the seventy-five people I was commissioned to interview, only
nine came through. Men and women were scared to go on record
(who could blame them?) and speak out against the industry that was
flooding the state with money.

I did talk with a retired couple who had sold their home on the scoria-strewn north shore of Lake Sakakawea after pumpjacks, the metal structures that rock up and down, pulling oil from deep underground, began to keep them up at night, moving some two hundred miles away from the boom to the small, south-central North Dakota pothole-prairie town of Napoleon. The large steel-blue elevators along their new community's railroad tracks were the tallest structures for miles. Along Main Avenue were the Napoleon Floral and Trophy Haus, Weigel Hardware, Del's SuperValu, and in a small building the local newspaper, the *Napoleon Homestead*.

Back in the northwest corner of the state, I spoke with Brenda Jorgenson, a tall egret of a woman with long silver-brown hair. Brenda showed me water samples from her tap in varying shades of gray and black—the same tap that had supplied the water she used to brew the coffee she offered me.

I met with a pair of sisters who cried when they told me that godwits, the small balls of brown-buff feathers with long upturned bills, no longer nested near their home. They wondered: if it wasn't safe for the birds, was it safe for them?

When interview after interview fell through, whether it was because of needing to get the crop in, some family emergency, or the simple "I've changed my mind," I began to escape from Dickinson, a town clanging with iron and semis, to Medora, the Wild West tourist trap thirty miles to the west.

EARLY IN THE MORNING I would zip out of Dickinson and dive deep into the craggy badlands. I clambered up Camels Hump Butte, a loamy lump near Beach, the closest town to the Montana border, where there was authentic Chinese food. I hiked up Bullion Butte, a mammoth butte over a mile wide, or I'd shoot up the steep incline of Teepee Butte, scrambling to climb the gloopy clay sides, praying to get a solid grip to reach the top, where a welded iron cross stained with bird shit was secure in the soil. Atop the buttes, I gazed around the mottled wash of silver sage, a landscape that time and water and fire and ice whittled into physical poetry. Now, that landscape was being broken by steel, fracking fluid, and explosives—all blowing up an ancient seabed nearly two miles underground.

I traded the screech of oil tankers blasting along two-lane highways and the bright blaze of burning flares for the bustling madness of Medora's summer tourist season: droves of cotton-candy-fueled families in flip-flops desperate to see lumbering bison or hear the yips of the black-tailed prairie dog towns that dot Theodore Roosevelt National Park. Children walked the hot pavement of Medora, smacking on their saltwater taffy.

Drenched after a morning of hiking, I'd sit at a mahogany bar in Medora, where I'd be waited on by a bevy of bartenders from Taiwan, eastern Europe, or South America—teens and twentysomethings spending their summer serving plump RV owners French fries and bison burgers.

The global flare of Medora is fueled by the reality that Medora is, essentially, owned by the Theodore Roosevelt Medora Foundation. Droves of young internationals, desperate for a taste of the mythic American West, arrive in one of the most remote regions of the country only to realize that this isn't Arches, Zion, Olympic, or even Yellowstone. In fact, Medora is more akin to the celluloid mystique of an Old West movie. It's a semiarid sagebrush steppe of rattlesnakes and pronghorn antelope—a wash of brown barely containing any trees, with one gas station and no train depot. An oasis where daily temperatures burn to over 100 degrees.

After my morning saunters up buttes, I'd crave a frosty pint of beer and fleischkuekle—the local German-from-Russia meat patty, wrapped in dough, and deep fried, served with a pickle spear and French fries on the side. In Boots, I'd eavesdrop on conversations, listening to moms and dads tick off another national park on their list.

Early in the summer I'd installed Grindr, an app with profiles of gay men that tells the user how far away the nearest gay man is from their phone. On previous visits to family in Bismarck, nearly two hours to the east, Grindr would list a smattering of brave souls in the state capital city but then list only, perhaps, a handful of men over one hundred miles away. North Dakota, Grindr confirmed, was no place for gay men.

Except in summer.

As I kept my phone close to my chest, man after international man populated my screen. Medora, as it turned out, was a gay Mecca. Profiles of men from Chile—their washboard torsos and that sultry line cleaving down their chest—flooded my screen. I took another sip of my cold beer.

And then a curly-haired bartender asked me if I was doing all right, if I wanted anything to eat. He had arctic eyes, a welcoming grin. I turned my phone over and set it down on the bar.

With interviews falling through left and right, my days suddenly were free to see the bartender, whose name I now knew was Jakub. Eventually, I drove sixty miles every other day to see him.

He had an easy laugh and confided in me that he was studying

oil painting back home in Poland. When I asked why he was spending his summer working in Medora, he said he thought he'd be able
to take weekend trips around the region.

"But Americans don't believe in trains," he said. I found out in
the month he had been in Medora he hadn't left—and Medora takes
all of ten minutes to circumnavigate on foot.

When I offered to drive Jakub through the badlands, or farther,
when his or my schedules allowed, he smiled. He'd love that.

On Jakub's days off we climbed Pretty Butte, where you could
throw a football into Montana. We packed lunches of tomato sandwiches, cucumbers, homemade chocolate chip cookies, and coffee.
Atop the sage-speckled butte, Jakub pulled out a small canvas and
paints and took off his shirt, his golden skin darkening in the sun, the
tips of his hair lightening. I brought a notebook to write in, slipped
under the silver sage, and curled in the shade to nap.

Some days we'd watch the mantles of clouds build, the sky brew-
ing lavender, then indigo, the clouds miles high, swelling with the
weight of summer rain.

Jakub began joining me on my quest to visit North Dakota's
eighteen so-called Extraordinary Places—a group of man-made
or geological formations proposed by Wayne Stenjhem, the state's
attorney general, as worthy of special protections—namely, that no
pump jack could be developed within two miles of the site.

The bill passed, but stripped of any enforcement provisions, so it
was the law in name only. In reality, oil development could creep in
as close as the extraction companies liked.

Still, it was my goal to visit each site, such as the Elkhorn Ranch,
now known as the Cradle of Conservation, where Theodore Roosevelt lived in the 1880s; White Butte, at 3507 feet, the state's highest

point; and neighboring Black Butte, the state's second-highest point, which was more difficult to climb because of the large boulders scattered around its summit.

On each journey Jakub would paint and I would write, and, on each field trip we'd do our creative work inching closer and closer, until our shoulders touched. I'd look over at him: he was focused on his painting—the shape of a line, matching the right pigment with the shade of sage—only ever revealing a slight smile. I let him lead because I didn't know how to be coy with men, how to be flirtatious in a fractured land.

ONE DAY, WE DROVE the Custer Trail south and east of Medora, a gravel-road romp that follows Custer's path through the badlands before he had the worst day of his life at the Battle of the Little Bighorn.

Jakub rolled down his window and stuck his head out. His curls whipped about like lush brown waves; his mouth was wide open.

"I love it here," he said.

I laughed and shook my hand.

"Don't you?" he asked when he pulled his head back into the car.

He reached over and placed his hand on my thigh.

I took one hand off the steering wheel, kept my eye on the road, and squeezed his hand. It was supple.

Jakub threaded his fingers through mine.

WE PULLED OFF the road at Tracy Mountain, a low-level butte riddled with quartz.

When the sun strikes just right, the south-facing slope of bentonite shines like a mirror.

We parked the car, left a note with my name, number, and a message to the landowner, telling them we were just there to hike. I left a twenty-dollar bill as a sign of our good intentions. At every Extraordinary Place my money was always there when we returned.

At the base of Tracy Mountain is a decapitated pumpjack, the horse-head top rusting on the ground. When the oil dried up in the 1970s, after the second oil boom, the Southwestern Production Corporation abandoned its wells. From decades of neglect, coupled with freezing winters and scorching summers, pumpjack and oil drums had rusted and broken down, a type of postmodern fossil in a landscape filled with actual dinosaur bones.

I pointed out Custer's wagon tracks as we got closer to Tracy Mountain. Rumor had it, I told Jakub, that the area was named after an ex-Confederate soldier who escaped there to avoid being tried for war crimes, using the butte—which is really what Tracy Mountain is—as a lookout post.

I looked over at Jakub. He rolled his eyes.

"Yes, I know who George Armstrong Custer is," he said.

He bent over, examining the wagon tracks, and touched the ground.

"This place never heals," he said.

It's true—there's a reason the bluffs and buttes "look like how Poe sounds," as Roosevelt wrote in his diary. Warped, gnarly, bare.

Roughly sixty-five million years ago, North Dakota was a warm, swampy ecosystem of fish and dinosaurs. What is now Wyoming was an active volcano region, spewing ash into the air and swamps. Carried by ancient waterways, the ash and sediment from the forming Rocky Mountains settled, pressed into sedimentary rocks such as sandstone, limestone, and shale.

About a million years ago North America was in the midst of a long ice age with glaciers cruising south from Canada, pressing and reshaping riverways. What are now the badlands faced a new force of erosion: the Little Missouri River. The river carved away the soft layers of earth, which created clusters of towering hoodoos. Ancient plants transfigured into coal seams.

I told Jakub the history of Custer's presence in the region, how he was described as effeminate, an apparent dandy who wore purple velvet riding gloves. We looked at each other and sniggered. Then I mentioned how Custer trimmed his long yellow locks before the Battle of the Little Bighorn, temporarily confusing the Indians as to whether he was even there.

"Custer," I said, "supposedly kept a pet bobcat in the basement."

Jakub rolled his eyes. "That's a little dramatic, don't you think?" He laughed.

As sweat began to slide down our backs, we scrambled up the rock escarpment of Tracy Mountain. Clay and rock gave way under our weight. Jakub and I stopped partway up the slope and shared a swig of water. I pointed out other Extraordinary Places in view: Bullion, White, and Black Buttes. I fanned my hand between Black and Bullion, telling Jakub that, somewhere there, out of sight, was the columnar junipers, a collection of vertical shrubs that sweetened that pocket of the badlands.

"Some of the gays at work want to camp there. They call it Burning Coal Vein. We should go," he said.

I agreed. But, privately, I worried about a mini-gay-pride parade in southwestern North Dakota. What if other people were at the campground? What if there were oil-field workers or ranchers who heard there was a smattering of sissies camping at the columnar junipers? My worry about who I was—am—at home made me nervous.

"You know," I said to Jakub as we continued to the top of Tracy Mountain, "the name Burning Coal Vein is because the black layers of lignite coal get struck by lightning, catch fire, and smolder for centuries and become"—I bent over and reached toward the ground—"this bright scoria rock."

Jakub turned around, smiled, and stepped toward me. He held my chin in his hands and kissed my lips.

I sighed, then realized where I was, and I pulled away.

"What?" he asked.

"We're in North Dakota. We can't do that here. We could get fucking killed. What if someone's watching us?"

"No one's watching us. Look."

I scanned the vast horizon.

He grabbed my chin and kissed me again. "We can't even see a car for miles."

I shook my head.

"I know. I'm sorry. It's just that you're the first boy who's kissed me in public at home."

He guffawed, turned toward me, and swung his arm wide. "You call this 'public'?"

He stepped close and kissed me again, this time more passionately.

# 3.

WHEN I LIVED in the Bakken oil boom that summer, I broke a promise to myself once, the one rule I had: Do not go out and drink alone in boomtowns.

For weeks I had felt relatively safe in Dickinson—shopping during the day at Cashwise Foods and going to the new gym. My friends, all professors at the state university in town, took me out for drinks at Rusty's Bar, a dingy downtown dive with a jukebox in the back and karaoke every other Tuesday. It was clear that this was the unnamed gay bar in the region.

My shoulders relaxed, I breathed deeper. For a moment, it felt like an oasis in what locals at the time now called the Saudi Arabia of the Prairie.

Weeks later, while my landlords were out of town, I, with my newfound confidence, went to a bar called Burning Saddles.

It was past nine. There were two big-screen televisions behind the bar. One played soccer, the other the Twins' baseball game. Off to the side, men were playing pool.

I didn't stay long, spoke to only the bartender, who had a purple-yellow bruise blossoming under her eye. She smiled at me.

I ordered two IPAs, feeling awkward at a bar where no one talked. The buzz of the TVs in the background and the sharp crack of billiard balls were the only sounds around the bar. After I finished my second frothy beer, I paid my tab and left.

When I stepped out into the cool June night, suddenly I flew. I crashed against a brick wall. My glasses fell off my face. A knee cracked against my forehead.

A man yelled, "Faggot."

I clutched my eye. With my other hand I scrambled and found my glasses. The sharp sting of burnt rubber flared in my nostrils as a white truck sped away.

The bartender rushed out of the door and asked if I was okay. She crouched by me and said that no one had left the bar after me. I slumped against the cold brick wall. She sat beside me and held my hand. I was sweating and, slowly, caught my breath.

"I'll be fine," I said.

"You have to let me call the police."

"No, no, I don't want any trouble," I said, and slowly wobbled onto my feet. I held my forehead. It burned.


ON MY DRIVE BACK to my room, I rubbed my eye and felt ashamed. I walked through the door, flicked on the lights to the house, walked into the kitchen, and grabbed a dishcloth. I opened the freezer and pulled out an ice cube tray, twisted it, and plopped the small cubes into the cloth. I started thinking in a type of conspiracy-theory-fueled delirium. Maybe someone in the bar texted a buddy, I thought as I held the pack of ice against my eye and forehead, telling him to wait outside for a small redheaded man. That seemed improbable.

But now it also felt possible.

A FEW DAYS LATER, with the first black eye of my life, I swung west out of Dickinson, shot into Medora, and snagged Jakub. It was a quiet Wednesday morning—the sun had just peaked over the bluffs when I pulled off the highway and drove into town. A few groggy families were up, wrapped in sweatshirts, having coffee at their campsites. I turned off the main road, rumbled across the railroad tracks, and turned into the Elkhorn Quarters, a barracks-type living arrangement, where Jakub was staying for the summer.

I wanted this to be a surprise and hadn't told him I was coming to town. I called his phone three times before he answered.

"I want to take you to the Elkhorn Ranch," I said. "I've packed some lunches and snacks in case we get hungry. There's some coffee in a thermos."

"What? Where are you?" he asked through a yawn.

"I'm outside," I said.

"What?"

"I'm here. Just throw something on. You can sleep in the car if you want."

A few minutes later Jakub stumbled out the door. He feigned a smile and shook his head.

"Should I bring anything with?" he asked.

"Your paints?"

"That's okay. I'll just savor the time with you," he said as he swaggered over, wrapped his arms around me, and leaned in for a kiss.

"Christ—go brush your teeth," I said, laughing and pulling away from him.

"Oh, what, honey, you don't like how I smell?" He smiled, opened his mouth, and breathed at me.

I fanned him away.

"Thank god I have some gum for you in the car," I said. "Get in."

Now the sun shined across the beige- and strawberry-streaked bluffs. Ahead, in the Little Missouri River bottom, Jakub spotted an obstinacy of bison ambling down the riverbank. The forecast for the day was hot—into the nineties, clear sky, in a landscape with little shade. We drove onto the interstate and sped west.

At Beach, I turned off the interstate and headed north. As I drove, one hand on the wheel, while Jakub quietly sipped some coffee, the radio cut in and out. Jakub reached over and turned it off and then slid his hand over mine. I half looked at him, keeping one eye on the road. He stared straight ahead, lightly gripping my hand, and I turned both eyes back onto the road. Out of the corner of my eye I could see him smile as he slowly sipped his steaming coffee.

A FEW MILES LATER I ripped off the highway and onto a gravel road.

"Whoa! Where are we going?" asked Jakub.

"You'll see," I said, smiling.

Orange clouds of dust kicked up behind us as we sped between cleaved bentonite bluffs.

A large red semi barreled toward us in the distance and, as we passed each other, barely pulled over. A cloud of dust washed over my car. In the blur, it sounded like a shotgun had gone off. A rock hit the windshield.

"Son of a bitch," I mumbled.

"No chip, though," said Jakub. He rubbed the spot where the rock hit.

We kept driving. As we continued, we passed a few fracking sites.

"You can tell they're new—new to this boom," I said, "because that's a fresh scoria roadway. See how bright orange and red it is. It isn't faded dull orange like others."

Jakub nodded.

A large flare next to the well site flashed like the Wicked Witch of the West's fireball in *The Wizard of Oz*.

We drove on, winding and bending deeper into the badlands on the narrow road.

By now Jakub had taken his hand off mine.

"It's okay," I said. "It's just a little ways ahead. There's nothing to worry about."

Minutes later I turned off the main fracking road and shot down between two brown bluffs. Small patches of silver sage lined the roadway. A car from Massachusetts passed us. I kept my hand on the steering wheel but lifted my fingers up to wave at the driver.

"How'd you know him?" asked Jakub.

"I don't," I said.

"Then why'd you wave at him?"

I turned toward Jakub and smiled.

"It's the nice thing to do."

He shook his head.

A minute later we arrived at the trailhead in the Little Missouri River bottom.

"All right," I said. "We're here."

"Where?" he asked.

"The Elkhorn Ranch. Teddy Roosevelt's hideout after his wife and mom died in the same house on the same day," I said. "Can you believe it, it was Valentine's Day, 1884."

"Christ."

Ahead of us the stippled bluffs cut against the large wash of sky. Tallgrass swayed in what little breeze there was.

When we got out of the car, grabbing the two backpacks and bottles of water, the back of my neck was already beginning to sweat.

"Look," said Jakub as we began to walk the trail, heading toward the cottonwoods in the river bottom. "There's a flare up there."

No other car was parked at the trailhead, so I reached out and took Jakub's hand in mine as we began to walk the cut-grass path. Jakub held out his free hand over the florets.

"I love how they feel," he said. "Just like cat's fur."

"Do you have a cat?" I asked him.

"My mom does—he's named Gnojek."

"What's that mean?"

"Dipshit."

As we crossed the threshold into the cottonwood trees, there was a slight reprieve from the heat. A few starlings sang above us. Every now and then the cry of a pheasant broke the silence. There was still a trace of dew on the short grass near the base of the tree trunks. We stepped out of the thicket, into a shorn patch of grass lined with six large stones.

"Here we are," I said to Jakub.

"Where?"

"The Elkhorn Ranch," I said, spreading my arms.

"Where is it?" he asked.

I laughed and pointed at the stones.

"Wow," he said, gently shoving himself into my shoulder. "Impressive."

He rested his chin on my shoulder.

I turned my head, looked down my nose, and raised my eyebrows.

Jakub kissed me.

"Okay, Mr. Unimpressed," I said. "Let's go for a swim."

"I didn't bring my suit," Jakub said.

"I know." I smiled and winked at him. "C'mon, let's go."

We left the Elkhorn Ranch and walked east toward the Little Missouri River.

"Now be careful," I said as we got to the bank's edge.

We sat down in the grass and scooted toward the steep edge. I pressed my feet into the soft dirt as I gripped some grass. I slid down the dusty bank and dirt clung to my legs.

"There's a spot down farther that looks easier," I said to Jakub. "I'll walk in the water and meet you down there."

By the time I reached him, Jakub was sunning himself on a small soft sandbar, his backpack and pile of clothes next to him. I let out a laugh.

"What?" He furrowed his brow.

"It's just you're nearly as white as I am, at least down there," I said as I reached him, set down my bag, and began to strip.

I reached out my hand, grabbed his, and hauled Jakub onto his feet. We stepped into the water. A wave of goose bumps washed over my body.

"Not too cold, is it?" asked Jakub.

I shook my head.

"No, not too bad."

"How deep does it get?" he asked as we waded into the middle of the small river.

"It doesn't," I said, sitting down. "We'll have to float."

Jakub sat down next to me. We looked downstream, our shoulders rubbing against each other. Muddy water washing against our backs. We pushed up and off the silty river bottom and began to float. Jakub held out his hand. I gripped it. We began to swirl gently downstream on our backs.

LATE THAT MORNING we sidled up to a long bar for lunch in Watford City. The small 1300-person town that I knew growing up had, by some estimates, now exploded to over 10,000 people. In the wheat fields and hills beyond Watford City, man-camps dotted the prairie—such military-style housing had cropped up to accommodate the booming population of oil-field workers coming from around the country and world. New gas stations, new grocery stories, new restaurants, houses, and hotels all sprouted up in town.

The lunch rush hadn't showed up yet by the time Jakub and I arrived in the bar. There was one man nursing a beer at the end. When we sat, I glanced over at him and nodded.

"Don't do that," said a waitress with lowlights and highlights. Her name tag said Tammy.

"I'm sorry?" I asked.

"Don't look at him," she said behind a plastered-on smile. "He won't like that. He was in the other week"—she turned her back against the man so he couldn't watch her talk—"and picked up one of those high-top stools and threw it at another wildcatter."

Jakub leaned on the bar.

"Should we get a booth?"

"No—but what'll y'all have to drink?" Tammy asked in a chipper tone. "If you move, he'll know I said something and then we'll have trouble."

Jakub and I took the large plastic menus from her, crinkled them open, saying we'd each have a water, and hid from the man at the end of the bar.

"How do you feel about this?" Jakub asked through gritted teeth.

"Like we're at Disney World," I said, sarcastically.

Jakub laughed.

Tammy shot over toward us with sweaty glasses of water.

"Don't do that."

"What?" asked Jakub as he put down his menu.

Tammy flung her hair. Out of the corner of my eye I watched the man slowly take a sip of his beer and drill his eyes into the back of Tammy's head.

"Don't laugh. Try to not talk as much as possible. Keep this simple and we'll be okay."

The man cleared his throat. Tammy turned and looked at him. She smiled.

"All done, Hank?"

"No. I want another," Hank said and leaned back on his barstool. He cleared his throat, looked over at the television playing a ballgame, and rubbed his salt-and-pepper stubble hair.

Jakub placed his hand on my thigh. I swatted it away and quickly flicked my head.

"Don't," I whispered. "Not here."

Tammy delivered Hank's beer and came over to us.

"You boys know what you want?" she asked in a bright voice.

We did, and Jakub ordered each of us a beer. When they arrived, we slowly sipped from our frosted pints and stared straight ahead at the mirror wall lined with whiskey, vodka, and gin.

I put my feet up on the brass bar rail and rolled my ankles forward and back. I cupped my beer with both hands, watched the small bubbles rise as the beads of dew on the outside of the glass fell.

Hank drank his beer fast, let out a loud sigh, savoring his beer, wiped his mouth with the back of his arm, and slammed a fifty down.

"Keep the change, darlin'," he yelled at Tammy, though she was only five feet away from him, rinsing off plates before sending them back through the small window, into the kitchen for dishwashing.

"Take care, Hank," said Tammy. Her eyes stayed on him.

He pushed off from the bar and rocked back on his stool before turning to the side and sliding off and hopping down on the floor. He was wearing steel-toed boots and looked over at Jakub and me.

"Queers," he grunted.

Jakub turned. I quickly gripped his thigh and slowly lifted my beer with my other hand.

Hank moseyed out the entryway.



SUDDENLY, AS IF out of thin air, Jakub's burger and my chicken Thai salad arrived. Now we could take the full measure of Tammy. Her nails were lacquered in white, tipped with a strip of black. A bright silver cross hung down from her neck and, for better or worse, I glanced at her breasts. She wore a deep merlot lipstick that complemented her dusty eyeshadow and had large white teeth. Now, she came over to us and rested her elbows on the bar.

"How long have you two been together?"

"What?" asked Jakub, pulling the burger away from his first bite. I sat back on my barstool.

"Oh, c'mon, I love the gays. My hubby and I moved here from Vegas, and we miss going to drag shows and finding glitter you know where"—she winked—"later at night."

My eyes snapped wide.

Tammy looked between us.

"Oh, c'mon, sweethearts, it's clear as crystal you're queer as the day is long. I mean look at you"—she stuck her nose out at Jakub—"you must moisturize three times a day. And you," she said to me, "your vocal fry makes any chain-smoking queen jealous."

I poked at my salad and shook my head.

"You don't have anything to worry about now that that crusty old fuck, Hank, is out of here. No one will come in until about five and you sweet things just give me a holler if you need anything."

But Tammy didn't give us a chance. After Jakub's second chomp on his burger, as the juice slid down his chin, Tammy zipped back over to us.

"You know, my husband and I have been here for seven years. Well—he's been here for eight and I stayed back home in Vegas to have our baby. Sam's a bit older than me, has a grown son up here workin' in the boom with him, drilling holes, shootin' shit into the ground. I had the baby and waited a few months while Sam found us a house here in Watford. He and his son were livin' in one of those man-camps outside of town—y'all see that on your way in?"

Jakub nodded as he held his burger by the side of his face. I grabbed my beer and slowly sipped as Tammy sped through her life history.

"Goddam kids here in Watford call my son a foreigner in first grade. 'You're not from here. We've been here for generations.' Those little shits cluck like hens and little Henry comes home in tears some days during the school year."

Jakub frowned.

Tammy stepped back, flung her hands wide, and continued her sermon.

"I mean, you all," she said, pointing at us, "know what it's like to be oppressed."

Jakub and I looked at each other.

"This part of the world is oppression. We're just trying to make a decent living, come back from that recession, save some for retirement. But then you got these old cusses that come in off the fracking rigs that get blitzed out of their mind, haven't screwed anyone in months, raging and all testosterone flying around. The boss here says he's going to start having us close at eleven p.m. Nothing good happens in this place after ten p.m. I told you what old Hank did the other week—well, that ain't the worst of it. You don't want to cross that parking lot out there after dark. It's good you boys are here during the day."

Jakub slowly nodded and feigned a smile.

"Dammit, Tammy," Tammy said to herself. "I'm yapping your ears off and lettin' your food get cold. You sweeties sit tight, I'm gettin' y'all another round on me. Those beers must be warm and now your food's cold. Ya doing okay with that burger, sweet pea?" she asked and leaned in toward Jakub.

Jakub nodded.

"Yes, it's good, thank you."

"He's a real nice one, isn't he," she said, throwing a wink at me.

Jakub leaned back, giggled, and wrapped his arm around the back of my chair as Tammy grabbed our pint glasses, whipped her hair as she twirled away from us, and made her way back to the line of draft taps.

WE FINISHED OUR BEERS and paid our tab. Tammy came around from the back of the bar and flung open her arms.

Jakub raised his eyebrows.

"It's just so nice to have some homos here instead of oil workers," she squealed as she wrapped her arms around me.

I held my arms at my side as she squeezed me like an accordion. "Thanks," I choked out.

Jakub held up his hand as she let go of me and shimmied toward him.

"Poland. We don't hug," he said. "But thank you for a lovely time."

We turned and exited the bar and held our hands above our brows to shield the sun. In the parking lot Hank, the man who was in the bar when we had arrived, rested against the back of his truck. I grabbed Jakub's T-shirt and pulled him in the opposite direction.

"Let's go for a walk," I said. "We'll take our time and come back in a bit."

"What—it'll be fine," said Jakub.

"It might not be," I said. "And I don't want to find out if it isn't."

We walked down the street, away from the bar, as trucks and tankers rumbled past. Ahead, at the one stoplight in town, a three-way intersection next to a gas station, semis snaked miles toward the horizon, hauling water, oil, and fracking waste to god knows where on god knows what time schedule. Every now and then a honk broke through the gunning of gears and gas, the sharp sting of diesel puffing out from the semis as they shifted and rolled down the highway. Jakub and I kept walking along the sidewalk, and I shoved my hands in my pockets as I looked out at the horizon.

EARLIER IN THE SUMMER, I had met my parents in a restaurant in Dickinson. I had let them know I was living there for the summer, that I was working, and that maybe we should have lunch.

We met in a 1950s throwback restaurant—an old gas pump was at the entrance, some tin Route 66 signs hung from the wall, a fishtail fender jutted from the wall.

As soon as we sat down, I asked the waitress for a gin and tonic. Dad looked over at me—it was barely afternoon.

The waitress said, "I'm afraid we don't serve hard liquor here anymore, sir, due to the oil workers."

I ordered a beer. I needed something to temper my anxiety.

The waitress placed three large plastic menus in front of us, smiled, and left us. Mom, Dad, and I snapped open our menus and hid our faces. I took in slow breaths. Four years into my exile, a stiff silence flowed between us.

We put in our orders—burgers for Dad and me, a taco salad for Mom.

When the waitress left, Mom began to cry. She ran a finger under her glasses to wipe her tears.

Months before, I had sent my parents a letter outlining my pain—my suicide attempt, my continued suicidal ideation, how my being gay wasn't a big deal. How, if they went to counseling and learned to accept me for who I was, I would be ready to rebuild our relationship.

I never heard back.

When I told Tanya that I had sent them this letter, she said she had heard.

"Dad read it," she said, "and then threw it away. He didn't want Mom to see it."

I didn't know why my mother was crying in Dickinson.

But that's not quite true. In the nearly four years since my parents learned I was gay, I had distanced myself from them. I had gone to therapy while I was a student at Hamline and learned that it was okay to set boundaries.

I texted them only on their birthdays.

Whenever one of their names flashed on my screen, my body lurched. I was late for my student loans. When was I going to be done with school. Why wasn't I coming home for Thanksgiving, Christmas, the Fourth of July. Merry Christmas. When was I getting a job. Happy birthday.

The texts were electric surges through my body.


WHEN MY BEER ARRIVED, I gulped, hard, wiping the foam from my upper lip. I ordered another one and Dad looked over at me.

We were the only people in the restaurant.

"Did you ever think, Mom, that there are other gay people here?"

"Keep your voice down," Dad said.

"Did you really think the 'right woman' never came down the driveway?" I continued.

The waitress returned, set down my beer, feigned a smile, and quickly left.

I chugged my second beer hard, too, and shook my head. Dad and I both looked out the window at the traffic zipping by on I-94—him in his typical black Harley-Davidson shirt with Harley-Davidson hat, me in my polo and Chacos.

I shook my head.

Mom let out a sniffle and continued to dab at her eye.


WHEN OUR FOOD ARRIVED, Dad slid his credit card over to the waitress.

We ate in silence.

When the waitress returned, she told us to have a nice day.


WE LEFT THE RESTAURANT and walked into the parking lot. Heat rose from the pavement as we went to our separate cars.

"Bye," I said.

Their car doors slammed shut.

It was my last time seeing my parents for years.


WEEKS AFTER my and Jakub's trip to Watford, a group of his gay coworkers announced that they would be gathering at the columnar junipers.

Junipers grow in southwestern North Dakota because of sulfur. For centuries the region was used as a rendezvous point for Native Americans, explorers, and pioneers because, when struck by lightning, coal seams lit and smoldered, in some cases for centuries, creating the conditions for juniper trees to take root and shoot skyward.

Jakub's coworkers picked an obscure Tuesday in July, one when they were sure the eight-site campground would be empty. Seven of them were going in the midafternoon to stake a claim to each site, and Jakub and I would come after his afternoon shift at Boots.

When I picked him up, he feigned a smile—it was a slow day and he had two sets of customers who said they wanted an *American* waiter. Jakub lowered his head and tried to look away. I reached out and held him by the shoulders.

"We don't have to go camping. We can go another time. I know you've had a rough day."

He shook his head and said no. He had taken the next day off and had been looking forward to this trip for weeks.

We went to his barracks, where he changed, washed his face and the back of his neck, and grabbed his backpack. We got into my car and barreled into the badlands.

As we snaked our way between the buttes, we rolled down the windows, waved at whoever we passed. Jakub propped his feet up on the dashboard.

"It's so beautiful here," he said, "but some people are mean."

I took my eyes off the road and looked over at him.

"Not you," he said, his arm hanging out the window, rolling up and down like a wave. "Just other people. And North Dakotans eat shitty food."

We laughed.

BEFORE WE ARRIVED at the campground, I stopped the car at a patch of ponderosa pines.

"Let's smell them," I said, opening my door. Jakub asked me why we would want to smell trees. "C'mon, just give it a try." I winked at him.

We bounded up a slope, dusted with crisp pine needles. We picked the same tree, its ruby, papery bark veined with black char.

"The trees need fire to scatter their seeds," I said as I pressed my nose against the bark and inhaled. "Try it."

Jakub pressed his nose against the tree and inhaled. He smiled. His eyes widened. "It smells like vanilla. Oh my god, that's lovely."

We smelled more trees—vanilla, coffee, burnt caramel. While we both pressed our noses to the last one, Jakub wrapped his arms around the trunk, wiggled his fingers back and forth, and wanted to hold hands. When we locked, he peeked around the trunk, pulled me in, and kissed me. He looked me up and down. "Now you smell like vanilla."

WE ARRIVED AT the campsite to shirtless gays cackling. They were around a small, smoky fire, nestled next to one another in nylon camping chairs. It was around six o'clock and one of the guys, Roberto, gathered larger sticks to build up the fire. We were having brats for supper.

I hadn't met the gays, as Jakub called them, not really—only in passing, or when Jakub would point one out on our drives out of Medora to climb buttes. This, now, was the most international gathering—much less the largest gathering of gays—I had ever been a part of in North Dakota. Jakub from Poland, Roberto from Italy, a pair of men from the Czech Republic, a man from Chile, one from Latvia, another from Spain, and another from Hungary.

As we stepped out of the car, a wave of catcalls rolled toward us. "Oh, look at the lovebirds!" the Spaniard, Carlos, squealed as he spun, wrapped his arms around himself, and made loud kissing and moaning noises. "You're just in time for dinner."

I looked at Jakub and flushed red.

"They're harmless," he whispered.

As the brats crackled, Roberto asked if anyone wanted his bun toasted. A roar rolled across the sage steppe.

"You can toast my buns anytime," Carlos said as he lifted his leg up and smacked his ass.

I kept my eyes on the entrance to the campground and gave a hollow chuckle at each flirtatious joke. I couldn't shake the notion of where we were.

"What's wrong?" Jakub whispered.

I waved him off. "How about I go grab that wine we brought?" I asked for everyone else to hear.

"Oh, Jakub, you got a good man," sassed Carlos. "You better not let him go—he drives you around, you 'make your art together,' he brings you wine. I need a man like him."


I RETURNED FROM the car with two bottles of Côte du Rhône in one hand and blue Solo cups in the other.

"We're glad to know you're a liberal," Roberto said, pointing at the cups. "Thank god you didn't bring those red ones."

As twilight sank across the stippled scoria buttes, the nine of us sat in a circle around the fire. The sky fired fuchsia, then orange, then husk and lavender before simmering into a sweep of stars.

———

LATER, I HEARD SOMETHING. I bolted up from my chair. Jakub's hand pressed on my thigh.

"Someone's coming," I said.

Earlier in the evening some of the boys had strapped on high heels, others had smeared their faces in foundation and rouge, doing a type of improv, rugged Wild West drag show.

Headlights appeared down the road.

"Put on your shirts," I said.

Roberto hurled packages of facial wipes around the circle, the boys scrubbed as if to rub their skin off their faces.

It was a truck—a large truck, rumbling toward the campground.

I felt my jeans tighten as Jakub's hand gripped me harder.

"It'll be fine," I said over and over. "If it comes to it, I'll talk to whoever it is."

"Carlos," whispered Roberto, "take off your fucking heels, you idiot."

Carlos whipped off his shoes and flung them under a sage bush.

The truck passed the first few campsites. The tents some of the boys set up were flooded with light. I breathed deeply. The headlights circled the top of the hill.

"Jakub, fill everyone's glass with wine, try to look natural," I said as I kicked at the ground, crammed my hands into my pockets, looked down at my feet. The truck's light now climbed my legs.

When the truck got to me, it stopped. I could see a gun rack in the back. The driver, a middle-aged man, leaned over and rolled down his window.

"Howdy," said a booming voice from the dark cave of the truck.

"How's it going?" I stiffened and asked, in my best Dakota twang, walking to the window, resting my forearms on the cold door.

Only one rifle. But I couldn't see if there was anything on his hip or in the glove box. The cab smelled like cigarettes and bourbon.

"You boys having a good night?"

"Sure are. Just out here for a bachelor party. Visiting from Center."

"Center? No shit! I used to go to Center." The man let go of the wheel, shifted toward me, his arm on the back of his bench seat. Tufts of silver hair shot out from his cowboy hat. He had a packet of cigarettes in his breast pocket. I couldn't tell if he reached for something as he shifted to look at me. "Lot of big-ass girls I used to date in Center back in the day."

"Oh, you mean my grandmas?" I said. The man got the joke and roared. His gut bounced as he smacked the southwestern woven blanket that draped across the bench seats. I chuckled and rubbed my finger back and forth on the truck door. I glanced at his side mirror and saw the gaggle of gays slowly sipping wine from their Solo cups. The fire snapped.

"Bachelor party, huh? Sounds fun." He turned, hoisted his arm across the seat, and looked out his back window. He grunted as he twisted to look back at the boys. His shirt stretched and I could get a better look at him. In his other breast pocket was a pack of snus; a buck knife glinted along his leather belt. There were sweat stains under his arm. Now I caught the sharp, sweet smell of onions.

"We're having a good time," I said, as I slowly looked back at the boys.

"Hey," said the man as he pointed at the group, "why's that one in those short shorts?"

"Oh, him," I said, pointing at Carlos, who took a deep pull from his Solo cup. "Well, he's the bachelor. We stole him away from his fiancée, and well, you won't believe this"—I looked back at the man, leaned in, and lowered my voice—"he and his bride-to-be were, well, you know. . . ." I nodded.

"No shit," snorted the man.

"And here comes our happy crew and breaks up the fun! By the time we were on the interstate, he realized he put on her damn shorts!" I walloped the site of the rusty truck door.

I looked back at the boys, who pretended to laugh. The man picked up a bourbon bottle from beneath the bench seat.

"Well, shit," he said as he uncorked the bottle and took a pull. "She must have been one of those big girls for him to wear those—and, shit, look—" the man yelled, his finger now pointing at Carlos as he handed me the bottle. "He still has her lipstick on!"

"No shit!" I laughed as I took a pretend-pull from the bottle.

Everyone now glared at Carlos.

"Well, I don't mean to stop the fun. Congratulations!" shouted the man as he waved at Carlos.

I handed the bottle back.

"Take care," said the man as he rolled up his window.

"You, too," I said.

The truck began to pull away and bucked down the gravel road. I watched those red taillights until I couldn't see them anymore. I let out a deep breath.

When I returned to the fire circle, only the wood crackled. I sat down next to Jakub, who filled my cup with more wine. We all sat there, looked into the fire, sipping, staring. The flames shivered. In a trance, we all sat silently as, every now and then, we heard a pheasant cluck. A coyote cried in the distance.

# 4.

As the sweltering heat of July turned to the humid nights of August, I refused to acknowledge that Jakub would be leaving soon for Poland and I would be going to Iowa, back to school for another graduate degree. A quiet sadness entered our relationship—on our hikes Jakub painted less, I wrote fewer words. He'd smear his burnt sienna, yellow ocher, and indigo across his palette. If we sat apart, I'd sometimes hear him tap the blunt end of his brush against the hard back of his canvas. Sometimes we'd sit atop a butte and hold hands, the smell of sage the only thing between us.

A person is laid bare in the badlands. Eons of erosion carve the world down into its basic element: dust. There is no hiding here, even from ourselves.

When we'd watch the sun sizzle and slide below the horizon, I'd often weep, my face turning into Jakub's shoulder, him staring ahead, his hand around my head. He'd press his mouth toward my ear and make a gentle swishing sound like the switchgrass. I'd heave, grip his knee, and spread out farther on the ground, turning my head toward the setting sun, rest my head in his lap, and begin to rub his leg. For a while, all we did was breathe and watch the light lower.

Nearly in mid-August, Jakub and I drove in silence from Medora to the Bismarck airport, past the shelterbelts bookending gleaming fields of wheat, the lemon-colored fields of canola. Jakub kept looking out his window, south toward the dusky buttes. The only time he laughed or made any noise at all on our way to the airport was when we passed Salem Sue, the "world's largest Holstein cow," atop the one hill west of New Salem, a small town of two gas stations just off the interstate. We held hands.

Eventually, in Mandan, we passed a waterslide park and heard children shrieking as they shot water into the air as they sped down the slides, before crossing the wide Missouri River. Pontoons parked on coffee-colored sandbars. Seagulls flew near people in swimsuits picnicking along the riverbank. We crossed into the cottonwood river bottom of Bismarck and passed the Riverwood Golf Course.

"When I was little, I thought this looked like a perfect place for dinosaurs," I said.

Jakub only squeezed my hand.

We hit a red light. I tapped my fingers across the steering wheel. Tears welled in my eyes.

We passed Kirkwood Mall, and I mentioned that there must have been a sale at the sporting goods store because of all the cars. Then we turned south and passed the blocky Wachter Middle School and ranch-style houses.

"My cousins went to school there," I said.

Jakub kept looking out his window.

We curved past the last stoplight in town, turned left, and drove into the small, single-terminal airport.

Jakub kissed me quickly in the car before we stepped out. I popped the trunk. He gathered his bags.

I had a coal burning in my throat—couldn't catch my voice—and turned my head to the side.

"I have something for you," he said.

He pulled out a mason jar and cradled it in front of his chest.

I looked at it and smiled. Small sprigs of silver sage filled the jar.

"I thought you'd like it," he said, blinking back tears.

I nodded my head quickly. My lip quivered.

We hugged. My hands gripped the back of his shirt.

We let go of each other.

Jakub picked up his bags.

I watched him walk through the automatic doors.

He didn't look back at me.

I walked around to the driver's side, slid into my seat, blasted out of the loading zone of the airport, and barreled south out of Bismarck, driving to the bluff high above the Missouri at the University of Mary. I parked my car, walked around to the back of the bluff, sat, and grabbed a bunch of stiff prairie grass. I clenched it. The brown buttes across the river were in faded relief.

I opened the jar, held it to my nose, and inhaled the sweet smell of sage.

# BLADE

# 1.

THAT FALL, I MOVED to Ames, Iowa, a university town surrounded by fields of corn and soybeans, for another master's degree. I was returning to graduate school a second time to get a terminal degree, so that I could have some semblance of stability and a future career as a college professor—and to have eight hundred miles between me and the oil boom I wanted to now write about.

In December, during my first semester, while reading the *Des Moines Register*, a headline caught my attention:

OPPONENTS TO DAKOTA ACCESS
PIPELINE TO MEET

In the article, I learned that the Dakota Access Pipeline would be 1172 miles long, 30 inches in diameter, and, at capacity, would carry nearly 24 million gallons of oil every day from western North Dakota to an existing pipeline in Patoka, Illinois, where it would then be sent through another pipeline to the Gulf of Mexico for refinement and distribution on the world market. The pipeline would begin near Tioga, North Dakota, cross the Missouri River twice, clip the northwest corner of South Dakota, and slice through Iowa diagonally before entering Illinois.

My home was coming home again.

A FEW DAYS LATER, I attended a public meeting at Ames City Hall. In the vestibule, graduate students from Iowa State University had me fill out a name tag and then, on a nearby poster board, write why I was for clean water and soil, rather than oil.

I walked into the cavernous auditorium, where the stage was filled with an economist from Iowa State University, various non-profit representatives, and lawyers.

When the program began, I listened to each person give their perspective on why we needed to stop this pipeline.

I, too, wanted to stop the pipeline. Over the preceding few months, when I wasn't traveling through western North Dakota with Jakub, I had monitored the development and progress of what was at the time the country's major shale play, the Bakken oil boom. I had been reading the six major North Dakota papers every day for the previous three years. I kept a file called Bakken Project on my computer with articles about sex trafficking, oil spills, man-camps, drug trafficking, and infrastructure development. I'd lifted weights with roustabouts and wildcatters in Dickinson and had seen blaze orange hats with Big Cock Country written in black across them, as well as T-shirts that said Going Deep and Pumping Hard or Frack That Hole. I had had Americanos at the Boomtown Babes Espresso, a pink drive-thru coffee shop in Tioga that advertised it had "the Bakken's breast coffee."

———

For the next three years, in graduate school, I wrote letters to the editor and traveled around the country to speak at colleges, universities, and libraries—to anyone who was willing to listen to what I knew about the oil boom back home.

I produced an anthology about fracking with contributions from some of the most noted environmental writers in the country, while I was finishing my own poetry collection about the oil in western North Dakota. I called senators and local officials. I attended meetings of the Bakken Pipeline Resistance Coalition in Ames. I taught fifty college students a semester as part of my teaching fellowship, had my own graduate classes to attend, and was looking for teaching jobs around the country.

In November 2015, during my second year of graduate school, I headed to the Boone County Fairgrounds for the first day of what would become more than a month's worth of hearings for the Iowa Utilities Board. That day, the public could give two-minute-long testimonies either for or against the construction of the pipeline. The muddy parking area was packed, the cars with license plates from Missouri, Arkansas, Illinois, South Dakota, Nebraska, and Minnesota.

Police officers greeted me as I stepped into the cinder-block building.

"Sir, let's have a look at your laptop."

I was carrying my computer.

"Why?" I asked.

"We need to make sure you don't have any weapons."

As he turned over my laptop case, opened it, and felt around inside, he asked, "Why do you have this?"

I lied.

"I'm part of the media."

"Who are you with?"

"The *Huffington Post*," I blurted out. I wasn't—not really—having only published a few op-eds on its news blog.

The officer handed back my laptop, let me pass, and said, "Next."

I WALKED INTO the large room. News reporters lined the wall. At the front, up on stage, were the three members of the Utilities Board. The room was divided into two sections of hard metal chairs. On the left, most people were dressed in blue and wore Stop the Pipeline T-shirts; on the right sat men in orange union shirts. The hearing already had started. Two large television screens shined in front of the stage, one on each side. In front of each TV was a microphone, where people could give their opinion on the pipeline.

I looked around the room and saw a few of my undergraduate students. They waved to me. I waved back and walked over to the corral where members of the media were gathered along the wall.

A few minutes after I arrived, a man with glasses and silver-brown hair approached one of the microphones with his guitar. He began to sing.

"Bakken pipeline, just say no, dirty oil has got to go," he crooned.

The left side of the room, the anti-pipeline people, began to clap along.

"They want to build a pipeline right through the vast Midwest," he strummed. "Through eighteen Iowa counties, but it's not in our interest. Bakken pipeline, just say no, dirty oil has got to go."

The man sang louder as he approached his two-minute limit. He looked back at the audience, which joined him for one more round of the chorus.

"Bakken pipeline, just say no, dirty oil has got to go." The left side of the room clapped and cheered while the union workers folded their arms.

I stayed for hours, listening to each side. For each person who favored the pipeline, another opposed it.

"I need this job," said one man on the right half of the room, "to help provide for my family."

In that moment, I thought of my dad, himself a lifelong union worker who built boilers for plants in the Midwest when I was a newborn; until I was two, he was largely away from home, welding shiny sheet metal to build ethanol plants and coal power plants across North Dakota and here in Iowa.

A minute later, an Iowa farmer approached the microphone on the left side.

"Why should I have to give up my land, jeopardize *my* livelihood, for someone else to have a job? Can't these union workers get a job somewhere else?"

Union faces burned crimson.

My mother's father, Grandpa Hatzenbihler, was a lifelong farmer. I wondered what he'd say if he were here and faced with someone building a pipeline on his land.

As I looked around the room, I kept thinking it was like medieval Europe: two groups arguing between each other while the king—or, in this case, the pipeline company Energy Transfer

Partners—was not in the room. The peasants bickered among themselves for a few scraps.

Minutes later, I gathered my things, went out and got into my
car, and headed back to Ames.

I kept wondering whether the pipeline would be built.

# 2.

NINE MONTHS LATER, in late August, 100 people gathered in the small 250-person town of Pilot Mound, the midpoint of the Dakota Access Pipeline in Iowa. Bulldozers overturned dark Iowa soil. Pipeline was being laid from North Dakota to Illinois.

In Pilot Mound we stood or sat in a circle on the alabaster-tiled floor of the community center. Hard metal chairs squeaked. The room went graveyard silent as we listened to Delbert Hutchins, a large bald man with soil-stained denim jeans, tell us why we were there: we were there to signal this pipeline was not good for Iowa, that it abused Iowa's farmland, risked polluting the state's waterways, and perpetuated a system of extraction that fueled climate change. We were there to send a message to the governor, who had threatened to send state troopers to arrest protesters, that the people of Iowa did not want a pipeline breaking through their communities, across their farms, or under their rivers.

There came a moment where Delbert fell silent—it looked like he was about to pray. He told us the coalition had picked out two sites where we could protest.

"To choose which one, we need to know how many of you are willing to risk being arrested."

The room went silent again.

"Would those of you willing to risk getting arrested please stand?" asked Delbert.

When I stood up, I saw thirty-five other people standing with me.

"If you're not risking arrest today but would be willing to risk arrest in the future, would you please stand?" asked Delbert.

Twenty more people stood. Hoots and clapping filled the community center.

I wiped my eyes. For years I had felt alone—alone in my writing, alone in my speaking engagements at colleges and universities around the country. My home in North Dakota, the nation's sacrifice zone for its dependence on oil, seemed more like spectacle than a place to save. No one had been there—not really. No one would go there, except to the national park beyond the heart of the oil boom.

Now, in Iowa, there were others with me. Now, I could put my pen down and stand my ground with my body to protect my home.

But I also wanted to protect my nephews: eleven-year-old Logan, eight-year-old Noah, and the five-year-old twins, Alexander and Oliver. They were drinking toxic Missouri River water. A Duke University study had confirmed that the Missouri was radioactive. I wanted to test my mettle, to see if I could stand up to the oil industry and help stop a pipeline.

Throughout the morning in Pilot Mound, we simulated what might happen to us while protesting. We were reminded that we were there as peaceful protesters. Delbert reminded us that although we did not want to be arrested, we were willing to go to jail if the governor would not stop the construction of the Dakota Access Pipeline.

When we broke for lunch, and I stood in line for the bathroom, a white-haired man said he saw that I was willing to risk getting arrested.

"Thank you," he said.

I lowered my head and looked at the ground.

"Is this your first time?" he asked.

I nodded.

"That one's always the hardest."

I asked him if this was his first time; he said no.

"My first time was in Selma."

LATER, AFTER LUNCH, I sat on a swing outside the community center. I kicked at the gravel and focused on my breathing. A small girl ran over and slid down the metal slide next to me. Her parents came out of the building to pick her up.

"Jane, do you see that nice man there?" her father asked, pointing to me. "He's going to do a brave thing today and try to stop the pipeline."

Jane looked me up and down—me, in my Chacos, blue Stop the Pipeline T-shirt, and Minnesota Twins baseball hat. She smiled and waved at me.

"Thank you," she shouted as she ran off the playground.

Her parents smiled.

"You're welcome," I tried to yell back, my voice breaking.

THAT AFTERNOON, after we blocked access at the first of four entrances to the Dakota Access Pipeline construction site, a state trooper told the nine of us that this was our final warning, that if we did not move, we would be arrested. We squeezed our hands tighter and stared straight ahead.

I looked to the far horizon, north and west toward North Dakota, and replayed, in my head, the voicemail my nephews had sent me earlier in the day: *Keeping fighting the good fight, Uncle Taylor!*

On the gravel in Boone County I silently chanted, *You're not here out of anger.*

Behind me boomed a voice.

"Sir, please put your arms behind your back."

My chest puffed forward as my shoulders shot back. Cold steel stung my wrists as sweat slid down my brow. I lowered my head and smiled.

When the handcuffs clamped around my wrists, when I was arrested, instead of feeling brave, I felt alone. There was no one who could do this for me, no substitute, no one—even if I had wanted—to stand in for me. It was *my* body I had to put on the line, to slow down the destruction of the buttes and sage and symphony of grasses.

"You're the first arrest, Taylor!" a friend called from the small crowd that had gathered to witness our arrests.

I tried smiling through gritted teeth.

I NEEDED MY ARREST to be more than protest against my fossil-fuel heritage. I needed it to test me, to see what I was made of. I wanted to see what I was willing to lay my body down to protect. I kept thinking about the plundered prairie pressed for black gold, pump-jacks rocking atop buttes, pipelines bursting under the Yellowstone

River, farmland oiled in early fall because of lightning strikes in Williams County, North Dakota, German shepherds with bloodstained mouths nipping Native protesters back in North Dakota. Grinding memories of strip mining, flaring, pumpjacks in the distance, and exploding oil tankers shot through me when the cold steel snapped against my wrist.

My home.

The home I wanted to protect.

# 3.

Two weeks after being released from spending an evening in the Boone County jail, I went to Iowa City to be a part of an evening presentation entitled "Fracking and the Iowa Divide." A historian at the University of Iowa had invited me to present alongside a sociologist, a city planner, the state geologist, and two musicians in the university's music building. The evening was recorded in front of a live audience, moderated by our host, Joan, a woman with sharp auburn hair who wore a long black dress, and was broken into three segments. I would be speaking during the second and third parts.

Backstage, I sat in the greenroom and attempted to meditate. My stomach churned. I stood, stretched, shook my arms, and walked around stacks of folded metal chairs.

I left the greenroom and walked through a high, alabaster hallway inside the music building, and circled to the front, where the event was taking place. I opened the door and peeked in. There were about sixty people in attendance.

I heard the historian who'd invited me.

"I imagine where we'd be without fracking," he said, "and this is what I imagine: Without fracking, oil and gas prices would be three times higher than they are today. We'd probably still be in the recession. We would be producing more coal and carbon dioxide. The dollar would be weaker. The power of Vladimir Putin's Russia would be stronger. Our ability to restrain Iran's nuclear ambitions would be weaker. So, there's a huge impact. Iowans have benefited hugely from fracking. Iowa ranks fifth in energy consumption."

I SLOWLY CLOSED the door and walked back to the greenroom.

On my way, I stopped and took a sip of water from a fountain, and wiped my mouth. I was up next with the city planner and the sociologist.

A minute later, I was onstage.

"Welcome to the World Canvass series 'Fracking and the Iowa Divide,'" said Joan. The city planner and the sociologist would speak before it was my turn. In my mind I considered what I would say, while pretending to listen to them.

"Next is Taylor Brorby," Joan finally said. "You are from North Dakota, are a writer, an environmental activist."

I leaned back on my stool.

"Tell us what you have seen in your own state. I mean, North Dakota now has all these new jobs, all these new houses, it seemed like—wow!—North Dakota has struck it rich," said Joan.

"Sure," I began. "Well, you all know where North Dakota now is, for instance."

The audience laughed.

"I grew up in coal country," I continued. "My entire upbringing was supported by coal, so I'm not just a crunchy-granola activist for ideological reasons. My parents somehow produced one—I mean, lignite coal paid for our bread and butter, literally."

I then painted a picture of the prairie I grew up on. I wanted the members of the audience to love my place, to love my home, even if they hadn't been there. I wanted to paint a picture of what the place was like during my childhood and what it now was. I began listing statistics about Watford City, a town that had doubled in size every two years during the height of the boom.

"You can now see my home state from outer space. It gives off more light pollution than Minneapolis–St. Paul, except North Dakota's is from the burning off of natural gas. It's the largest bonfire on the planet."

I looked out into the audience, but the only familiar face I could see was my friend Joel. He was Kirsten's dad: Kirsten, the first friend I made at St. Olaf, in the book line more than a decade earlier. The rest of the audience was washed in darkness as the stage lights shined in my eyes.

I told the audience about Steve Jensen, a farmer in western North Dakota who had seven football fields worth of oil ooze across his land from a nine-inch-wide pipeline. At the time, it was the largest inland oil spill in the country's history.

When I mentioned that the Dakota Access Pipeline was over three times the size of the pipeline on Jensen's land, and that at full carrying capacity it would push 24 million gallons of oil each day across Iowa, I said that, when the pipeline breaks—and if it leaks for only an hour—it would spill over 1 million gallons of oil.


AFTER THE PRESENTATION ended, I sat in the lobby autographing copies of my fracking anthology. Kathy, whom I had just met two weeks before in the back of the police van while we were getting arrested, came and gave me a hug.

Once I sat back down, I continued with the signing while my friend Joel waited for me.

The historian who'd spoken walked up to me and smiled. I took another break from signing books and stood to speak with him. He continued smiling as he shook my hand. He leaned in to whisper in my ear.

"You don't really believe all that bullshit you said out there, do you?" he asked.

He pulled back but kept shaking my hand.

"Thanks for a great event. Good to see you again," he said before letting go of my hand.

Shaken, I returned to my seat and continued signing books and tried to brush off what just happened.

A woman with cropped silver hair, dressed in a black turtleneck, black-and-white checkered pants, and a silver pendant was next in line.

She stepped up and said, "You did *so* well."

"Thank you."

I drew a sketch of the badlands, complete with pumpjacks and flares, in her book.

"Do you live here in town?" I asked her.

"No."

"Do you live in Iowa?"

"No."

"Oh," I said. "Are you here visiting friends?"

"No, I've never been to Iowa before."

I stopped drawing and looked up from the book.

"Pardon me, ma'am, but why are you here?" I asked.

"I'm from Texas, took time off from work. I've been following your work. I flew here because I needed to hear you in person."

I looked over to Joel and leaned back in my chair.

"Ma'am, I don't know what to say. Thank you. Thank you for coming," I said.

"Thank *you*. Keep doing this work."

She took her signed book, turned, and walked out of the lobby of the music building and into the Iowa City night.

I turned to look at Joel, who raised his caterpillar eyebrows, smiled, and giggled.

# 4.

THE FOLLOWING JUNE, after receiving my MFA at twenty-nine, nine months after my arrest, I learned Grandpa Hatzenbihler had entered hospice. I loaded my Prius with my suitcase and a lunch of tomato sandwiches, sliced cucumbers, cold brew coffee, and a small kale salad that my landlady, Donna, made me. It was a cool morning in Ames. The leaves softly whirred against the branches.

I pulled out of town, turned onto I-35, and zipped north. Iowa spread from horizon to horizon—farmers were out in their fields; seeds had been sewn into the soil. A few sparrows flicked out from under the overpasses. I turned on the radio, tried to sing along to Madonna and Britney Spears, tried to take my mind off where I was going, what I was about to see.

TEN HOURS LATER, when I pulled off I-94 into Bismarck, I passed by a strip mall with a Perkins, Paradiso, and Kmart before turning down more quiet, residential streets, arriving at my grandpa's assisted living facility. I sat in my car and focused my breath. *There's Uncle Kevin's pickup*, I thought. *That looks like Aunt Jill's car. Oh, there's Aunt Gail's van from Canada.* I opened my car door and walked across the sweltering parking lot.

Once inside, I turned right, as I had always done since Grandpa moved there, and made my way to his apartment. I walked by doors decorated with tropical fish, some with knickknacks or with GRANDPA AND GRANDMA'S HOUSE or THE JOHNSONS' RESIDENCE on little wooden signs featuring two bluebirds. The door for a woman named Miriam had cardboard palm trees, toucans, and tiki torches.

I got to Grandpa's door, gave a gentle knock, and walked in, shoulders up to my ears.

"Oh, hi, Taylor," said my aunt Jill, a short woman with tight blond hair. She reached up and wrapped her arms around me. I gently patted her back.

Mom and Dad were there, and I gave them a quick hug.

Dad whispered in my ear.

"Good to see you."

I nodded and walked into my grandfather's room, where he was lying in his bed, protected now by shiny metal rails up along its side.

The room was dim, the blinds drawn. Aunt Raylene was in the room with Grandpa.

"Hi, Taylor," she said softly.

"Hi, Raylene." I moved to the opposite side of the bed, away from her.

"I'm glad you've come."

"I knew I had to come, I couldn't miss this," I said.

"Hi, Grandpa," I said, and his eyes snapped open. He grumbled and cleared his throat a little bit.

"Taylor's come to visit you, Dad," said Raylene, firmness in her voice so that he could hear. She looked over toward me. "They say hearing is the last to go, so we've been playing him some gospel and country music."

"I might play him something else, Raylene," I said. And I began looking for Lawrence Welk polka music on my phone.

"I'll let you have some time with him," she said and walked out, drawing the bedroom door to a crack so I could be alone with him.

"Hi, Grandpa, it's Taylor," I said.

His eyes looked at me, and when he pulled back the curtain of his cheeks, a coffee-stained wall of teeth shined at me. He was swaddled beneath thin white sheets. His skin was sallow, his dusting of white hair clipped short atop his head. He closed his eyes and nodded.

He kept nodding, and I heard a gentle whistle escape his mouth. He had fallen asleep.


THERE'S A MEMORY I have of Grandpa Hatzenbihler at his seventieth birthday party in our backyard in Center. I'm eight and the chokecherry trees have finished blossoming; our garden of onions and carrots and potatoes and peas has just been planted. Dad has just finished building me a tree house, which I proudly show off to a few of my cousins. "Look," I say, "Dad even put in a rope ladder so we can feel like pirates as we climb up." My cousins are impressed. Aunts, uncles, and many of my grandpa's siblings are there. Grandpa is in blue jeans, a checkered blue and merlot shirt, a trucker hat perched on his head. And Grandma is in powder blue slacks and a cutoff blouse striped with rose, teal, and white. Eddie Hilzendigger, a neighbor one street over from Grandpa and Grandma, sits atop a speaker on our back patio playing polka music. When he starts "Roll Out the Barrel," Grandpa hops up, snags Grandma (who, at sixty-nine, has begun to slow down), and takes her to a patch of cement near Eddie. And then they're off—twirling and hopping, forty-eight years of marriage dancing the polka better than anyone I know, hopping like deer through the field as the rest of us hoot and holler.

IN HIS ROOM, on his deathbed, I asked my grandpa how he felt.

"I feel . . . I feel . . ."—he looked around the room—"I feel like an eight-pound trout."

Over my shoulder, just in view from his bedroom into his kitchen, was a mounted eight-pound rainbow trout he had caught in the Missouri River.

"That must feel pretty wonderful," I said.

My voice broke.

"Wunnerful, wunnerful," said Grandpa between breaths. "Wunnerful, wunnerful," and a whistle slipped out of the side of his mouth. "Wunnerful, wunnerful."

I grabbed my phone, opened YouTube, and told him that I thought I'd have something he'd enjoy. I turned up the volume.

"It's so wunnerful to have you with us tonight. Here are our little Champagne Ladies to dance to the 'Beer Barrel Polka' for us all. Myron, take it away."

It was Lawrence Welk, the King of the Polka, Grandpa's favorite, clad in a dark suit with his brown hair slicked back. Originally from Strasburg, North Dakota, Welk, like Grandpa, was of German-from-Russia stock. Welk's stilted English, which made Grandpa smile whenever we watched reruns of *The Lawrence Welk Show*, was a holdover from being raised in a German-speaking household.

When the "Beer Barrel Polka" ended, I pulled up what I knew was Grandpa's favorite polka, "In Heaven There Is No Beer." As soon as it began, I saw the end of the sheet at the edge of the bed move. Grandpa's toe tapped. In his faint voice, he began to sing along.

"In Heaven there is no beer, that's why we drink it here . . ." His breath went in and out during the interlude.

The verse repeated and I joined in the crooning with Grandpa.

Then my voice broke. It was too real, watching Grandpa's breath go up and down, watching him locked in his bed, his body no longer able to move. He needed gentle sponge baths in bed. He couldn't roll, couldn't move his limbs, couldn't even drink anymore—he could take water only from a little purple sucker of a sponge.

Grandpa finished the song, and I wiped my eyes.

He sighed, turned to the side, and fell asleep. Soft light slipped through the blinds and washed across his face.

I walked over, pulled the blinds closed, and picked up his liver-spotted hand. I rubbed my thumb back and forth on it. His skin was so thin. His mouth was open; his lips were chapped. I walked into the bathroom adjacent to his room, filled a small glass with water, and dipped the purple sponge into it. I returned, lifted the sponge from the glass, gently shook it so no droplets fell on Grandpa, and rolled the sponge across his lips.


A FEW MINUTES LATER I left his room.

"There's some food over there, Taylor, if you want any," said Raylene, kindly.

"Thanks."

Dad moved toward me. He looked heavier than the last time I saw him, a few years earlier. His handlebar mustache was nearly all white, but he had his usual Harley-Davidson cap atop his head.

"How long are you back for?" he rumbled in a low, guttural voice.

"As long as it takes," I said.

We stood there then in silence.

LATER, I SPENT a few hours at Tanya's multilevel house, playing with my nephews, jumping in the pool, and recovering from seeing Grandpa and the little conversation I had with relatives.

That night, after dinner, Tanya, Logan, who was now eleven, and I went back to Grandpa's. Mom, Raylene, Uncle Kevin, and Uncle Dean were playing cribbage. When we arrived, we went into Grandpa's room to greet him. He was asleep. A soft yellow light from the lamp on his headboard illuminated his face.

"Hi, Great-Grandpa," said Logan.

"I think he's sleeping right now, buddy," I said.

Logan nodded his head and went into the other room to watch his grandma and great-aunts and uncles play cards. Tanya and I sat on the edge of another small mattress at the end of Grandpa's bed and watched him ever so gently breathe.

A FEW HOURS LATER, while the cribbage players had distributed some bars, some licorice, and some cookies for dessert, Grandpa began to sputter. Tanya and I jolted.

"Something's going on!" Tanya said, her voice rising.

Raylene and Mom rushed in. Mom grabbed a suction device as Grandpa coughed up a gelatinous dab of blood, so dark purple it jiggled like jelly.

Logan rushed out of the apartment, and I raced after him.

WHEN I FOUND HIM at the end of the hallway, sitting in a stiff chair, he was staring at the multicolored carpeted floor.

"I lost my appetite, Uncle Taylor," he said, his head hanging down, not looking at me.

"Oh, buddy, don't worry," I said, crouching down to look into his eyes. "We can take that dessert home later, if you like." I rubbed his knee.

"That was so scary in there," he said, his voice breaking.

"I know, buddy, I know," I said. I lifted both of my arms up and he hugged me. "Should we go get Mom?"

Logan nodded. As we made our way back to the apartment, I wrapped my arm around Logan, rubbed his shoulder, and gently whispered, "It's okay, buddy. It's going to be okay."

Logan didn't go back into Grandpa's apartment. He waited in the hallway.

I poked my head through the door.

"Hey," I said to Tanya. "Logan wants to go. What do you think?"

"Yeah, that's fine," cut in Mom, who was once again sitting at the card table.

Tanya and I looked at each other and nodded. Tanya stood up from the rocking chair, slipped out the door, and the three of us walked out into the dark North Dakota night. In the distance, a chorus of peepers chirred.

———————

THE NEXT DAY, a Sunday, Tanya and Mike had opened their house up to cousins and second cousins who had arrived so they could swim in the pool, a momentary distraction while death lingered at the door.

Tanya, Logan, and I made our way over to Grandpa's again.

It was a quiet day—Uncle Dean played cards with Raylene. Tanya and I went into Grandpa's room and sat together.

I began to cry.

"Stop it," said Tanya, who could not control herself and began to cry, too.

"I know. I'm sorry."

"If you start crying, then I'll start crying," she said, half crying, half laughing.

I put my head on her shoulder.

"I'm going to miss him so much," I said.

"I know, me too."

We sat for a few minutes in silence, tears on our faces.

Tanya cleared her throat.

"One of my favorite memories is dancing with Grandpa and Uncle Pete," she said. "We'd do 'The Butterfly,' and when the music would speed up, I'd do-si-do and they'd shoot me up off the floor," said Tanya.

"How about that time when Grandpa and Uncle Frank, acting like little boys again, decided to put firecrackers between two metal pie tins, lit them, and shoved them into the room at Uncle Frank's cabin where all the kids were sleeping?"

"You know they were drunk off of red-eye."

And we began to giggle, and then to snort a little bit; eventually our shoulders jiggled.

Grandpa's eyes snapped open and suddenly looked around.

"Oh!" said Tanya, stifling a laugh. "Is he up?"

We couldn't stop giggling.

Grandpa's eyes closed and he went back to sleep.

"Guess not," she said, and we continued to laugh and hold each other's hand.

LATER THAT NIGHT we returned with Logan. Tanya stayed out in the kitchen to talk with the aunts and uncles while they played cards. Boxes of opened Chips Ahoy, a veggie platter with cauliflower, carrots, celery, and ranch dressing, and a meat and cheese tray lined Grandpa's small kitchen counter.

I went into his room, shuffled over the side of his bed, and kissed his forehead. My lips went hot. I hurried back to the kitchen.

"Hey, Grandpa feels like he's pretty warm in there," I said.

"There's a pan that you can fill some cold water and do cold compresses on his forehead and the inside of his elbows," said Raylene. "That's what the nurses told us we could do to try to keep his temperature down."

I went into Grandpa's bathroom and began to fill the pan. Colgate toothpaste, Brylcreem, Cetaphil, and some pill bottles lined the sink. I turned off the faucet and went to Grandpa.

FOR THE NEXT FEW HOURS, I dipped the washcloth into the pan, lifted it, wrung it out, and dabbed my grandfather's forehead and arms. There was a type of rhythm, a type of dance, to it. Partway through, I pulled out my phone, turned the volume low, and played some polkas.

My aunt Arliss, who always gave me a good squeeze and told me that I needed to come and visit her and Uncle Joe on the coast of Oregon whenever I walked out into the kitchen, came into the room. We pulled back Grandpa's bedsheets. The tips of his fingers were now dark blue. We pulled the sheets farther off him and his feet were darker still. I noticed Grandpa's torso: throughout my entire life he'd had a round, firm belly filled with cream and dough and beer, but it was now deflated, and his thighs were the size of my arms. His once full head of silver hair was thinned like the stubble of a wheat field. Arliss and I pulled the sheets back up.

AROUND ELEVEN O'CLOCK Tanya came into Grandpa's room and told me she was going to go home.

I stepped out into Grandpa's kitchen-cum-living-room.

"I want to stay with you, Uncle Taylor," begged Logan.

"Buddy, I'm going to stay really late tonight." I said in a firm tone, looking at Tanya.

"That's okay, I want to stay with you," Logan pleaded.

I thought back to the previous night, when Grandpa began to cough and the blood started coming. When I first arrived and noticed so many large, red towels in Grandpa's bedroom. Aunt Gail told me that it was in case he started hemorrhaging.

"Buddy, I'm going to be here real late," I repeated, looking Logan in the eye. "How about we come over first thing in the morning?" I looked back at Tanya; my eyes begged her to take him. I couldn't manage both my grandpa, if he died that night, and Logan, if he was there to witness it.

"Logan, let's go. We'll come back over in the morning."

Logan let out a sigh.

"I'll leave the front door unlocked for you," Tanya said to me.

"Thanks," I said. "Good night. Love you."

I WAS NOW ALONE with my two sets of aunts and uncles—Uncles Dean and Kevin and Aunts Arliss and Raylene.

Eventually, around 12:30 a.m. Arliss came in.

"How's he doing?" she whispered.

She moseyed over to the opposite side of Grandpa's bed and looked at me. Her eyes glistened against her cerulean blouse.

"His breathing's getting shallower," I told her, feigning a smile.

"Hi, Dad," said Arliss gently. She rubbed his head.

We stood in silence, Arliss stroking Grandpa, and me rotating the compresses.

GRANDPA'S BREATHING slowed further; now, there were more than twenty seconds between a breath.

"Arliss, I think we're getting close. Can you keep time on your watch, and I'll tell you when he takes a breath?"

Arliss's eyes widened. "Yes—yes, Taylor, I can do that."

"Okay," I said, "I think this is it."

This would be the first time I had ever seen someone die.

I watched Grandpa's mouth, but sometimes his breathing was so shallow it didn't move. A vein twitched in his neck. My eyes darted between his neck and his mouth.

"Breath," I said to Arliss.

And the seconds ticked by.

"Breath."

"That was forty seconds."

The timings got further apart; Grandpa's shallow breaths got shorter, quicker. I could tell his lungs were failing. He was leaving. The body was shutting down. I gripped the sheet near him tighter.

"Breath," I said more firmly, documenting whenever it seemed his body or mouth moved.

"That was a minute fifteen."

"Okay."

I had forgotten to remove the cold compress from his elbow. I whipped the wet washcloth away and dropped it in the bin beside the bed. There was a gentle splash. Some water wet my feet. I picked up Grandpa's hand.

"Breath," I whispered as if I was giving some type of military command. As if I was willing my Grandpa to hang on, as if I said it only loud enough that he'd take a breath. I thought that I could make his lungs fill, somehow, and he'd pop up, telling us he had a good nap. That's all it would take, one good breath, one deep breath to bring him back from where it was he was going. I wanted him to tell us that he was ready to go fishing, to snag the poles out of the closet, that we'd have to stop and get some minnows.

"Breath."

"A minute forty-five, Taylor," Arliss said, her voice cracking.

"All right. We're close," I said.

"Come on, Dad," said Arliss as softly as she could.

I wanted him to snap out of it. To stay put, to not leave me. I wanted another big hug. I wanted to hold him tight, smell his coffee-scented breath as we rubbed each other's backs. I wanted more pumpkin pancakes, more memories of picking juneberries. I wanted more—more of him.

"Breath."

"Two minutes thirty."

And we watched and watched. The vein stopped twitching. The seconds turned to minutes. A lump burned up my throat.

We passed three minutes. It was like a leaf slowly falling from the tree in autumn, lingering here and there on the wind on the way down.

"Taylor?" asked Arliss, her voice just shy of breaking.

I took in a breath, lowered my head, and closed my eyes.

"How long has it been?" I asked her.

"Four minutes and thirty seconds."

I looked up at her. Tears fell from my face onto Grandpa's sheets.

"He's gone, Arliss."

A sob erupted from Arliss as she crossed herself. I wiped my eyes and moved to the doorway. Raylene and Dean looked up at me from their cards.

"What is it?" asked Raylene, the devoted daughter who didn't yet know she had lost her father.

"Grandpa," I said. And before I could say anything else their cards fell like petals from a flower. They rushed into Grandpa's room. I walked over to the loveseat.

"Kevin," I said, gently rubbing my uncle's shoulder. "Kevin, you have to get up. Kevin, get up," I commanded, a bit firmer.

Kevin's eyes shot open. He grabbed his glasses from the coffee table and cleared his throat. He reached over for his hat, rubbed his salt-and-pepper beard, and sat up.

"What? What's up?" he asked.

"Grandpa's dead," I choked.


LATER, SOMEWHERE AROUND three in the morning, after we'd called family members, I drove the dead streets of Bismarck back to Tanya's house. The parking lots of Red Lobster and Space Alien's Grill and Bar were empty, the Fairview cemetery was unlit, and the KOA campground was quiet.

When I got to Tanya's, I stumbled into Alexander's bed. He was asleep, on the floor, a herd of stuffed animals around him; a red blanket was pulled up to his neck. His twin brother, Oliver, waddled into the hallway light, dazed, and asked where I had been.

"Checking on Great-Grandpa," I said. "But I'll tell you about it in the morning. I love you."

"I love you, too, Uncle Tay-Tay," said Oliver. He rubbed his eyes, walked up the stairs, and snuck back to his bedroom.


THE NEXT MORNING, before the boys were up, Tanya and I zipped over to Grandpa's apartment. His body had been removed. After some hugs, someone asked who wanted to go over and tell Aunt Frances, Grandpa's sister-in-law.

I volunteered.

On the way over to her assisted living facility, I thought about how I was going to break the news to her.

I arrived, signed in at the front desk, and made my way to Aunt Frances's apartment. I heard music flow out from the chapel.

I got to her door, plastered with pictures of her grandchildren and great-grandchildren, and knocked. No one answered. I stepped closer and knocked a little harder.

When a care attendant walked by, I informed her that I was Frances Kary's great-nephew and wondered if she was home.

"Oh, she's probably at morning chapel," said the attendant. "She's our favorite, you know," she smiled.

"She's everyone's favorite," I said. "I'm sorry to ask this, but might I be able to get her? I want to tell her that her brother-in-law, my grandfather, died earlier this morning."

"Oh, I'm so sorry." The care attendant frowned.

"Thank you," I said with a forced smile.

"Let me go in there and snag her—what's your name again?"

"Taylor."

"Okay, just a minute, Taylor."

A minute or two later the door creaked open. The attendant held it, and my ninety-one-year-old great-aunt emerged, her hair dyed brown and curled on her head. She gripped her walker tightly.

"Oh, good morning, Taylor."

"Good morning, Aunt Frances," I said as I leaned down to hug and give her a kiss on the cheek.

We moved into Aunt Frances's one-bedroom apartment before I told her.

"Sorry to take you out of chapel this morning," I said as we sat down at her mahogany table.

"It's no trouble. It's good to see you." She smiled.

"It's good to see you, too," I said. There was then a wide gap of silence. I looked out her window as she stared at me. I then looked down at the floor before my eyes came up to meet hers.

"Aunt Frances, Grandpa died this morning," I said with tears in my eyes.

"Oh, oh god." She held her hand against her mouth, closed her eyes, and sharply shook her head. She let out a cry. She slid her hand up to her forehead and pressed. She cleared her throat and quickly composed herself.

"Who knows?"

"All of his children, and they're spreading the word to their children."

"When will the funeral be?" she asked as she rolled her fingers across the table.

"We're not sure yet. I don't know who's taking care of the arrangements."

"I'll call my girls this morning and tell them. How about Tanya's boys?" she asked.

I looked her in the eyes.

"Oh," she said.

I cleared my throat.

"They don't know yet. I'm on my way to get Logan after seeing you."

"Don't let me keep you," she shot her hands into the air. "You have things to do and those nephews to look after. That's going to be hard. Good luck, Taylor."

I stood up and sidled over to give her another hug. She reached her arms up, gripped me around the neck, and stretched to kiss me.

"I love you," I said in her ear.

"I love you, too. Make sure someone calls me to keep me updated. It takes an army to get a funeral in order."

I laughed, nodded, and walked out of her apartment. As I slowly closed her door, I heard sniffles before the door latched shut.


WHEN I GOT TO TANYA's, I parked the car and took a breath.

"Hey, Logie, are you ready, buddy?" I yelled as I stepped into the house. My brother-in-law, who worked from home, was one floor below Logan's room.

"Logan?"

I walked downstairs into Logan's room and found him, for once, folding his own clothes. I sat on his bed and watched him shuffle back and forth between pile and dresser, an eleven-year-old going on twelve trying to be stoic, breaking out every word with an axe.

"Daddy told me Great-Grandpa died," Logan said in a quiet voice.

"He did, buddy," I said softly.

Logan tried to put another shirt in his drawer.

"Were you there?"

"Yes, I was. I got to hold his hand and tell him I loved him and that I was going to miss him so much."

Logan stopped at his dresser. He looked over toward his closet, away from me.

"Come here, buddy," I said and patted the place next to me on his bed.

Logan came over, sat down on his Star Wars bedsheets, and rested his head on my shoulder. I wrapped my arm around his shoulder and pulled him tight against me. I rubbed his back.

"I'm going to miss him so much, Uncle Taylor."

"I know, buddy, me too. Me too. We're all going to miss him—Grammy, Grampy, Great-Aunt Arliss, Great-Uncle Dean. But we all have each other."

Logan began to cry. Pools of tears welled in my eyes. I kissed the top of his head.

"You know," I whispered, "it's a really good thing to cry when you're sad." I rubbed Logan's back. "We can take all the time we need. There's no rush to go over there."

Logan nodded.

I kept rubbing his back.

# INFLORESCENCE

# 1.

Forks, Washington, is a town of around four thousand people—a town with two gas stations, one stoplight, a hardware-clothing-grocery store, an auto parts store, and a Subway. Though it was surrounded with Sitka spruce and ponderosa pine, I knew this town—in its way, Forks reminded me of the small towns I grew up around in North Dakota, ones desperate for any tourist money to help support the local economy. While driving through Forks, seeing pictures of the cast from the movie series *Twilight*, I thought back to the Enchanted Highway of North Dakota, a series of multistory metal sculptures—grasshoppers, northern pike, ring-necked pheasants—that shot south from I-94 to the 150-person town of Regent, where visitors could wrap up their tour of the sculptures by staying in an old school redesigned to look like a medieval castle.

For a summer, I rented a dome house on the Sol Duc River, fifteen miles outside of Forks. The house was a mile off the one highway that traces the perimeter of the peninsula, twenty minutes down the road from the Lake Crescent Lodge, where FDR had stayed on his tour to consider the Olympics as a new national park. The house was nestled among spruce and pine; purple bell-shaped foxglove was painted against the world of green—moss, needles, dewy grass. The Sol Duc gurgled across smooth stones in the distance. Forest plantations dotted the highway.

I had never been to the Olympic Peninsula, a lush world of ferns and cedars, of pine martens and agate-strewn beaches. At thirty-one, I did not know at first that for my summer of recovery from the hangover of five years of activism against the Dakota Access Pipeline and two years after my grandfather's death, I had chosen to live in the self-proclaimed logging capital of the world.

When I arrived on the peninsula, I savored the scars of long-gone glaciers: the jagged Olympic Mountains jutting against the tarp of the sky. I pressed my nose against pine trees, breathing deeply. Each afternoon, I heard the anemic call of a juvenile bald eagle and its parent. And, each day, while driving to get the mail or on the thirty-mile round-trip to exercise at the gym in Forks, I passed a wooden sign with chiseled words painted in white:

---

FOREST PLANTATION
FIRST HARVEST, 1930'S.
SECOND HARVEST, 1984.
PLANTED, 1986.
NEXT HARVEST, 2036.
JOBS GROW WITH TREES.

---

Seventeen years from now, the trees I drove past would be sliced to their bases. 2036—it haunted me. The sign felt like a cautionary letter from the future—seventeen years until the rips of chain saws would echo in this part of the peninsula.

———————

IN FORKS, when I shopped for groceries, I always checked out with a woman named Carol, a small, sixtysomething with a perm who asked me how my writing was going and if I caught any trout.

"You must love it here—far away from people, time to focus. I'm glad you can spend your summer here."

I was glad. In its own way, Forks was quaint—a kind of throwback to my childhood, a town where children still roamed freely, and where you could still rent DVDs a decade after places like Blockbuster and Family Video had gone bust.

And, each week, I'd drive out to the coast, to Rialto Beach, an agate-strewn mosaic of ocean spray and gulls where I'd find a bonewhite spruce on the beach, then hunker down, close my eyes, and listen to the salt water slosh against the sand.

After a while, I'd get up, dust the sand from my legs, grab bunches of washed-up kelp, and hurl it back into the foam. On calm days I'd wade into the ocean, up to my knees, and race against waves as they rushed after me.

Tourists with their dogs ambled up and down the beach and, in the late afternoon sun, I'd watch the kelp loll in the brackish waves. And that's when I met Sean.


ONE DAY, while leaning back against a tree, a yellow lab bounded toward me. A man in his early thirties in running shorts and a tank top came bounding after her.

"I'm so sorry," he said, snagging her bright blue leash. "This is Penny—she didn't shake off on you, did she?"

I laughed as I petted Penny, who now pressed her snout against my cheek and licked my face. She pressed closer to me until I heard the clang of my thermos: I had knocked it over.

"Oh my god, Penny! I'm so sorry," he said.

I said it was no problem, and I introduced myself. I said he and Penny were welcome to join me, if they liked.

He introduced himself as Sean and when I told him I was visiting the peninsula for the summer, he asked how long of a drive it had been for me to come out west from the East Coast.

"Five days—but I broke it up, and took longer," I said. "I went to the Chicago Institute of Art to look at Picassos, danced at clubs in Minneapolis, stayed for a few days with family in North Dakota, before staying with friends in Lolo and Yaak, Montana."

Sean and Penny sank down on the sand next to me. Penny rested her head on Sean's thigh. He scratched behind her ear.

"You've been to the Yaak? I hope you weren't dressed like that," he said, looking me up and down.

I scanned myself: Chacos, khakis, a bright blue Patagonia jacket, a wide-brimmed hat.

"Why, I think I was wearing *exactly* this outfit," I said.

When Sean laughed, he threw his head back. His shoulders shook.

"There's only two bars in Yaak," I said. "There are even Confederate flags flying in that valley. I thought, 'Christ, we're nearly to Canada and you're flying *that*.'"

Sean shook his head. "Don't I know it. The Yaak is one of the worst places in the country for logging—but now, here, you're actually in *the* worst place," he said.

I soon learned that Sean was spending his summer working for the national park, and in the winter, he was a ski bum.

When I mentioned that some of my first memories were of being on skis, he leaned in. I told him that I was originally from North Dakota.

He cut me off.

"But North Dakota doesn't have mountains."

I mentioned how we'd stay with family in Billings to ski at Red Lodge or Bridger Bowl, how some weekends, we'd head south after school on Friday, my parents driving into the night to get us to the Black Hills, six hours south of Center. We'd ski there all day Saturday and Sunday, getting home late Sunday night, and my legs would burn in school the rest of the week. I said how, as a child, I loved roaming through the casinos of Deadwood, imagining Wild Bill Hickok playing poker, or Calamity Jane breaking in, challenging any man to test his marksmanship against her.

"There'd be these large silver dollars that the casinos used," I said. "I loved whenever my parents would let me keep one.

I also said how, at night, if my sister would chaperone me, Mom and Dad would let me go to one of the arcades to play Pac-Man and how much I loved watching the bumpers blast the steel ball around an Addams Family–themed pinball machine.

Sean told me how he trained in his teens and twenties, trying desperately to qualify for the Olympics. He dislocated his knee at twenty-two and never fully made a comeback. So now, as he said, he was a bum, teaching tykes to make pizza pie slices to slow down while they wobbled on their skis.

"I've bummed at Steven's Pass, Breckenridge, but my favorite is Big Mountain in Whitefish, Montana."

"Scary place," I said. "Lots of neo-Nazis."

"Can be, but you have to know how to act, how to dress." He

laughed as he again looked at my outfit. "It's why I know the Yaak. I was in a bar one night, passing through camping. Some guys roughed up an out-of-towner just because, just because they could. They asked where I was from when they came back inside the bar. When I said Whitefish, they bought me my next round of bourbon."

We laughed. I knew that feeling well: altering your personality, learning the local ways of fitting in—or at least trying to, hoping you could dodge any hint of trouble.

As Sean and I continued to talk, I kept noticing how he shifted his hand and gently rubbed Penny under the chin. He had an easy laugh and I wondered, if only for a minute, if Sean might be like me.

EACH DAY AT THE GYM in Forks a large, lumbering twentysomething named Erik manned the front desk. He'd sometimes pass by me as I pretended to exercise, spraying and wiping down the equipment. It took Erik three weeks to say hi to me after I got my gym membership. One day, Erik sprayed a machine next to where I was exercising and asked me where I was from. I told him western North Dakota.

From then on, Erik began talking to me.

Erik shared stories about how local loggers once chased the Hells Angels out of town with their chain saws. "Threw some of those assholes right into the creek," he said. And I learned how the peninsula was populated with Vietnam veterans. "Some of them live off the grid, back in the woods, grow all of their own food. My dad and I once visited a guy who, after Nam, hid away and didn't see another person for three years."

I mostly asked Erik questions while I huffed on the stair climber: how often he got to Seattle, where the best burger was on the peninsula, if there were parts of the national park no one knew about that I should explore.

Because of our conversations, the peninsula changed for me. Forks now looked grittier, and I noticed how the low hills that I could see out of the gym windows were buzzed to different heights.

"That's to prevent mudslides—they cut the trees in sections instead of all of them in the same year so that the soil stays put. It's just a bigger version of agriculture," Erik said.

After the gym, I'd often stop at the Forks Public Library to check my email. One day, while I was reading the obituary for Gloria Vanderbilt online, a pack of four elementary-school boys broke the silence.

"Back that ass up, bitch," said a boy with fuchsia tube socks. He had a tight-to-the-skin haircut, with a tuft of curls on top looked like swirled frosting.

"Gonna crack that pussy's back," said the second boy, who was wearing a blue-and-gray camo sweatshirt.

I looked up from my laptop and stared at them. The third was a blond with a scuffed skateboard. The fourth boy's backpack bounced off his butt. They slumped into the thin cushioned seats and scrolled on their phones.

"Dude, that ho's fucking whack."

His friend giggled.

The man next to me pulled out his ear buds. He watched the boys but didn't blink.

A Native girl in a periwinkle T-shirt tromped toward the boys, her hair pulled back in a ponytail.

"Bitch, where you been?" asked the first boy.

A larger boy, maybe twelve or thirteen, swaggered in; his denim jeans had a hole in the left leg. His gray baseball cap was pulled close to his eyebrows, and he cradled a lump in his sweatshirt.

Then the third boy shot over to his larger friend. The larger friend looked around. They passed a small white kitten between their sweatshirts. The kitten yawned and I saw the glistening pinkness of its mouth.

The larger boy pivoted and shot out of the door. The pack of boys gathered their things.

"What the fuck—where we goin', Max?" said the blond boy.

The librarian at the help desk stared out the windows, not turning toward the boys. She clenched and unclenched her jaw.

Two blocks down the road was a section of a large tree. The sign on it read:

WELCOME TO FORKS.
LOGGING CAPITOL
OF THE WORLD.
THIS SITKA SPRUCE LOG CAME FROM A TREE WHICH
WAS 11'8" IN DIAMETER, OR 37'1" IN CIRCUMFERENCE,
AND 256' TALL. THE TREE WAS ALREADY 259 YEARS OLD
IN 1776 WHEN THE DECLARATION OF INDEPENDENCE
WAS SIGNED. SITKA SPRUCE IS NATIVE TO THE FOG
BELT OF NORTH AMERICA'S WEST COAST.

The section of tree was mounted like a fish for the town, for all the tourists, to see.

I wondered about the boys, wondered if hard language comes in hard places, places forgotten by cities, places where little precious things die—which later, a friend on the phone informed me, was certainly what happened to the kitten—where death isn't a noun, but a slow-trickling verb.

FOR A WHILE during our first meeting, Sean, Penny, and I sat and listened to the sonorous sound of the waves washing over the rocks.

When I stood and told Sean I better make my way back to my house to get supper going, he asked if I fly-fished.

I was a bit surprised. Did I look like I fly-fished? Maybe he assumed my Patagonia jacket gave me away.

"Of course," I said. "That's one of the reasons I'm out here this summer."

"Good, then we should set a date to fish together."

He smiled at me and kept rubbing Penny.

We made plans to meet at the Beaver Post Office, two miles down the road from the dome house I was renting, and then we'd go onto a pool where, Sean assured me, we'd find some trout.

As I walked away from Sean and Penny, I wondered what he meant by "date." Was it safe to go on dates at the edge of the continent, on a peninsula with only one highway wrapping around its perimeter? Sean was a short man, like me—what would that mean if a larger man came upon us in the woods?

I watched the sand wet and the water recede as I made my way toward my car. When I looked back, Sean was casting kelp into the sea and Penny was bouncing over the waves, into the brackish water. My stomach warmed, and I bent down to pick up an agate to help me remember the moment.

———

WHEN WE GOT to the pool two days later, after breaking through some brambles and branches, it was a slow, gin-clear hole, fifteen to twenty feet deep. Sean, in a gingham green oxford shirt, rolled up his sleeves and unbuttoned his shirt to his sternum. Upstream was a long, meandering channel that sharply cut against rock; downstream, beyond the pool, the stream bed rose, and gentle riffles flickered in the midmorning light.

To get to the pool, Sean had taken me down what I now saw were company-owned roads—roads we had trespassed on. I had left my Prius at the post office, and we had rumbled past perfectly planted rows of pine in Sean's Subaru.

"Do you like owning a stick shift?" I asked Sean.

"Of course I do—do you know how to drive one?" he said, smirking.

"Of course I do," I protested. "I had to learn by driving around the block. I was working a summer for a food supply warehouse and had to run this thing called a rescue mission—small restaurants in western North Dakota ran out of chicken strips or ice cream and I'd have to drive supplies to them."

"Aren't you the little hero." Sean laughed.

I shook my head.

"Anyway—this guy loaded this large F250 with what I had to take on this four-hundred-mile round-trip. When he opened the door, I saw the shaft—"

Sean laughed again.

"—and I asked, 'Is that a manual?' The guy said it was. 'Do you know how to drive one?' he asked me. I shook my head. He told me to hop in. We went around the block, he said I had the hang of it, and sent me on my way. Son of a bitch, you should've seen me buck at those four-way stop signs in those small towns."

Sean laughed again as I shook my head and looked out his window. Suddenly, I felt his hand on my thigh. He squeezed me slightly. I kept looking out my window, at the passing pines. Goose bumps washed across me.

As we continued to rumble down the road, I told Sean this reminded me of living in the oil boom: trespassing to see well sites up close, hoping no one tore down the road to . . . well, to what? In extractive economies anything can happen, people can just "disappear."

When I told him how I'd leave a note with a twenty-dollar bill on the windshield whenever I trespassed, he laughed.

"I do that, too."

Standing in the middle of a trout stream in the West is akin to getting a massage—the glacial water cools your tubes after a day of writing. The wider world fades away as eagles, elk, fishers, and insect hatches come into sharper view, the gentle ten-two motion of shooting a copper John through the air, the tiny fly submerging in riffles or in slack water behind a boulder only to feel the *wham* of a cutthroat trout—it's a type of sensual, spiritual experience.

At the pool, Sean said he'd take the lower section.

"This part, where you'll fish, is usually better."

The sun cut through the purple clouds and a gleaming line of gold cut up the Sol Duc River.

I began casting, my line folded across the top of the water.

"Get the fly to the far bank and strip it to you," Sean shouted.

When I looked downstream, Sean had removed his shirt. The

suspenders of his waders pressed into his rounded trapeziuses. I shivered as I traced with my eyes the line cutting down from his clavicle, cleaving his chest in half. Sean waved and smiled at me. I shook myself back into the rivered world and waved back. He laughed and cast his line.

To be attracted to another man in a violent place seems akin to a ticking bomb. Logging, strip mining, fracking. The American West is the playground for the country's obsession with exploitation and destruction, with most extractive economies near Native American reservations. There are increased rates of birth defects, higher rates of cancer. Violent people who mimic the violence done to the land.

Boom.

And where there's danger, there's room for trespassing—and where there's trespassing, there's room for mischief.

As LATE MORNING folded into early afternoon, Sean and I packed up our things—the water was too clear, the trout too discerning. We got skunked. We began to make our way through the remnant of uncut spruce before the rows of pine appeared on our way back to the Subaru.

While walking side by side, Sean's arm slid against mine. I stopped, looked at him—him with that sly gaze, his shirt still off, my eyes following the vein from his rounded shoulders down his bicep. I got a lump in my throat. My shirt was still on. I had told Sean earlier how I, the ultimate redhead, always get sunburnt while showing my translucent skin, how people at the beach think I'm the White Light at the End of the Tunnel and start walking toward me.

Sean had laughed.

Now, he stepped toward me and pressed me against the cool bark of a spruce. The smell of its needles flared in my nostrils as Sean kissed my neck. My fishing net dug into my back.

"Sean, Sean," I said, as he pulled away, his hands still clasped around my arms. "My net," I said, and jerked my head.

We both laughed.

I flung off my wide-brimmed hat, unzipped and tossed off my fly-fishing vest and net, and held Sean's face in my hands as we continued, the silent forest around us.

A WEEK LATER I was followed.

A man left the gym in Forks with me. He revved his jacked-up black truck as I turned on my Prius.

I had come into Forks at twilight, after another day of fishing with Sean, to exercise. Earlier in the summer I would exercise at noon to avoid the evening rush at the small gym. Spending mornings and afternoons with Sean meant I needed to adjust my exercise schedule. Suddenly, I was surrounded in the gym by unfamiliar faces. Some men exercised in camouflage shirts or changed out of their Carhartt's in the locker room. Like in all small towns, they knew I wasn't from there—or that I had recently moved to the area. I'd keep my head down as I quickly changed out of my oxford shirts and dark denim jeans into athletic shorts and shirts. In the gym I wouldn't make eye contact as I hopped from machine to machine.

As I turned my headlights on and pulled out of the parking lot, the truck followed me. Its brights were on. I turned down the dimly lit side streets in Forks. I backtracked. All the while the truck never lost sight of me. I bit my lower lip, tapped my finger on the steering wheel, shut off the radio. I knew no one in Forks.

I kept turning onto side streets off the main highway, hoping the truck would continue onto the highway and on out of town, letting me drive the fifteen miles back to the dome house in peace.

But the truck didn't turn onto the highway. It followed me.

I took roundabout ways through town and, at each one, the truck followed.

This was my fear: alone on the peninsula, Sean at work doing campfire talks at the national park, my nearest friends over an hour away in Port Angeles.

I drove out of Forks toward the dome house.

I tried slowing down to let the truck pass me. He'd slow down to stay behind me. If I sped up, I could hear him gun his engine to stay on my tail. Eventually, I set my cruise control at five miles under the speed limit. As cars passed me, I knew it was too dark to signal that I needed help, that I was worried I was being followed, that I might be in danger. The bright headlights burned my eyes. I hunkered close to the steering wheel. My eyes watered.

The miles passed. My palms sweated.

Beaver was the last blip of civilization—the post office, a general store, a lonesome bus stop—before the dome house. I knew I couldn't go back to the house. The forest-choked road turning down the gravelly hill, off of Highway 101, me slowly lumbering through the dark trees to the house. The neighbors—even if they were home—lived out of sight. I had never met them, had never even seen them.

I pulled off the highway and parked under a large streetlight by the post office. I kept the Prius running and got out of the car. I breathed deeply and stepped toward the truck.

I stepped out of the wash of his bright lights. I could see he was smiling, even laughing. I clenched my fists and started yelling.

"You goddam motherfucker, what in the hell are you doing? Why the fuck are you following me? You're a certified asshole, do you know that? Fifteen miles with your fucking goddam brights on!"

The man didn't yell back, didn't gun his engine. He put his truck in drive, and slowly turned back onto the highway. I could see the ashen profile of the man's face. He was still laughing.

"You goddam fucking son of a bitch!" I yelled after him.

The taillights illuminated his license plate, and I kept screaming until I couldn't see the truck anymore. I bent over, my hands on my knees. I heaved under the flooded light of the gravel parking lot.

And then I threw up. My eyes burned.

I stood up, wiped my nose with the back of my hand, locked my hands above my head, and went back to my car. I grabbed my cell phone and left a voice message for Sean, asking him to meet me at the post office once he got off work, that I would stay there and wait for him.

I had no internet reception to look up the Forks police number and, instead, dialed 911. I told the dispatcher that it wasn't an emergency anymore, but that I needed to be patched through to the Forks police station.

When I described the pickup and license plate to the officer on the phone, he cut me off with a laugh.

"Oh, that's Terry Johnson. He's harmless. Iraq War vet, a little loony. He'd never hurt a fly."

"Then why the fuck did he follow me?" I yelled.

"Probably thought it was just something fun to do."

My jaw clenched; my arms flexed. "Fun to harass someone?"

The officer chuckled. "It's okay. Is he still there? I'll talk to him if he is."

"No," I said. "Thanks for your help." I hung up.

The bitterness welled in my throat, and I threw up again. If anyone drove by on the highway, I didn't want them to see me. I burned with anger at myself for choosing to come out to a remote part of the world for what I thought would be a restorative summer in the lungs of the world, the rain forest of the Olympic Peninsula—a place where now I found it difficult to breathe.

When Sean arrived, he ran toward me. He hugged me, patted my head, and made soft cooing sounds. I gripped the back of his soft flannel shirt.

I said we should go to the dome house, and I asked him if he would spend the night.

He agreed.

When we arrived, and as I unlocked the door, Sean placed his hand on my shoulder.

"I'm sorry I'm so worked up," I said, my voice breaking.

"Are you kidding? That's horrible, what happened—but you're safe now."

He rubbed my back.

Inside, I showed Sean the room I slept in.

"Holy shit," he said. "Is that a mural?"

It was. In my room, the owner had constructed a ten-foot-wide wood and ceramic mural of salmon spawning. The foreground was a wide river that cut to the side, narrowing, giving the mural a sense of depth.

"This is incredible," said Sean. "'So briefly he roamed the gallery of marvels'—that's Ted Hughes?"

I nodded. In the low center of the mural, stamped on the body of a spawned salmon, was the line from Hughes's poem "An October Salmon."

"Do you know it?" I asked as we left my guestroom and headed upstairs to the open-floor living room, kitchen, and master bedroom.

"Yes. I learned it in college. I was an English major."

I smiled as I opened the freezer and grabbed my bottle of gin.

"So was I."

"Of course, you were," he smiled. "You're a writer. Do you mind if I make us a fire?" he said, nodding toward the fireplace.

"Go right ahead," I said as I dropped lime slices in our glasses.

I asked Sean if he'd like to listen to one of my favorite Jim Harrison interviews.

"Sure," he said as he built a tepee of kindling around wadded newspaper. "He seems a bit outdated to me, but we can listen."

I turned on some lamps and shut off the overhead lights. I set our drinks on the coffee table.

The fire began to crackle as Scott Carrier, the host of my favorite podcast, "Home of the Brave," and Jim Harrison began to fill the room.

Sean scooted over and sat next to me. We listened and slowly sipped our cocktails. I began to nod off, my head slumped across Sean's shoulder.

# 2.

Toward the end of the summer, I met my friend Colleen, who worked outside of Port Angeles at an environmental educational nonprofit, at the Lake Crescent Lodge for an afternoon of beers.

Inside the lodge there was a blazing fire in the large, cavernous fireplace. Mission chairs and large leather sofas dotted the lobby, while at the end stood a small bar, the bartenders smiling and flitting among customers. I dodged between passing tourists, hopped up to the bar, waited for Colleen, and imagined FDR rolling through here, singing his praises about the splendor of the Olympics.

Colleen arrived around one. She hugged me so hard I coughed.

"I've been worried about you," she said.

I had told her about my being followed weeks earlier—and, since then, an imprisoned person had escaped for three days from the Olympic Corrections Center, twenty-five miles south of Forks.

"I know," I said. "I've started to feel uneasy at night out at the dome house. The other day, walking back from fishing to the house, I thought I saw a person—it was just the heat—but I'm worried I'm getting a little paranoid."

We ordered our beers and settled into an afternoon of the sun slipping through the side windows, admiring the shimmering aquamarine water of Lake Crescent.

A blond Liberace, complete with large rings on each finger, was our bartender. We nicknamed him Lavender Lemonade because of the drink special that day, which made him blush. Colleen and I learned that he was working this summer at the lodge through a connection of Susan, from whom he rented a room in Taos. Susan herself, another bartender at the lodge, waved and came over to shake hands.

"We both work at northern national parks in the summer to get out of the heat of New Mexico," said Lavender Lemonade.

"And then we bartend in Taos in the winter—have y'all been?" asked Susan.

Colleen and I shook our heads and listened as Susan regaled us with a litany of reasons we *just had* to come and visit.

While Susan chatted away, Lavender and I would catch each other's eyes and smile.

Later, when Susan and Lavender left us alone, Colleen began to talk about being nearly thirty and being dissatisfied with work. A decade of EMT and outdoor educational work left her feeling uprooted and exhausted. For the past several years Colleen had ping-ponged between Washington, Maine, and Minneapolis–St. Paul for jobs.

"What if you picked a city and said, 'I'm going to move here and figure it out'?" I asked. "Where would you go?"

She said Minneapolis.

Throughout the afternoon, Colleen and I concocted a plan—which she would later go on to execute—to get her to Minneapolis.

"Hey, Lavender Lemonade," Colleen said.

Lavender skittered our way and smiled.

"Have you ever been to Minneapolis?"

Lavender shook his head. "But I hear it's a great place for the arts . . . and good food."

"Yes," I said. "And for dancing."

He smiled and went back to another set of customers.

We sighed.

"I think you should leave Lavender Lemonade your number."

I shifted.

"Oh, come on," Colleen teased. "He's cute, and it'd be fun. Imagine: a little gay fling where FDR slept."

"Is that supposed to be a turn-on?" I asked.

We sipped our beers before she summoned Lavender again.

"Do you live in Port Angeles?"

I kicked Colleen under the bar.

"Oh, no—they give us housing here around from the lodge. Quaint, a little tight, but it's okay for the summer."

Lavender left to refill other customers' drinks.

Colleen took a sip of her beer and smirked.


LATER THAT NIGHT, after parting ways with Colleen and going back to the dome house for supper, I came back to Lake Crescent, its deep aquamarine water now black, flickered silver from the moon as I drove along Highway 101. I had left my phone number on the back of our receipt. Lavender had texted me and invited me to a bonfire some of the staff were having.

I met him at the lodge, under a large Roosevelt elk head mounted above the hissing fire. We walked outside, past the bright white veranda, and I looked west at the deep, glittering glacial lake. I thought of him, President Roosevelt, in that moment when I looked over the lake, taking a drag off his long cigarette, content with his itch for conservation. The water mottled with moonlight; the curtain of night was cut with pines high atop the ridges. I could hear children skipping stones in the distance.

We got to the bonfire, where ten or so people were singing along to a guitar player. They passed around a bottle of bourbon.

"Hey, you!" hollered Susan, who gave two big thumbs-up to Lavender Lemonade, who had changed out of his work clothes into a hoodie, a small lock of blond hair flowing across his forehead. Susan gave us a big wink.

Lavender looked at the ground. "You want to go sit by the lake instead?" he asked.

I told him I did.

We crunched across pine needles that gave way to a pebbled shore, where Lavender, earlier, had apparently laid a blanket and left a small cooler.

It seemed a bit much, but I was leaving the peninsula in a week, and Sean and I knew whatever we were doing was ending. What did I expect, anyway, by coming back to Lake Crescent?

"I brought some of that special lavender lemonade since you didn't get to try any today," he said.

We sat down, cracking open the mason jars he presented. The herbaceous punch washed across my tongue.

Lavender Lemonade told me he had worked in the national park system for a decade, that he had been to lodges in Glacier, Yosemite, Yellowstone, and Estes Park—but that, so far, Olympic was his favorite.

"I feel safer here," he said. He stared across the lake. "The people who come to Olympic are nicer, more appreciative. It's a journey to get out onto the peninsula, so we don't get as many tourists, as many crazy families, as Yellowstone or Yosemite."

He asked me why I was out here.

I told him that I was working on my writing, spending a summer in solitude before returning to teach out east.

"You certainly came as far as you could," he laughed.

I mentioned how I had lived in the oil boom. I described the buttes of the badlands, the smell of the sage, the yolk-yellow breasts of the sage grouse. How if you sat long enough, waited for the golden hour, then the entire sweep of the badlands surged into a riot of reds and purples and golds. I told him how there were ponderosa pines tucked into the southwestern pocket of North Dakota, but that they looked shrimpy compared with the ones here, in the rain forest of the Olympics.

"It sounds beautiful," said Lavender.

"I guess I like a little danger in my life," I said, "living in logging country, in oil booms—"

Lavender Lemonade leaned in and cut me off by kissing me.

When we stopped, he asked if I wanted to go back to his bunkhouse.

"Susan said she's going to sleep at a friend's tonight anyway. She said it's all right."

We gathered the blanket and cooler, and walked away from the shimmering lake, back through the pines, and into the cedar-scented bunkhouse.

———

THE NEXT MORNING, I rolled over and woke to the smell of cigarette smoke. Susan had slipped into the bunkhouse; she held her finger up to her mouth, grabbed a bottle of shampoo, and snuck back out through the door. I poked Lavender Lemonade's shoulder.

"Good morning," he said, smiling, his eyes still closed. "Last night was fun, wasn't it?"

"It was," I said.

I felt his warmth as I nestled next to him. I kissed the side of his cheek and pulled him toward me. I was leaving soon—leaving the Sitka spruce and whatever romance smoldered with Sean. I knew I was part of the economy of the West: take something, anything you can—coal, pine trees, parts of your life never fully realized—and leave. It was the history of the West.

It was my history, too.

# 3.

A FTER MY SUMMER STAY in the Olympics and my encounter with Lavender Lemonade and summer with Sean, I traveled to Colorado for a conference on literature of the American West in Estes Park. On a late September night, I wandered into a local dive bar where academics sang karaoke. I squinted through the purplish haze, the bar counter far in the distance. Off to the side, on a red-lit stage, a man with a butt cut wailed away to "Free Ride."

I spotted my new friend Josh, whom I had met hours before at a conference, a beer in hand, smiling at me.

Earlier in the day, during the question-and-answer portion of the panel I was on, a woman told me, after hearing me read a piece about North Dakota, that one of her graduate students, here at the conference, was from there. This wasn't the first time I had been told that I should meet someone's friend/student/partner/aunt/cousin twice removed because they, too, were from North Dakota.

I suppose it's so rare, such an oddity, to know *one* person from the least-visited state in the country that, met with the spectacle of another, there's no stopping the bubbling desire to make introductions.

It doesn't shock me that I am often the only person people know from North Dakota, a state with well under a million residents, because it's so difficult to get out of there. Residents of the state will often chime their favorite mantra: the cold keeps the riffraff out.

So, when someone offers to introduce me to a person they know from North Dakota, I politely feign interest and move on.


AFTER THE QUESTION-AND-ANSWER session, I sunned in an Adirondack chair next to my friend Kathleen, a philosopher and one of the keynote speakers at the conference. I hadn't seen Kathleen, a woman old enough to be my mother, in a long time. Four years earlier, we toured around North Dakota together with other contributors, promoting our fracking anthology. I had taken Kathleen to the columnar junipers, where Jakub and I had camped years before.

Kathleen and I had ambled through the juniper, winding our way between the bentonite bluffs, which were scratched with the names of previous visitors.

Now, sitting in the sun, high in the Rockies, Kathleen and I reminisced about our time touring around North Dakota. We asked each other how the writing was going.

Out of the corner of my eye I noticed a man, close in age to me, lumbering in boots, and dressed in black. He was hulking, and he had shortbread-colored hair tussled atop his head.

As he swaggered by, I tried not to stare, stammering back into my conversation with Kathleen. I regained my composure by pointing at the herd of elk in the distance.

Even then, in that fleeting moment, I hurried to crush the lingering hint of attraction. I was, after all, in the West.

Growing up, while watching professional wrestling with neighbor boys, I'd pretended to be attracted to the female valets—Sable or Ms. Elizabeth, who accompanied Macho Man Randy Savage—when really it was the oiled men in their short shorts that made me silently squirm.

I grew up in the world of men with bodies like the man who swaggered by Kathleen and me—large bodies built by fixing fence posts, hurling hay bales high into barn lofts, breaking in horses. There was no need to curl dumbbells in gyms where I came from. The men I knew had bodies built by necessity—barrel chests, hands the size of hubcaps, prairie-hard thighs wedged into tight Wranglers. That's how the man dressed in black looked—like the men I first gazed at in middle school, the type of bodies I knew it was risky to be attracted to. There's so much strength in those bodies, as well as the ability to hurt me if they knew what I secretly thought about them.

THAT EVENING AT DINNER, the lumbering man in black plopped down beside me, telling me his old teacher had said that I was from North Dakota and that he needed to meet me. He leaned in as he spoke. I leaned away, at first. I moved closer to my cadre of friends. I knew North Dakota men, knew I should keep my distance to stay safe.

He said his name was Josh, that he was from Park River, a town in the opposite corner for the state from Center. Park River was in the eastern part of North Dakota, a place where there was enough water, more trees. The world there was lush. Josh told me that he taught Native American literature at a small Catholic university in Connecticut.

---

LATER, IN THE BAR, Josh and I didn't stop yammering. While Josh faced the stage to watch the butt cut academic sing his next song, "Walk This Way," I turned toward the bar to make it easier for us to talk in each other's ears. I nodded as Josh's breath warmed my ear. He'd then turn his head away and wait for me to reply.

At some point I made a grave error. After a few rounds of close, back-and-forth conversation, I felt comfortable with Josh—here was another man who had gotten out, who was a writer and teacher, like me. Someone my age, some unicorn of a human I wish I had known in childhood. At some point during our conversation, I raised my hand and pressed on Josh's bicep, a sign, some type of acknowledgment that I agreed with whatever it was he said.

Suddenly, I came back to myself. I remembered hurtling through the air, slamming against the brick wall in Dickinson. I remembered the one thing I wasn't allowed to do in the American West: touch other men.

I scanned the bar I didn't know, where I stood next to a man I had just met.

Josh told me about the breakup with his ex-girlfriend, which forced him to flee back to North Dakota, as I scanned the room and tried to recover from what I worried was a fatal error. Had anyone seen what I did?

Josh kept talking.

It wasn't him I was worried about, it was the men I didn't know, the ones who could punch me, smash my glasses when I stepped out of the bar, the ones I might not notice keeping an eye on me—those were the ones who sent an icy chill down my neck.

On a phone call months later with Josh, I asked if he remembered my touching his arm. He said he did.

I told him how scared I was in that moment, how I worried my action was going to cause trouble, how we were just across the state line from where Matthew Shepard got assaulted after visiting a bar, beaten on the backroads of Laramie, hanged on a fence. In the morning, cars passing by thought he was a scarecrow, his body mangled, barely breathing.

Matthew, of course, was—still is—a scarecrow. His bloodied body is a semaphore, a signal to gay people: this will happen to you, too, if you come here.

Josh told me how he could weep. I told him how much I'd like to act like the composer Leonard Bernstein, a hero of mine, a flamboyant man who hugged and kissed everyone. A man whose children, before he met the Pope, said, "The ring, Dad! Remember—you kiss the ring, not the Pope!" I wanted to be that open with others, be able to express myself without fear.

Spare emotions fester in a landscape where the only way capitalism has made sense of the American West is to fence it in, break it into 160-acre parcels, frack, mine, dam, and cut it to a stubble.

As I listened to Josh, I went back in memory to Center, back to the bars, wood paneled and filled with blue cigarette smoke. Old women playing pull tabs, maybe some young men racking pool balls, a few old-time miners sipping Lord Calvert along the mahogany bar. Their belt buckles glistening in the low light, Hank Williams piping through the speakers.

It's a familiar scene in the West, a quiet, easy scene. A safe scene. Until it isn't.

I VISITED JOSH a few months later at his home in Connecticut. Over two days—from the time we sipped our morning coffee at his dining room table until we brushed our teeth for bed—we traded stories from North Dakota.

Josh told me about being a truck driver, about working in a cubicle in Fargo after graduate school, about growing up poor, about going to bonfires in high school, getting into fistfights with friends.

"With your friends?" I asked. "How'd that happen?"

"We just—I don't know. We just sat there; the room would get quiet. Then there'd be this tension. And we'd just wail on each other."

In some small part of me I found that violence alluring. I had never gotten into a fight, had never been hit or had thrown a punch, but I romanticized what that would be like—whether my small frame was sturdy against the hulking men I knew from my childhood.

But Josh didn't intimidate me, not in that way, not in a bodily way. He had done his PhD on missing and murdered indigenous men. He lit up when I told him about painting with pastels in the wheat field behind my childhood home. We swapped stories about reading Louise Erdrich's books.

"Oh man," he said, "I can still remember the first time I read her story 'The Red Convertible.' There was this little old woman who had moved back to Park River and opened a bookstore. My mom told me she was selling off everything in her store and that I should go and take a look. I got to talking to this old lady and she handed me that collection and said I should read the title story—the book was on her, I could have it for free. I drove out of Park River, pulled over into a field, and read that opening paragraph and was knocked out. Someone got me."

I told Josh about making sugar kuchen with Grandma Hatzenbihler, learning to polka with my mom, and about how I felt like I could breathe easier when I left North Dakota for college.

"I'm so glad you got out," he said.

I swallowed and felt a bit embarrassed about how easily it came out of me, my admission that I felt safer away from home.

We stared at each other. We knew the weight of not getting out, of not escaping, of being trapped. We had seen it. High-school classmates pregnant. Few colleges or universities to attend. Minimum-wage jobs in small towns. Limited hospitals. No professional sports teams or orchestras.

The pressure to stay home.

The pressure to stay home.

"But I miss home," I said to him. "I miss that landscape."

"I do, too," he said.

It was the first time I had opened up so deeply to another man from North Dakota. The type of men I knew growing up shared Josh's body, but their tenderness—if they had any—was hidden, tucked away in some private part of themselves. Josh's eyes flared whenever he got excited over one of my stories; his head snapped back as he cackled over a joke. He didn't pull away if I bumped into him while we were tugged along by his Catahoula leopard dog, Libby.


By the time I left his house, my voice was hoarse.

Inside my car, I opened a pack of throat lozenges, and as I put one in my mouth, I thought about how happy I was: I had lost my voice, not out of fear or being silenced, but by finding a friend who knew where I came from, and had felt what I had felt. And that was a type of healing from a place where I had spent so much of my private life hiding who I was, of living in fear.

# 4.

ONTHS LATER, the pickup doors screeched as Logan and I got
out to go visit the North Dakota Heritage Center. Logan,
then thirteen, wore shorts every day, his legs exposed to the ice-
tinged wind. The Heritage Center, expanded since I was his age,
now welcomed us with large cannonballs—circular formations of
mudstone swirled together at the meeting of the Cannonball and
Missouri Rivers, south of Bismarck—and a modern glass rectangu-
lar entryway. Inside, we gazed at great prehistoric sloths, taller than
both of us, baby pteranodon perched atop a wall; a portrait of Sitting
Bull slashed in half by the butt of a Winchester rifle; and agates,
quartz, and amethyst glistening behind Plexiglas. I rolled around the
lump in my throat, told myself *not yet not yet not yet.*

I remember, too, coming to the Heritage Center as a child,
smelling the same container of bison shit that everyone thinks
won't smell anymore, curling my nose when I opened the lid,
inhaling something akin to a boys' locker room. With classmates,
I looked at tar-paper shack and sod house recreations—the homes

of our ancestors. The Mandan, Hidatsa, and Arikara exhibits were shoved in the corner, tucked out of view, which, in middle school, was how I felt.

After an hour or two of wandering, Logan and I left and hopped in his parents' blue Ford truck and drove back to their house.

The words came.

"Buddy, I think you know this already, but I want to tell you something."

In typical thirteen-year-old fashion, my nephew stared straight ahead and played it cool.

"You know I'm gay, right?" I blurted.

He continued to stare ahead and sighed.

"Yes, Uncle Taylor."

And me, the teacher that I am, shoved my foot further into my mouth and asked this stupid question: "And what does that mean to you?"

I saw him roll his eyes.

"It means that you're attracted to someone of the same gender, Uncle Taylor."

For Logan, times had clearly changed, and his mother and father had helped and encouraged his enlightened sensibility. My nephew already knew who I was—at thirteen, he had the language I had yearned for, the grasp of a world I always felt was out of reach for me. And here he was, all twenty years younger than me, and the world felt changed. I felt seen.

"And what do you think about that?" I continued, praying to God my nephew—who sang in choir, who pitched in baseball, who played tackle football and defense in hockey, my nephew who still let me tickle him, who just was learning the intricacies of sarcasm, who still slept with a stuffed orca called Whaley and a small powder blue blanket called Blankie—I prayed he wouldn't reject me.

"I think it's fine, Uncle Taylor," he said in the newfound bass voice. And then, after a pause: "Uncle Taylor, what's your favorite pasta?"

I smiled. "Tortellini, obviously. Only peasants like anything else."

Logan laughed. We drove on.

My grip loosened on the wheel—or was it the world? It was such a small, passing moment, which is where many of our monumental shifts happen. It is not the grand stage, but the quiet kitchen, the silent dining room, the bedrooms, the drives home where gayness—my gayness—reveals itself. Drag shows are spectacles. Television shows provide a comforting illusion that life progresses, that we no longer need to live in fear.

But we do. We do live in fear.


MONTHS AFTER COMING out to Logan, I was back in North Dakota, again teaching creative writing—this time in Mott, a small town of seven hundred in the southwestern corner of the state. People from around the world travel to Mott to hunt for ring-necked pheasants; it's known as the pheasant capital of North Dakota. There's one school, a main street with a few restaurants (the Pheasant Café and Lounge, Bottoms Up Bar and Grill, Scorpion's Bar and Grill), Hot Dogs Pet Grooming, and the Commercial Bank of Mott. The town is subsumed in a camel-colored world of wheat and dry buttes as the Cannonball River squiggles against its southern edge.

In late October, when harvested wheat fields, trimmed to a

stubble, prickled gold in the slant light, I brought my second-oldest nephew, Noah, along. I taught my workshop in a building that served both as city hall and the Mott Public Library. While I taught, Noah played on one of the two computers in the library.

The workshop was filled with retired women—I only ever get women in my creative-writing workshops in North Dakota. But, this day, there was also a high-school junior named Desiree.

Desiree wore glasses, her blond hair pulled behind her black sweatshirt. She had the day off from school because of a statewide teacher convention and, instead of doing whatever high-school students do for fun in Mott, was attending my workshop.

I knew her, at least in some faraway corner of my mind. I was she—a person hungry for something I wasn't getting in my small town, even if I didn't know what that *something* was.

With those women, while circled around a shiny cherry table in the local library, I felt like I was back in Center, back in those painting classes, back in the car with my mother, barreling toward saxophone lessons in Bismarck. I felt the hunger flowing from Desiree. I had it, too.

In the workshop, we read a short piece of nonfiction by a writer from Minnesota who returns to her hometown twenty years after leaving. She takes the reader through a litany of memories—who slept with whom, where she worked, how she loved listening to Metallica and Skid Row.

But when everyone laughed and related to the story, as they always do with this piece, an eerie silence filled the workshop because of the final sentence of the first paragraph: "Pastor Dan wasn't out of the closet yet."

I continued reading on. "We were Laura Ingalls, but wilder." The women resumed their chuckling, reminded of the noted author who wrote the *Little House on the Prairie* series of children's books.

Later, when we broke down the piece, everyone avoided the sentence about Pastor Dan. When I brought it up, Desiree looked at me. I knew that look. I know that look. The look of praying to God no one knows what you know, of not being found out, of knowing there's no way you can stay home and survive.

AFTER THE WORKSHOP, the sun slid toward the burning horizon as my nephew and I shot back toward Bismarck. At eleven, Noah had become my elementary-school-aged research assistant. Earlier that year, he had accompanied me to the spot where the Dakota Access Pipeline slipped under the Missouri River, near Standing Rock; we then traveled to Sitting Bull's grave, before swinging north to trace the river to the bend where Sakakawea met Lewis and Clark at Fort Mandan.

Full on French fries, chicken nuggets, and deep-fried fleischkuekle, Noah and I rumbled along and watched the wash of North Dakota prairie crackle amber, sienna, orange, and sage. The buttes and bluffs were velvety as the horizon behind us simmered before sweeping into a deep indigo. We played I Spy and Would You Rather. I quizzed Noah who, earlier in the year, learned North Dakota history in school.

As we edged closer to Bismarck, while fidgeting with his Batmobile, Noah asked, "Uncle Taylor, why don't you have a wife?"

"I'm not going to have a wife," I replied.

"That must be lonely," he said.

I peeked over at him. He was looking down, focused on his Batmobile.

"It's not that lonely because I have a lot of friends," I said.

"Uncle Taylor, do you date women?"

"No." I gripped the slick steering wheel and rolled my knuckles back and forth.

"Do you date men?"

I looked west toward the stippled sunset before refocusing on driving.

"Yes."

There was a silence, if only for a half second—that silence that any gay person knows, the silence between acceptance and exile, where tension brews, tears flow, where breath quickens; the silence that births us from the chrysalis of what people thought we were into who we really are; the silence of a quiet door opening or closing.

"You're gay!" he shouted in a tone that took me back to eighth grade, back to the school hallway where I kept my head down. It was a slam, a knockdown, said with enough energy and surprise, tinged with that underlying euphemism: you're different from me.

I turned my head away from the quiet highway, looked him directly in the eye: "That's right—I'm gay, Noah."

He didn't expect it. He looked at me, then returned to the Batmobile, his small fingers shifted along the car's shiny black body.

"Uncle Taylor, would you rather eat only Chinese food or only cheesecake?"


WHEN WE RETURNED to Bismarck, Noah asked me if I'd like to play Super Nintendo. We mashed our small gray and purple controllers as we battled each other in *Streetfighter*. We laughed as we spun and hopped around corners on battle mode, shooting green and red turtle shells at each other while playing *Mario Kart*.

Sometimes, when we finished a round, Noah stared at me. His eyes widened a bit behind his glasses, and I wondered what that meant, what that *look* meant, what he thought, if I was being planted somewhere else in his mind, placed in some faraway corner.

Later, we sat on the couch and watched cartoons together as stars glinted in the night sky.

Slowly, bit by inching bit, Noah snuggled up next to me before resting his head on my chest.

A FEW DAYS LATER, on a bright cobalt day in October, my sister and I hopped in her large red truck and rolled ourselves north out of Bismarck on Highway 83. Cirrus clouds streaked the sky, and a light wind flicked the few remaining leaves on the trees. The previous week buckets of snow had whitened the still green lawns in Bismarck—now, breaking out of the city, the hills rose and the coulees fell. Breathing space.

A few miles out of town we turned right, passed a billboard, one still standing from childhood. Painted blue with a heartbeat line it read, ABORTION STOPS A BEATING HEART.

We passed new houses in a new development—black, white, steel gray. We curved around the road and eventually turned left.

Ahead was an unfinished house, wrapped in lime Tyvek polyethylene, which slowly disappeared as it was swallowed up in the claret-colored siding.

"There it is," said Tanya, "Mom and Dad's house."

They had asked Tanya to take pictures of the siding. They had sold the lake house but were still living at the lake, renting a small house while their new home was being finished. A massive four-stall garage reached out to the unfinished driveway. Plywood planks led from the road toward the house—one plank shot off to the left toward a Spiffy Biffy, a brand of portable toilet.

Tanya reached across from the driver's seat to snap pictures. I leaned farther back so I wasn't in the frame. I hadn't told them I was back home, back visiting the nephews. I no longer tell them I'm home, tell them I'm traveling through, ask them to meet me.

I stared at my parents' house, what would become their home—a home I feared I would never enter.

To LIVE IN EXILE is to be separated, unwelcomed, burdened. Burdened by the weight of history, by the weight of memories, by the weight of what was said or what wasn't said.

Before growing upward, prairie grasses shoot down their roots—they test the soil conditions to see whether this place, this spot, is the right home for them. With each visit to North Dakota, to home, I test the conditions, send down my roots, and find that there is no place for me.

The weight of sharing this, of holding my feelings like a burning ember against my sternum, is too much. I am transplanted. I am displaced. I yearn for home and yet, when licking my finger, testing to see which way the tempest of memories blows, I find I am caught in a whirlwind of emotion that reasserts itself: You have no home here.

My heart remains in western North Dakota, among the clouds that billow on humid July days. It is in the silver sage that scents the prairie. It is in the splayed body of a pronghorn antelope as it shuffles under rusty barbed wire fences.

THEN, IN FRONT of my parents' home, I contemplated texting my father. Father, my father, whose voice I've inherited, who seemed like Hulk Hogan in childhood, who had heavy eyes from the grave-yard shift, whose anger always seemed to smolder at the surface— my father, from what I heard through the grapevine, was mellowing with age.

I had mentioned this—my idea of texting Dad—while having coffee with Aunt Shelia a few days earlier.

"That would cause you to have another seizure, Taylor," she said. "You can't do that."

A month before coming to North Dakota, on the trip to Colo-rado where I met Josh, I had my first diabetic seizure in twelve years. My first seizure since spending summers living with my parents in college. My first seizure since living openly as a gay man. The first one since dropping out of seminary, moving around the country. The first seizure since living alone. The seizure, a reminder that my body is bound to my mother's diabetic body. There is no escape, no denial that with each finger prick to check my blood sugar, my mother, too, pricks her finger, our disease, our shared bond across distance.

I'd like to write that I do not think about her, that I do not think about *them*, my parents—but how can I, when each sharp prick reminds me of the pain I feel in my body. Or when I unconsciously find myself rubbing my maimed thumb, a type of unconscious wor-rying over the nub, the missing appendage, the life that could have been, a type of loss built of amputation and scar tissue.

———

ON HALLMARK CARDS we slurp down the clichéd phrase that *Time heals all wounds*. But I've found that wounds fester, scar tissue builds. Shoulders sink with the silence on birthdays, Christmas eves, in quiet moments when memories slip in like small streams into the larger river of myself. The memories disrupt the current of my life and bring me back to my origin, a place rooted in love and pain.

In so many ways, I thought on this last trip to my parents' house that I had killed off the part of me that yearned for them, that it had withered on the vine of my body. But how can a person live with a dead relationship when the family members are still alive? I had had this conversation with my sister before—how, if I were a worse person, I would just default on my student loans, and my parents' credit (since they were my cosigners) would plunge with mine, the last link between us. It would be a type of revenge for their never saying "We're sorry. We love you *because* you're gay. We were wrong."

AFTER TANYA AND I finished visiting their house, I slipped away to a bluff overlooking the Missouri River. Indian grass shot through the snow drifts, cut copper against a carpet of white. The grass shivered in the wind. I pulled my scarf tighter around my neck and gazed out at the river, reflected blue from the sky. It came from the north and flowed south. Across the river, buttes carved a sharp profile against the sky, and I closed my eyes: I saw the sweep of prairie roll before me, before the prairie was ripped apart by draglines, before pump-jacks pulled oil from a landscape deep below the surface of stippled grass. I saw the time before Lewis and Clark plowed against the strong current of the river, sweeping before me, in their keel boat, before they met Sakakawea in a fire-licked earth lodge. Before the Mandan bricked the river bottom in their large earthen homes, before the massive glacier shaped three rivers into the vast Missouri River Valley. Before North Dakota was a salty, shallow sea filled with trilobites that fell to the ancient seabed, were dusted with sand and, slowly, over time, transfigured into oil.

Before the stories I now know were possible.

It is biblical, how my memory of home swirls into a tempest, knocks me out with the weight of everything I now know. I cannot let go of home. The mantle of stories streams across the horizon.

# FLORET

# 1.

THERE IS A DREAM I've had, different in variation, the family members changing depending on the season or time of year. There's one version of the dream where my father and I meet in a river-bottom park in Bismarck, walk the winding cement paths and watch the veined cottonwood trees shimmer in the late afternoon sun. He's heavier and older—white hair has replaced the red hair we shared. I am older and heavier myself, white hair beginning to frost my temples and break through the prairie patchwork of my beard.

I imagine us being silent, our determined steps pushing against the ground, against the weight of what has passed—the missed birthdays, Christmases, Thanksgivings, the missed graduations—against the weight of the space between us. I imagine my tears trailing behind, me wiping my eyes. In the dream, there are questions I want to ask him: Why he let me go? Why his love for me—the love I know he still has for me—cannot transcend the limitations of our shared heritage?

But in my imagining, in my dreaming, there are no words, there are no hugs; the questions are never asked. In my dream, there is a fracture—and then a pivot where we stop walking and I turn toward my father. I begin to roar. I begin to point. I begin to thunder.

There is, in my dreaming, no happy, satisfying ending. There is no completion of this circle of pain, sadness, and rage. There is only separation, a growing chasm as time passes.

There is, in my life, no happy, satisfying ending. I have not seen my parents since my grandfather's funeral. I often wish I could, but I cannot find my footing on the path toward reconciliation when, on that sunny night in August after I graduated from college, I was told it was not okay to be this way, that it is not okay for me to be gay.

I no longer feel ashamed for the person I am.

# 2.

WHEN I STRUGGLE, I close my eyes, breathe, and go *there*—
to the bend in the Missouri River where, when the light
strikes the surface of the water just right, it sparkles, and the wind
and leaves and orchestra of the prairie snap into sharp relief. There's
the croak of the northern leopard frog; the cut banks slough into the
sepia-stained river; the piping plover trembles across the wet sand,
searching for its nest.

In my mind, there's an eagle, sharp and lean, perched against a
backdrop of the darkening cottonwood river bottom. In the bottom,
somewhere, a lynx slinks among the lush grass. A log, stripped of
its bark, smoothed to marrow, is submerged in the river, and then
the armored ghost comes into my imagination—larger, more fully
grown now than when I saw it years ago, it's whitened with old age,
its barbels trace the murky river bottom, its small eyes barely detect
any light; the sturgeon hunts, as it always has, for seventy million
years. It's here, in the dark bottom of things, where I have gone
in my journey. Like a grain of sand pushed by the current, my life

has meandered, slowly shifted farther downstream, where it inches toward a new beginning as I continue to search for the deep current, to find the place where I am meant to be.

# CAPROCK

To finish this story—for a beginning begets an ending—we must return to where we started: the wide, shallow sea. Now dark and imperiled, hardened but hidden, we don't think about it—but it's there, beneath our very feet. We press down upon it every day.

Below the lake that never freezes—past aquifers and saline formations—lies a plain of caprock, a hard frosting of rock icing a soft lump, like crust on a cake. More than a mile below threaded grass roots is a landscape no human eye has ever seen, a world of fissures and crevices in ancient rock. Here, too, is where the primordial sea resides. Caprock has held salt water in place for millions of years. Porous—there's space down there, and it's waiting to be filled.

The world above, stripped of coal, cut to a stubble, is suddenly not enough. It already seems so congested, the air included.

Now, we must drill down.

There's room below for what we can no longer handle.

Deep underground, unless we can act with the most extraordinary measures, we'll complete the story of a land that is fractured with the destruction of every living thing.

# ACKNOWLEDGMENTS

MANY PEOPLE SUPPORTED me in completing this book. Below, I offer them my thanks.

Charlotte Sheedy saved me, encouraged me, and continues to buoy me along the river of writing.

Robert Weil, dream editor, whose work tendencies mirror my own, reintroduced me to the genius of John Steinbeck—without Bob, this book would not be in the world.

The entire Liveright dream team—Haley Bracken, Peter Miller, Carine Zambrano, Nick Curley, Steve Attardo, and Amy Medeiros, along with Trent Duffy, Allison Johnston, and Jennie Miller—kept me on track and made this book a reality.

My English teachers, Kathy Lord-Olson, Jennifer Montgomery, Jane Pole, and Jonathan Hill, helped me understand that a life with literature was possible—and necessary.

The congregation of Christ Church Lutheran kept me going during a very dark period in my life—in particular, Kristine Carlson, Kevin Olsen, Will Stark, and Howard and Erla Polsfuss.

Jim Farrell taught me to see the world as it could be.

Kari Lie saved me.

Brenna Gerhardt brought me back home.

Steve Semken made it possible for me to become a writer and told me to dream big.

Gayle Burdick and John Jensen have given me much more than a place to call home.

Fayette Harrison taught me how to hold an audience, and the importance of storytelling.

David James Duncan and Todd Davis welcomed the "breadcrumbs" that became this book.

Katie Yale, Jeremy Schraffenberger, and Debra Marquart stepped in and told me not to give up on myself or this project.

Kathryn Rhett's attentive eye and constant support never let me waver from the path of completing this book.

Scott Boddery, Ari Isaacman-Beck, and Chas Phillips make the Mason-Dixon Line, and life, one hell of a good time.

Thomas Christian and Andrew Kingsriter supplied the title for this book, though they didn't know it at the time.

Anna Schattauer Paille, Katelyn Larson, and Benjamin Henschel trained my ear in rhythm and meter.

The Bakken "Dirty Thirty" made getting arrested one of the best days of my life.

David and Libby Christian kindly gave me a summer of quiet and solitude on the beautiful Olympic Peninsula.

Sandra Steingraber reminds me just how lucky I am to have a friendship where nothing is off limits.

Terry Tempest Williams knows just what I need to hear at just the right moment, including coyote calls.

Donna Prizgintas, the Gertrude Stein of Ames, took me in, taught me to cook, and kept me going through grad school and keeps cheering me on now.

Mary Swander, birthday twin, always picks up the phone and shows me how to raise hell.

Steve Kuusisto helps me understand the importance of being tenacious.

A legion of friends, through conversation and support, made writing this book possible: Wendell Berry, Nick Neely, Clint Peters, Toni Jensen, Pam Houston, Diana Babineau, Mark Odden, Caroline Nitz, Kathryn Cowles, Joe Wilkins, Geoff Babbitt, Josh Anderson, Sean Hill, Derek Sheffield, Simmons Buntin, Elizabeth Dodd, Camille Dungy, Amy Weldon, Mimi Pond, Mary Evelyn Tucker, Anders Carlson-Wee, Athena Kildegaard, Diane LeBlanc, John Price, Michael Branch, Kathleen Dean Moore, Rick Bass, Kerri Arsenault, Angie Carter, Alison Hawthorne Deming, Kenny Cook, Rachel Morgan, John Christian, Paul Bogard, Colleen Foote, Richard Salter, Antonia Felix, Phil and Barb Eaves, David Anderson, Kali Fajardo-Anstine, Fred Kirschenmann, Carolyn Raffensperger, Cynthia Barnett, David Orr, Andrea Peacock, Lawrence Lenhart, Ann Carrott and Jim Odden, and the entire Brown family.

Blue Mountain Center, Mesa Refuse, the Collegeville Institute, and the MacDowell Colony gave me needed time and nourishment, in the fullest sense, for self-restoration.

My colleagues at Gettysburg College, Hobart and William Smith Colleges, and Wofford College have made a life in academe not only possible but rewarding.

My students remind me what I'm fighting for.

Thank you to the colleges and universities who have hosted me over the years, where many of the early ideas in this book were first explored through lectures, panels, and classroom visits.

Beethoven and Brahms, without whose sixth and first symphonies this book would not have been written.

The Minnesota Orchestra's public radio broadcasts remind me that music is my deepest love and that I still want to be a symphony conductor.

Paul Gruchow, Carol Bly, Bill Holm, and Louise Erdrich taught me that my home was worthy of literature.

Kelsey Ward and Baxter Datt, who are always up for adventure, help remind me how beautiful life is.

Ashley Hatzenbihler and Michael Welch remind me what good work looks like and the goodness of family.

Kirsten Brown keeps me in line and loves me in only a way a sister can.

My nephews, Logan, Noah, Alexander, and Oliver, make being an uncle one of the most exciting parts of my life. I love you.

Mike Sampson once let me know that he was always there to pick up the phone when I needed it—I've never forgotten that.

Consuela, Sheba Queen, Mary Lou Jo Bob Henner, my big sister, traditionally known as Tanya, whose love, support, and laughter in only a way a sibling understands, is as bedrock to me as the soil of North Dakota.

My parents, who've had a difficult journey, but who tried.

To the little boy who roamed the stacks, looking for a book that reflected his life: this one's for you, as are all the rest.

# ABOUT THE AUTHOR

T AYLOR BRORBY is the author of *Crude: Poems About Place, Energy, and Politics* and *Coming Alive: Action and Civil Disobedience* and is the co-editor of *Fracture: Essays, Poems, and Stories on Fracking in America*. His work has been supported by the National Book Critics Circle, the MacDowell Colony, the Stone Barns Center for Food and Agriculture, and Mesa Refuge.

Taylor's work has appeared in the *Huffington Post*, *Orion Magazine*, and *North Dakota Quarterly*, and it has been widely anthologized. He is a contributing editor at *North American Review* and serves on the editorial boards of *Terrain.org* and Hub City Press. He regularly speaks around the country on topics related to extractive economies, queerness, disability, and climate change.